Illuminating Fiction

Illuminating Fiction

A COLLECTION OF AUTHOR INTERVIEWS
WITH TODAY'S BEST WRITERS OF FICTION

Edited by

Sherry Ellis

RED HEN PRESS | Los Angeles, CA

Illuminating Fiction
Copyright © 2009 by Sherry Ellis
All rights reserved

No part of this book may be used or reproduced in any manner whatsoever without the prior written permission of both the publisher and the copyright owner.

Cover art:
Edward Hopper 1882-1967
Soir Bleu, 1914
Oil on canvas, Overall: 36 x 72in. (91.4 x 182.9cm)
Whitney Museum of American Art, New York;
Josephine N. Hopper Bequest 70.1208
© Heirs of Josephine N. Hopper, licensed by the Whitney Museum of American Art.

Photography by Jerry L. Thompson

Layout by Sydney Nichols

ISBN: 978-1-59709-068-1 (tradepaper)
ISBN: 978-1-59709-247-0 (hardcover)
ISBN: 978-1-63628-192-6 (library binding)

Library of Congress Catalog Number: 2009924820

The Annenberg Foundation, the National Endowment for the Arts, the California Arts Council, and the James Irvine Foundation partially support Red Hen Press.

Published by Red Hen Press
www.redhen.org

First Edition

Acknowledgements

With heartfelt gratitude to my agent Jenoyne Adams, whose dedication and determination helped me bring this book to fruition, and to my editor Kate Gale, whose attention to detail assisted me in making this the best book it could. With thanks to my niece Laurie Lamson, who conceived of gathering these interviews into a collection; to my sister Phyllis Shinder, who in the very beginning helped me develop the form for these interviews; to Sarah Anne Johnson, whose workshop I took on conducting author interviews; and to my loving and supportive friends Sharon O'Halloran and Maeve Moses, who encouraged my efforts and were always there to help me along the way.

Some of the interviews collected in this book were previously published in the following publications: *Agni* online: "Creature of Habit," Interview with Jill McCorkle (2003), "Blindfolds, Hypnotism and Chairs," Interview with Lise Haines (2003); the *Bloomsbury Review*: "Coming to Elvis," Interview with Chris Abani (Vol. 25, Issue 1, Jan/Feb 2005); *Glimmer Train*: "What I Will Follow," Interview with Mary Yukari Waters (Issue 57, Winter 2006), "Novels as Omnivores," Interview with Matthew Sharpe (Issue 58, Feb 2006); the *Iowa Review*: "Memories That Reach Back into Consciousness," Interview with Lan Samantha Chang (Vol. 36, No. 2, 2006); the *Kenyon Review* (online edition): "A Little in Common," Interview with Margot Livesey (Nov 2005); *New Millennium Writings*: "A Palette of Words," Interview with Julia Glass (2005/2006); *Post Road*: "Mistress of Ceremonies," Interview with Elizabeth Searle (Issue 8, Spring/Summer 2004); *Provincetown Arts*: "A Chat with Paul Lisicky," Interview with Paul Lisicky (2003/2004), "Growing the Story," Interview with Fred Leebron (2004/2005); and the *Writer's Chronicle*: "Imagined Worlds," Interview with Edward P. Jones (Vol. 37, No. XX, December 2004), "An Inventory of Ron Carlson," Interview with Ron Carlson (Vol. 38, No. 6, May/Summer 2006), "Revealing Your Characters," Interview with Steve Almond (Vol. 39, No. 6, May/Summer 2007).

This book is dedicated to the memory

of my beloved mother Jeannette Sokoloff

Contents

xi   Introduction

1   Foreword to Early Draft
    from The Known World, *by Edward P. Jones*

2   Stamford
    A Short Story by Edward P. Jones

9   Edward P. Jones
    Imagined Worlds

20   Julia Glass
    A Palette of Words

31   Arthur Golden
    A Sense of Urgency

45   Jill McCorkle
    Every Town Has Its Stories

56   Matthew Sharpe
    Novels as Omnivores

66   Mary Yukari Waters
    What I Will Follow

78   Ron Carlson
    Inventory of Ron Carlson

90   Amy Bloom
    Characters That Won't Go Away

98   Lise Haines
    Blindfolds, Hypnotism, and Chairs

107 Paul Lisicky
Looking for Surprise

118 Lan Samantha Chang
Memories That Reach Back into Consciousness

128 Steve Almond
Revealing Your Characters

138 Joan Leegant
The Life Around Them: Animating the Inanimate

149 Kathleen Spivack
Pulling Yourself In

158 Chris Abani
Coming to Elvis

169 Elizabeth Searle
Mistress of Ceremonies

178 Margot Livesey
A Little in Common

190 Fred Leebron
Growing the Story

199 Yiyun Li
Tell, Don't Show

Introduction

As a child, my weekly pilgrimages to the local library were among my favorite parts of the week. I loved reading books of fiction and when I was only four years old I tried to get my first library card. As I grew older I continued to be an avid reader.

The next step in my fiction pursuit began when I was in my mid-forties. I wanted to write a fictional account of a family that I worked with in my role as a social worker. Never having studied writing before, I began to take summer workshops led by well-known writers. At that time I never imagined I would conduct interviews with several of the authors who led these workshops.

My fascination with the study of fiction writing expanded. The idea to conduct author interviews was spawned one day when I decided to take an author interview workshop. I had already spent the last twenty-five years conducting interviews in my role as social worker, with substance abusers and families in need. I thought that perhaps my already existing skills as an interviewer would transfer, in part, to the role of author interviewer. While there are key differences between the two types of interviews, the ability to ask pertinent questions and give focused attention to detail is similar.

At first I requested interviews with authors with whom I had studied: Jill McCorkle, Ron Carlson, and Paul Lisicky. As I developed confidence in my interviewing abilities my circle widened. I had the wonderful fortune to secure interviews with other such highly renowned authors as Edward P. Jones, Julia Glass, Arthur Golden, Amy Bloom, Yiyun Li, Chris Abani, Steve Almond, and Lan Samantha Chang, as well as several other writers.

It has been a unique and marvelous experience to peek into the minds of these writers. As you read these interviews I hope you will enjoy learning about their work habits, how they conceived of their novels and stories, how they refined and enhanced them, how they developed their styles, what they consider to be their strengths and weaknesses, and who their mentors are. As a student of fiction I learned that every writer is different and that there is no one path to becoming an author. What is essential is to have drive and tenacity, a commitment to developing your authentic voice, a good story, and self-empowerment.

All of the authors I interviewed were generous with their responses and their time. I thank them all for gracing the pages of *Illuminating Fiction*.

A Note About the Order

The interviews in *Illuminating Fiction* are organized with the goal of emulating the vigor and flow of a gripping novel or short story. Interviews with well-known authors are interspersed with interviews with writers who are newer to the literary scene, to form a complete whole. Rather than handpick authors from an alphabetical listing, it is hoped that the reader will be interested in all of the interviews in *Illuminating Fiction* and read the book from beginning to end.

Foreword to Early Draft

from *The Known World*, by Edward P. Jones

It is with great delight and appreciation that I introduce the following excerpt from an early draft of the Pulitzer Prize–winning novel *The Known World*, by Edward P. Jones. This early section is included in *Illuminating Fiction* with the objective of showing not only the importance of the art and craft of fiction writing, but the importance of revision and the sculpting of a piece of work. One of the many things I've learned through conducting author interviews is that what an author chooses to keep in his work, the editorial path that he or she chooses, is as essential, if not more so, than the author's initial vision.

Jones initially planned on having a very long piece in *The Known World* about the character Stamford and Stamford's life after slavery. In this section Stamford would live in Richmond with his wife Delphie and they would run an orphanage for black children. A poor German couple would perish in a fire and leave their infant daughter behind. No white family would take the baby in and Stamford and Delphie would care for her. They would ultimately travel to Germany to bring the child to relatives too poor to travel to America. Jones intended to concentrate on Stamford's emerging sense that he was put on the earth to care for children. One can only imagine how *The Known World* would have been altered if Jones had chosen to include this passage and develop Stamford's life in this manner.

I thank Mr. Jones for his generosity for contributing this early draft of *The Known World* to *Illuminating Fiction*.

Stamford

A Short Story by Edward P. Jones

The day and the sun all about him told that was true. Now, it mattered not how long he had wandered in the wilderness, how long they had kept him in chains, how long he had helped them and kept himself in his own chains; none of that mattered now. He saw Ellwood turn onto the street where he had business, the same street he would come back on to get to the Richmond Home for Colored Orphans. No, it did not matter, Stamford told himself. It mattered only that those kind of chains were gone and that he had crawled out into the clearing and was able to stand up on his hind legs and look around and appreciate the difference between then and now, even on the awful days when the now came dressed as the then. He was standing now on the very corner where more than a hundred years later they would put that first street sign—STAMFORD AND DELPHIE CROW BLUEBERRY STREET.

HERE IS WHERE HE BEGINS TO SING TO THE BABY.

The white child, having found the safety of sleep, released Stamford's little finger. He would miss the little darling and he would worry that the place they had waiting for her in Germany would not make her happy and healthy. If the money could be found, he might have to send Delphie back with her to see what kind of place that Germany was. He might have to go himself. It was a pity that the child herself was not old enough to write back a letter that he would have to get someone to read, a letter saying, "I have found home, Papa Stamford, and I am settled in at last." So somebody else would have to investigate how Germany treated her children.

Delphie turned and sighed in her sleep. Stamford stood, waited to make certain she was fast asleep and then placed the child in her crib. He knew how much she loved that crib and some way would have to be found for them to take it with her to Germany. He checked on Billie in his own crib and was satisfied that all was right.

In the hall, he looked up beyond the second floor, up to the ceiling on the third floor, and saw that nothing was out of place. In all the house there was only the sound that angels made when people let them sleep in peace.

He knocked on Delphie's door and she opened it before there was a need for a second knock.

"I been puttin my mind to studyin on why you and me don't get together," Stamford said.

Delphie said, "What?"

Stamford grinned. The road to young stuff takes you through the forest of wide grins, the man had advised him. He grinned some more. "You and me. Us together. Me and you puttin up together and bein as one human bein, is what I'm sayin."

Delphie stepped out of the cabin. She was not smiling because she was not very happy. "I would not want that, Stamford. I would not want that at all."

"Sure you do. You sure do. I'm tellin you I got what ails you, honey. Got that and more to spare. Just gimme one chance to show you what I gots, honey. Just one chance."

Delphie looked up and down the lane. The rain was gentle, not hard, and she could see that just by how the sparse patches of grass did not lean and complain when the rain hit them. Her eyes came back to Stamford and she realized that she pitied him more than she had ever pitied any human being. More than even a dead child laying dead and motherless in the road.

Stamford reached up and touched her breast. Now the titty, the man had advised, is the real talker on a woman, see. You have to tell it what you want even when that damn woman is saying you don't really want that young stuff. Talk to the titty first and the door will open just like that.

Delphie took his hand from her breast, firmly, and let it drop down to his side. The rain stopped and, still grinning, he looked around to see what the commotion was all about. When he returned, she was waiting. "I would not ever be with you," she said. She stepped closer to him and for just that moment he was hopeful, forgetting her words and taking in the smell of her. Delphie put her hands to his shoulders, grasped them. "You too heavy a man for me to carry, Stamford. I done carried men and I know how they can break your back. I ain't got but that one back and I don't want to give it to somebody like you." She stepped back, turned and went into her home. She was used to nursing people, trying to heal them, and so it was it was a long moment before she shut the door.

Stamford stepped out into the lane, into mud. The man, the adviser, was silent in his head. He walked absently toward Caldonia's house as the mud tugged on his shoes and pulled him down. When the rain started up again, he understood that he was actually walking away from his own cabin and he turned around and through the heavy rain tried to make out just which cabin was his own. He went down the lane. The mud pulled at him. He walked on and gradually became aware of his surroundings. He passed Celeste and Elias's cabin. He stopped. It's rainin, he thought. It's pourin down rain out here.

He went on. He had no more heart for the world, and if God had asked him if he was ready right then, Stamford would have said, "Take me on home. Or spit down to hell, I don't care anymore. Just take me away from this." ??? cabin door opened and ??? came out carrying a bucket. At the lane she slipped and fell into the mud. Stamford saw her and reached down and picked up her and the bucket. "What you doin out here in all this mess, child?" If he knew once what her name was, he had long ago forgotten it.

"Goin to get some blueberries," ??? said. In one part of the world, way off to their right, lightning came and went quickly before the man or the girl knew what had happened.

"What?" Stamford said. The thunder came and both people knew it was not just rain but a storm as well.

"Some blueberries. Gonna pick me and my brother some blueberries."

"You ain't got no business bein out in all this mess. Ain't you heard that thunder and lightnin."

??? said, "Whatn't no thunder and lightnin when I came out. Just rain. All there was some rain." The bucket now had some rain it and she turned it upside down. She looked a bit disgusted with herself that she had added to all the water on the ground. Her face seemed to say, "I really didn't mean to do that."

"Gimme that thing," Stamford said. "You get back on into that house." He took the bucket and saw for the first time that her little brother was standing in the door. She saw what he saw in the door and said, "???, didn't I tell you to keep that door closed."

The boy shut the door.

Stamford said, "Where you mama, child?"

"Up to the big house, helpin to clean up."

"Well, where your daddy be?"

"Out to the barn, helpin with that sick horse." She looked back to make sure her brother had closed the door. She said, "But we done had dinner, so that ain't it. Me and ??? just felt like some blueberries."

Stamford sighed. He wanted death more than anything but he could take a little detour now. He said, "Just go on back in the house and I'll go get some blueberries."

"Anough for ???, too," ??? said.

"Yes," Stamford said and emptied out what little bit of rain there was in the bucket. "I'll get some for both yall. You and him both." He knew he would have made Delphie a good man, would have made her happy until some real good young stuff came along and he had to tell her bye bye. He realized now that he had come to the end of his life. He just wished he was the kind of man who could throw himself down a dry well. "Go on home, child," he said to ???. "Please, go on home." ??? went to the door, opened it, went inside and shut the door.

He stepped toward where he knew the blueberries were, again the only person walking in the lane. He had heard of a poison plant one man had taken to get to the other side, but because he had never thought he would want to die, he had not taken note of what the plant was or where it could be found. The thunder and lightning were closer but he wasn't very aware of them. He was aware that it was raining and that, along with getting blueberries, was just about all his mind could hold onto right then. A woman on one plantation had sharpened a stone and cut both her wrists. Bled out into the ground. He had heard that she was a real pretty woman so that must have been a waste of good stuff. Maybe she was a cripple like Celeste. Pretty was good. Cripple, not so good. The man, the adviser, was still silent, and Stamford went beyond the lane out into a wide place not far from the useless forest where Moses went to be with himself.

He stepped and tried to make out where someone had said the sweetest berries could be had. He blinked and raised a hand to shield his eyes from the rain. The thunder and lightning were now even closer, about two miles or so beyond where he believed the sweetest things could be picked. Best hurry, he thought. Best get outta this weather. He wanted to die but he wasn't particular about catching a cold to do it.

The patch he found was priceless and he was done in less than a half hour. He hefted the bucket. Yes, that would satisfy a boy and a girl bellies until supper. He walked away from the patch, the useless forest on his right, the patch on his left, the lane and the cabins ahead. He was on a nice piece of ground that some women said had the prettiest baby's breaths and morning glories. He had picked some when he was courting Gloria. Beautiful flowers in a man's sweaty hands. But they got the job done. Yessiree bob. Maybe he could kill her before he died. That would learn her. Send her ass to hell so she could sit on one of the devil's wobbly two-legged stools for the rest of eternity just so she could ponder what she done to him. Kill her and then sit on a rise himself and watch her suffer for the rest of eternity. The rain continued and the storm was nearer than he realized.

He didn't pay very much attention to the first crack of thunder, but the second one turned his head around. He was in time to see the tree in the forest shake. Moments later, he could see the first crow flying as if upside down, heading toward the ground. The second crow flying upside down told him it wasn't flying but death that had hold of them. It took less time for him to blink before the second crow joined the first on the ground. Then he saw that the lightning was sitting on a tree limb, and Stamford knew that the crows hadn't been a satisfying enough a meal. He set the bucket of blueberries on the ground. Maybe someone would find it and take it to the children. He went toward the lightning in the tree, and while the lightning couldn't see him very well, it started down the side of the tree. It was purplish in the tree but before it reached the ground, it was quite blue, quite sleek, as tall as two tall men.

Before he had gone six feet, Stamford turned and looked at the bucket of blueberries. If someone was to find it and know who it was for, the bucket, he thought, should be closer to the quarters. He went back and moved the bucket three feet closer to the children back in their cabin. The rain never let up.

When he turned back, the lightning was at full power on the ground, quivering, one long blue blade of death. But the longer it stood waiting for the man, the more its eyesight improved. Stamford began to run toward it. Someone else would have to do the job on Gloria. He could wait for her on that rise in hell.

When the man and death were only about twelve feet apart, the lightning saw him and it began to dissolve into the ground. When it was one long streak on the ground, it moved away from Stamford. The man hollered at it. When he was only a few feet from the dead crows, the lightning stabbed another tree and split it in two. The man arrived at the forest in time to see the pieces separate and fall away from each other. The tree parts were silent as they made their way down. His heart sank, and then it sank some more.

He stood at the crows. If I could bottle that young stuff, I would be a rich man. Why hell, just one sniff of the bottle stopper would make me a prince. Stamford knelt down. The birds had fallen in very chaotic fashion, but somehow they had ended up on the ground as well laid out as a body in a coffin. Their glistening wings had been smoothed out, their eyes closed tenderly, and they lay side by side, just as they must have stood side by side before death snuck up on them.

Every single damn day was one unfair thing after another. Stamford licked the fingers of his right hand and rubbed the crow laid out on the left and then licked his fingers again. He closed his eyes and waited. When nothing happened, he did the same with the crow on the right. Neither bird seemed interested in sharing its little piece of death. He stood up and looked down at them. "All right," he said to them. "I won't grudge you that." He felt a heaviness hitting his head and thought it was just more rain. When it kept on, it touched the top of his head and pulled down what he began to realize was the yolks of eggs. To tell him that he was right, a piece of egg shell fell into his open hand. He knelt back down and placed the shell into the fold of the wing of the crow on the right and rubbed the yolk on the bird on the left. The ground opened up and took the birds in.

This was how Stamford Crow Blueberry began. In 1909 the colored people in Richmond unofficially renamed a very long street for him. Those colored people who insisted on calling the street what the white people had officially named it were considered ignorant and were put to shame. Letters to colored people with the official name of the street on them were returned and people had to find another way to send letters and whatnot to colored people living along the street. In 1987 the city of Richmond renamed the street for Mr. and Mrs. Blueberry and put up signs all along the way to prove that it was official. It was more than a hundred years before that, in 1878, that Mr. Blueberry reluctantly told a man from Howard University all about the crows and the egg shell and how he made his name, how the Richmond Home for Colored Orphans had its beginnings.

Moving toward the bucket of blueberries, Stamford held his hands out and bit by bit the rain washed away the last of the yolks. He came to the bucket and knelt and felt that maybe the bucket didn't have enough. But the children had been waiting a long time and he didn't want to disappoint them. He shook the bucket, thinking that might make it look fuller. It helped, but not by much. A young child might be fooled but not an older one. His shoulders dropped with disappointment. He saw one blueberry rolling down a little hill in the bucket and he caught it. He held the berry between his fingers, began to squeeze it. It bled a little juice. The blueberry was now useless and he regretted having squeezed it. Not to let it go to waste, he put it in his mouth. It was passable; God had given him a head full of good teeth, but not a one of them was sweet. The rain kept on and he began to worry that soon the bucket would have more rain than blueberries. He chewed and swallowed the berry, and then he raised his eyes to see the cabin coming his way through the air. It was not moving in any threatening and so Stamford was not afraid. But he did stand up.

All the cabins along the lane looked the same except to whomever lived in them. Stamford only knew it wasn't his cabin. The cabin settled down to the ground and rested a few feet before him. The door opened and ??? stood there, her hands behind her back, quite pleased with herself in that way little girls can look when they have a secret and are dying to tell it. She opened her mouth, her teeth, her tongue blue, a girl happy with her blueberries. Her brother appeared beside her and he opened his blue to show his happiness as well. The boy shut the door and the cabin and went back the way it had come. The closed door might have acted like a kind of eye because the cabin turned around so the door so see the way back.

After he had given the bucket to the children, Stamford stood in the lane in the mud and the rain and counted the doors to the cabins where children lived. He left out the ones with infants because he knew they weren't old enough to bite down and enjoy blueberries. And he had never heard of a sugar tit laced with blueberries. The rain kept up. Indeed, it got worse and worse and anyone walking in it felt the sting. It was a very painful rain. It was to lead to a flood, and one historian from Lynchburg College, without hyperbole, wrote that it may well have been the worst in the history of the county. Twenty-one human beings lost their lives, including eight adult slaves, five men, and three women. All the children, whether white or black, free or in bondage, were spared. No one counted the livestock and the dogs and the cats that were killed because there were so many and the land was covered with their bodies for days and days.

It was on the occasion of the opening of the first that the man from Howard University wrote the . . .

Edward P. Jones

Imagined Worlds

In the novel *The Known World*, Edward P. Jones explores the life and times of Henry Townsend, a former slave, who learns the ways of slave ownership from his former owner. Jones builds as his fictional stage the community of Manchester, Virginia, the town in which Henry was born and raised. After Henry dies an unexpected and untimely death, the thoughts and lives of several of the residents of Manchester are revealed through their complicated relationships and circumstances. In *The Known World*, Jones demonstrates the extent to which a narrator can be omniscient about the past, present and future, the extent to which a novel's platform can be shared by a multitude of characters, the extent to which a fictional world can seem real. Like Ravel's *Bolero*, it weaves back and forth and comes to a hypnotic and bold end.

Jones won the Pulitzer Prize for fiction for this novel as well as the National Book Critics Circle Award and the International IMPAC Dublin Literary Award. In addition *The Known World* was a *New York Times* Editors' Choice 2003, a notable book pick of the American Library Association, a selection of the Today Show Book Club, a September/October 2003 Book Sense 76 Pick and a long-term *New York Times* bestseller.

Jones made his literary debut in 1992 with *Lost in the City*, a collection of short stories that take place in Washington, D.C between the 1950s and 1970s. *Lost in the City* was a finalist for the National Book Award and won the PEN/Hemingway Award. *All Aunt Hagar's Children: Stories*, Jones's second short story collection, was published in 2006 to wide-spread acclaim. Several of the stories were originally published in the *New Yorker* magazine. Some of the characters that appear in these stories originally appeared in *Lost in the City*. Jones's stories have also been published in *Callaloo*, the *Paris Review* and *Ploughshares*.

Jones was raised in Washington D.C. by his mother. She was unable to read or write and when Jones received his report cards he had to sign her name. Jones originally was introduced to reading through comic books; and by age fourteen he had started reading novels and short stories. As a sophomore at the College of the Holy Cross he started writing fiction. In 1981, Jones earned an MFA in writing at the University of Virginia. He has taught creative writing at Princeton University, George Mason University, and the University of Maryland.

In 2004, Jones received a MacArthur Fellowship; in 1994 he was the winner of a Lannan Literary Award; and in 1986, he received a fellowship from the National Endowment for the Arts.

Prior to the publication of *The Known World* Jones worked as a proofreader and columnist for the trade journal *Tax Notes*. He has stated of this nineteen-year time period that what he wanted more than anything was a steady paycheck.

I met with Jones in a private room in the lobby of the Washington, D.C. apartment building where he resides, at a long and gracious mahogany table. This interview occurred two weeks after it was announced that Jones had won the Pulitzer Prize.

SHERRY ELLIS: You have said that for approximately ten years prior to the physical writing of *The Known World* that you thought about the characters and the plot, but that you did very little writing and limited research. Can you describe your process?

EDWARD P. JONES: I'm not really sure that I can. I didn't have an enormous amount of details and many things were very general. For example, Barnum Kinsey—when he reveals to Skiffington what happened to Augustus—I knew the framework but not in great detail. I knew what he would be doing and when it would be; I knew the gist of it. I simply worked out the specifics when I got to that point in the actual writing.

When I wrote my first book I kept notes; I might have been reading a magazine when a thought would come to me, and I would use the magazine inserts to write notes. The only things I had when I sat down to write *The Known World* were six pages of the first chapter and six of the final chapter. In the very beginning of the process, 1992, I had read some of the history and I had some written notes on small yellow papers. But in 2001, when it came time to do the writing I didn't want to do all the reading, so I just went ahead and began to write. How I kept it in my head I don't know.

ELLIS: John Vernon, in his *New York Times* book review of *The Known World* wrote, "Jones has an ear for speech now buried in the past, though its echoes remain. His own narrative style is doggedly declarative, slow, persistent, imperturbable, and patient . . ." Do you agree with this description and do you consider yourself a particularly patient writer?

JONES: No, I never think of myself in any sort of adjectives. The only thing I can say about what I do is that I don't like to use a lot of emotions or what I call "neon-lighting" because almost all the time whatever I'm writing about has enough emotion in it, and all I have to do is tell the story. I gave a reading last night at a library in Arlington [Virginia] and someone mentioned this, that all of these horrible things are told as if I was avoiding emotion. That's what I wanted to do, just state the facts. People can look at you and say things about you that you never think about your own self, because you are in your own skin. So you don't go around saying that I'm this, I'm that, I'm the other, because you are it.

ELLIS: In *The Known World* religion and thoughts about God are integral parts of the characters' lives. There's a passage in which Moses, a slave, wonders about God's presence. "It took Moses more than two weeks to come to understand that someone wasn't fiddling with him and that, indeed, a black man two shades darker than himself, owned him and any shadow he made. Moses thought that it was already a strange world that made him a slave to a white. But God had indeed set it twirling and twisting every which way when he put black people to owning their own. Was God even up there tending to business anymore?" Can you speak about the relationship between slavery and religion in the context of your novel?

JONES: That's one of those questions people talk about when they write papers. And I'm not a religious man at all. When Moses wondered if God was even up there tending to business, that's probably not something I would think; I know he's not up there. But I knew that almost all the people in *The Known World* were religious, that it was part of the times, and I had to inject that at every possible point that I could.

As far as religion and slavery are concerned, the only thing I can say is that the Bible and religion were both used to justify slavery. But I didn't go back and write these issues; I have to leave these weightier thoughts to someone else. They weren't on my mind.

ELLIS: In *The Known World*, when characters die, they have a dramatic separation from the earth in which they rise about it or see their former surroundings; they visit the people whom they have loved. Is this meant as a manifestation of religious belief or as metaphor?

JONES: At the time of death a lot of them go into houses. What happens to them is a comment on what their lives had been. When Henry dies for example, the last thing he thinks is that he's walking into a house that he's rented; that he was told had a thousand rooms, but only seems to have three. His head touches all the ceilings. His life has been confined in a certain way. When Mildred dies she goes into the house and finds her son sleeping, because he's dead. His wife is lying beside him, but she's awake and alive. In Mildred's own bed her husband is sleeping and she gets in beside him. She has a rather peaceful death because she's a very good person. Skiffington runs into the house and he ignores all the rooms where the people in his life have been. In a certain sense he was trying to live for the Bible. The Bible is falling over and he tries to put it upright.

The characters don't all rise up; many of them just go into houses. Augustus rises up because he is has to get to his wife who is in his house. I wanted to comment on how they lived their lives.

ELLIS: Robbins is a wealthy slave owner who tells Henry that he should "take hold of it all." He says, ". . . God is in his heaven and he don't care most of the time. The trick of life is to know when God does care and do all you can behind his back." How did you develop your characters, so many of whom have such rich complexities?

JONES: I knew the people because I lived with them for so long, and when it came time for me to put it all down, I just did it. I went through my mind and wrote down all the things that were in my head. The complexity comes because you're trying to make an interesting story that people will remember when it is all over. And that's it. They're very complex because you want to tell a good story.

ELLIS: The reader of *The Known World* often learns about futures and fates of characters at the same time. Inherent is the reader's knowledge that we are nearing the eve of the Civil War. Time moves back and forth. What impact do you believe the use of foreshadowing and the movement of time and future have on this novel?

JONES: I had a sense of what happened to people, twenty-five or fifty years later, and I wanted to share some of that. In some ways I think of myself as a God of that world. For example, in the Bible, they talk about someone living for hundreds of years; you meet people and you know what their beginning is and you know what their end is. I was writing that kind of story. Again, everything is going towards trying to tell a good story.

ELLIS: John Yardley in his review in the *Washington Post* states that *The Known World* is similar to a Victorian novel. I'm wondering if this was your objective, and if so, why you chose this model?

JONES: I wouldn't call it that, but there were things I read in nineteenth century novels that I liked such as chapter headings. I like the fact that they have an enormous amount of characters. But I wasn't trying to follow any Victorian model at all.

ELLIS: You use census figures and statistics as a means of emphasizing the era, instead of more traditional literary means such as clothing and technology of the times. Do you think your background in the world of mathematic sciences influenced your decision?

JONES: What happened was that once I knew I wasn't going to be using a real county as the setting, I created my own and I had to go about making it real to the reader. Also, I think, part of it was that I wasn't only writing the history of the people but also the history of the county, in an effort to make the reader feel this was a real place.

There are a number of things that I could do as a writer. One of them was talking about the census. I had to make up all the figures of course, because the place isn't real. I didn't go to any book to find out how many people were in Virginia; I just guessed. I made up numbers for Manchester County, which I called the largest of the area.

ELLIS: As you were writing *The Known World* did you concern yourself with the potential reactions readers might have?

JONES: No. The only reader that I cared about, that I wanted to make happy, was me. I didn't think, Well, someone's going to read this book and be shocked. The only thing I cared about was that I didn't want to have a lot of stupid black people; I didn't want to have a sitcom situation. I didn't want to have characters, even though they were slaves, be entirely powerless. No, I didn't have anybody else in mind but myself.

ELLIS: How did you choose the characters' names and were there any particular challenges or ironies in your choices?

JONES: Yes, I think choosing names is very hard. A lot of times I just sat there. For *Lost in the City*, I didn't think of the names as I was writing. I just put question marks there and when it was all done I went to the D.C. phonebook and looked at a first name from one page and a last name from another. But that took a lot of time, and I didn't want to face that procedure again.

So when I was writing *The Known World* I decided to sit in front of the computer and pick names on the spot. Skiffington, I remember I chose that name before I wrote any pages because I wanted a name that sounded English. The only name I consciously wrote down was Celeste. In the back of the dictionary there was a list of names and what they mean. I wanted Celeste as the name for that character as she's probably the most angelic person in the book.

ELLIS: According to Ralph Ellison, "The act of writing requires a constant plunging back into the shadow of the past where time hovers ghostlike." After writing *The Known World* were you better able to understand the phenomena of black men owning black slaves in the Antebellum south?

JONES: No, I didn't give that any thought. I learned about blacks owning slaves when I was in college. And then years and years later I decided to write about it. My only thought was about writing characters, and it just so happens that some of those characters were black people who owned slaves.

So I didn't have any issues in it, and I didn't think about it when it was all over. And I don't think I knew their motivation any better. Part of that is because when I know people I only know them in the book. Had I done research, it might have been a different story. Maybe I would have focused on something that explained them, but I didn't do research. All the people were made up; I didn't have to think about them and come to terms with who they are.

ELLIS: In the short story "The Sunday Following Mother's Day" there's no explanation offered about the man who murdered his wife, who years later, when he is released from jail, wants renewed contact with his children. To what extent is resolution a part of your stories?

JONES: Well, I think in some of them there is resolution. In "The Sunday Following Mother's Day" I think the resolution is that he can never be close to his daughter because of what he did, and the daughter cannot have her father in any way. In "The First Day," for example, this little girl comes to fully realize what it means to be illiterate and that her mother wants her life to be far different. The last line is something like "hearing all the voices of children all over the world, but hearing her mother's voice above all of that." It's just a simple statement that while she grew up and moved into the world and learned more and more, that she would never forget what her mother was and what her mother taught her. So, there might be some stories in which there is no resolution, but there's a tad even so, and in the others I think there is strong resolution.

ELLIS: In your older stories you frequently write from a female perspective. How do you get into the mind-set of a female?

JONES: I don't think about it. The character is there. She does certain things. She has a certain life. I just sit down and start writing. I remember that when I was starting out writing, I remembered to say "this woman is wearing a dress" and similar things, but I don't even think about it now. I just go right into it. I don't go into any mind-altering state at all. The woman is there, she has to do and say these things, and I just go and do the job.

ELLIS: In "All Aunt Hagar's Children," the protagonist, a black man thrust into the role of detective, gives mouth-to-mouth resuscitation to a white woman in the early 1950s. He recalls, "My mother had always told my brother and me that if she ever caught us kissing a white woman she would cut off our lips." Are there challenges you face juxtaposing the internal beliefs and attitudes of your characters next to their external actions?

JONES: I don't see any sort of challenge. There were a thousand things he could have been thinking when this happened. The one thing that would make sense and define both he and his mother was this statement, because this was the first time he had ever kissed a white woman. Again, I just did what I had to do. He's doing this to try to save her life, but his thoughts are almost always on his mother. He has women issues. He has mother issues too. So that thought was more appropriate than almost anything else I could come up with.

ELLIS: Here's another question about "All Aunt Haggar's Children." When the protagonist's family gathers for Sunday dinners, a different flavor of Kool-Aid is served each week, based on the family member who's making the choice, whose turn it is. Are there images and associations that you were hoping to elicit by your choice of Kool-Aid as this family's beverage, and this family's pattern at this particular time?

JONES: No. You're just trying to tell a story and make the readers see these characters. If I had just said they had soda for dinner, it wouldn't have been as interesting; saying all that he says about Kool-Aid, and how he doesn't like this flavor, and that's he worried when the twins come along that his chance to choose the Kool-Aid will change from every third week to every fifth or sixth week. The reader can see this and understand who this person is. That's all I'm trying to do.

ELLIS: How do you come up with the ideas for your stories?

JONES: I'm not sure. I think you just live your life and all of sudden something just pops into your head. And because my mind works a certain way as a storyteller, I immediately begin to think of the story possibilities; I create a world around this thought that came into my head.

ELLIS: More specifically, do you have any recall as to the genesis of "A Rich Man," the story of a man who has been unfaithful to his wife for many years and the life he leads after her death?

JONES: I had a friend who lived in a senior citizens' building, and she told me about this couple that lived in a one-bedroom apartment. One of them stayed in the living room and the other one in the bedroom. She didn't know anything more about them than that. And that's where I got that idea from.
    I started to think of these new stories and I wanted to have characters from *Lost in the City* come again as characters in *All Aunt Haggar's Children*. And so each story in *Lost in the City* will have a corresponding one in *All Aunt Haggar's Children*. In the story "A New Man" in *Lost in the City* it's Elaine Cunningham and then she reappears in "A Rich Man"; this is years later. So that's why she's there, to make the connection.

ELLIS: Do you have a particular place you write or any rituals attached to your writing?

JONES: No, I just get up. I don't care much for coffee but it wakes me up. So I have a cup and turn on the computer. My computer was on the kitchen table in my other apartment and now it's on a table my friend gave me, but it's not big enough for all the things I use, such as the printer; so I have to get a bigger table. I turn on the computer and start writing, and before I get to the chair I think about how I'm going to start, what the first lines will be, and I jump from there.

ELLIS: Do you believe there are benefits from taking time off from writing?

JONES: No, actually I don't believe you can ever really take time off from writing. You're not always busy writing, but you sure are thinking about it. You could be sitting in a movie theater watching a movie and you're thinking, How can I get a character out of the room? What statement can I use?

ELLIS: How do you select your titles?

JONES: Sometimes it's very difficult. And for every story I try to have a title that fits the entire story. But yes, they are hard. I suppose I tell students if all fails to give it the name of the main character.

ELLIS: Is there a particular point you stop writing at the end a day?

JONES: I revise and revise until it looks perfect at that moment. And the good rule is to stop before the well runs dry, so that you will have something to go back to, to start the following day.

ELLIS: Jorge Luis Borges said, "I have always imagined that paradise will be a kind of library." As a writer what is your idea of paradise?

JONES: It's getting up and writing in the morning, ten or fifteen wonderful pages, and then reading part of the afternoon and then watching videos at night.

ELLIS: I've read that you liked comic books as a child, or "funny books" as they were called in D.C. When you started reading regular books, did you love reading them immediately, and were there any writers who were particularly inspirational to you?

JONES: I was reading just about everybody. They all have been inspiring in one way or another. But I was rather unhappy when I went away to college, when people only knew about Washington D.C. in terms of government, but they didn't know about it as a community. I picked up a copy of James Joyce's *The Dubliners*, and of course I was taken by the quality of the work but also that Joyce managed to bring to life so much of Dublin. I was inspired by him, and did the same thing for Washington.

ELLIS: Do you believe your life experiences, in particular your early life experiences, have informed your writing?

JONES: When I write, aside from the people talking within quotation marks, I think I try to have the voice that my mother would use. I can't describe it. It's a Southern voice and there really are clichés that were used once upon a time. People really don't use these phrases anymore: "Every goodbye and gone" and "Every shut eye ain't sleep." I think the voice is almost always hers. Except in cases where the first person is male, but even then sometimes. Especially with a man like the "no-name man" in "Aunt Hagar's Children"; he is very influenced by my mother's voice.

ELLIS: What about your mother's values? Are they also a foundation of your work?

JONES: Yes. I try to treat everyone the way I want them to treat me. Last night I was at a reading. One of the librarians stood up and said it was time for me to leave, but I told her I wanted to be there as long as possible. And there was a long line, even to buy the book, and I tried to smile and be gracious with each and every person.

My mother was in the hospital once and this woman came in who was working with her in a restaurant, and she said to me that the reason she came to see my mother was because when she started working at the restaurant there were no lockers left and no one would share their locker with her, but my mother did.

My mother never stole anything. Well, actually she did when she was younger, before she had kids. She used to crochet and she went into a five and dime and she stole five or ten cents of thread. She said she was haunted for days. She was a very honest person. When she was working at that restaurant she used to have to vacuum the dining room, and one day she found some money. The woman who it belonged to gave her a reward and came back and shook her hand. There was no one around; I don't know how much money it was. The man who owned the restaurant had a room there. He kept change on a tray. And the only person he'd have clean the room was my mother.

ELLIS: Do you think writers need teachers?

JONES: No, I don't.

ELLIS: Do you have any advice for unpublished writers?

JONES: Just read and write, and read and write. That's what people do who are compelled to write. I could never give any advice to people who write because they want to be rich and famous. I generally read just for pleasure and I can rely on someone's work when I'm reading along, but I'm basically the same person I was when I was a teenager; I pick up a book if it looks interesting, and I just enjoy a good story.

ELLIS: Ha Jin said, "I think a writer can only write about what is close to his heart." Do you agree?

JONES: Yes, I guess that's true. I don't have any desire to write about Martians. I suppose I'll always write about black people. When I wrote *The Known World* my intention was just to write about slaves that were owned by Townsend and the story got away from me. I never imagined that I'd be writing about so many white people. As things moved along people just took on larger and larger roles. Skiffington, Mr. Robbins, people like that.

ELLIS: Are you working on something new?

JONES: I'm still working on the stories for *All Aunt Hagar's Children*. It's due in August. I've got six stories to finish.

Julia Glass

A Palette of Words

Julia Glass, winner of the 2002 National Book Award for Fiction, invited the characters in *Three Junes* to set up a home inside of her head. *Three Junes* is a lush and evocative novel told through the eyes of a grieving Scottish widower, a single pregnant woman, and a young gay man. It unfurls over the course of three Junes (1989, 1995, and 1999) and spans two continents. When she accepted the National Book Award for Fiction, Glass dedicated her speech to "late bloomers"; her first short story was published when she was thirty-seven, her first novel nearly a decade later.

Glass has always been a lover of books, and from fifth grade through high school she worked at the public library in her hometown. As an undergraduate at Yale University, she studied art and subsequently spent a year painting and drawing in Paris on a travel fellowship. A few years later, when she found herself drawn toward writing fiction, she felt guilty about devoting her time and energy to an art form other than the one she had studied. During the next ten years she faced many personal traumas, including the end of a marriage, breast cancer and the suicide of her sister.

In 1993, Glass was awarded a Nelson Algren Fiction Award for "My Sister's Scar." In 1999, her novella *Collies* won the Pirate's Alley Faulkner Society Medal for Best Novella. (*Collies* was the genesis, and ultimately the first part, of *Three Junes*.) In 2000 she was awarded both a New York Foundation for the Arts fellowship in Fiction and a Nelson Algren Fiction Award for "The World We've Made." In 2001, she won the Ames Memorial Essay Award for her essay "My Sister, My Surgeon, Myself."

In May 2002 *Three Junes* was a selection of the ABC/*Good Morning America* Read This! Book Club. *Three Junes* was also a May/June 2002 selection of Book Sense 76. In 2004 Glass was awarded a National Endowment for the Arts Literature Fellowship as well as a fellowship at the Radcliffe Institute for Advanced Study, which enabled her to finish her second novel, *The Whole World Over*, which was published by Pantheon Books in May 2006.

Julia Glass's stories have appeared in *American Short Fiction*, the *Bellingham Review* and the *Chicago Tribune* Literary Awards supplement. Her essays and feature articles have appeared in the *New York Times*, *Publishers Weekly*,

Gourmet, Redbook, More, Glamour, Parenting, Literal Latte, and in the anthology *Kiss Tomorrow Hello: Notes From the Midlife Underground by Twenty-five Women Over Forty,* edited by Kim Barnes and Claire Davis (Doubleday, 2006). Her paintings have been exhibited at the Brooklyn Museum of Art, the National Academy of Design, and various art galleries. She has also designed and hooked rugs, several of which appear in the book *Punch Needle Rug Hooking* by Amy Oxford (Schiffer, 2002).

In the fall of 2003 I met with her over coffee at Tartine, a café in Greenwich Village. The frames of her eyeglasses were spring green and emphasized her ginger-colored hair.

SHERRY ELLIS: In the *New York Times*, Katherine Wolff stated that *Three Junes* contains "fitting locales for a novel that illustrates emotional isolation." What do you believe is the importance of the locations you selected for *Three Junes*?

JULIA GLASS: People ask me about the locations, and certainly on a simple level I chose locations that I know to some extent. At the point I wrote the novel, I'd only been to Greece once, for two weeks, in 1979. I hadn't spent too much time in Scotland either; my mother had done genealogical research and found cousins of hers, and I was sent to visit them when I was seventeen.

Having finished the book though, and looking back on it, I see that there is a certain amount of symbolic resonance to some of the settings. I think of Greece, for example. What country is more steeply rooted in the past than Greece? And Paul MacLeod is of course reviewing his past. There are temples everywhere and goddesses preserved in alabaster, and there Paul MacLeod is, haunted by the memory of his wife whom he adored and had put on a pedestal. And Scotland is a place that I very much associate with family, and I don't just mean my family. Scotland seems like a very obvious choice symbolically, to set a family drama, the history being full of family loyalty on the one hand, and quite violent betrayal on the other hand. Actually I think that Mal makes illusion to it briefly.

However, it's also true that when I'm writing fiction, I love to sit by my computer in my little apartment and travel somewhere in my head that's almost embarrassingly touristy. I love the shore of Long Island. In some ways I may have done something that is easy for a beginning writer to do, to choose picture postcard locales. The one danger is that such settings may upset the events in a story—but I think I'm able to actually take a lot of control of description of setting. I'm able to take places that are very stereotypical and give them particular personality in my writing, because of my visual background.

ELLIS: Several of your characters long to change themselves. In "Boys," the third section of *Three Junes*, Anna says to Fern, "When it comes to life, we spin our own yarn, and where we end up is really, in fact, where we always intended to be." Can you discuss the character you had the most challenge developing and explain why?

GLASS: That's interesting. Of the major characters, I think Fern is the biggest challenge for me and I think that is because outwardly she is the most like me, although she is not an entirely autobiographical character. However, I did go to Paris and paint for a year on a fellowship for independence; I did go through a struggle changing what I was doing, a little bit more radically, as I made the change from painting to writing; and I think that her very intense, intimate feelings about mistakes she has made in love, and her hopes and fears—especially as someone who is about to become a parent—are similar to emotional crises I've gone through. I had to be careful to draw a line between my own experience, having had a failed marriage before the relationship I have now been in for thirteen years, and the experience I invented for Fern. In general, I had to keep a firewall between some of the characters' hearts and mine.

Also, Fern's part of the book is the part I really had to do some significant revision on after the book was bought by my publisher. I know that some readers are disappointed in a way, after Fenno's part of the book ends, because they feel he has the strongest voice—though I've met a few readers who like the Fern section better. The challenge was to maintain the strength of that middle section despite the fact that Fern is simply not as large or daring a character as Fenno. The other characters were easier for me because they truly were fabricated and it wasn't so messy working inside their heads.

ELLIS: As you were writing *Three Junes* what were the things that you most wanted to learn?

GLASS: How to get through incredible loss, how to go forward when a lot of things in life have made you stumble emotionally, crippled you, and when you have terrible regrets about mistakes that you have made or ill fortune that's befallen you. There's a kind of determination in the book to create a happy ending or reasonable resolution for the three principal characters, to see them blossom even though they've been deeply, even inconsolably wounded. But I don't think I knew that beforehand. I was really just setting out in the dark and I was looking forward to the story just a little bit at a time. I never had much of an overview until I was close to the end, and that's when I thought to myself that I'd better take stock of the whole story or I'd be lost. I really don't write from a plot line; I write from characters. Who those characters are, and how they interact, is what creates the story. Just to finish the book was incredible, to sell the book was incredible, and of course, what has happened with it since is incredible; I pinch myself every day.

ELLIS: How do you think your writing relates to your painting?

GLASS: I majored in studio art when I went to college, even though I loved reading fiction and I wrote good papers, in part because writing was more of a challenge than painting—not to say that I didn't have talent. I loved working with color, and I experimented with everything from still life and portraiture to big abstract canvases depicting arrangements of dark floating shapes. I won a fellowship after graduation to paint in Paris for a year, and that's when I turned seriously to figurative painting and drawing. I ended up in New York in the early 1980s, doing large oil paintings of people in rooms. I'm not sure how to describe them except to say they were definitely narrative, suggested odd goings-on. I'll admit I was greatly inspired by Balthus at the time, though my work wasn't quite so sexual!

I started to write fiction in my late twenties, and eventually I had to choose between my writing and my artwork—because I was also making a living. Until I published *Three Junes*, I often felt regretful that I might have "wasted" all those years on art, but what I've realized is that my writing is intensely visual, that I would never write the way I do had I not been trained—and trained myself—to look at the world as a painter.

I had wonderful English teachers in high school at Concord Academy, a school that has turned out a lot of writers, and it made me a solid wordsmith and a good reader, but I didn't study creative writing after that. And so I believe I work, not exactly as an outsider, because with my education I certainly wasn't an outsider, but as someone who didn't go through the system of taking workshops and getting an MFA. I'm sorry I didn't get to hang out with writers, get an earlier start, and have mentors the way a lot of people do after they get out of writing school, but I got to make my own rules rather than following those set down by a group of teachers.

ELLIS: A border collie named Rodgie and a parrot named Felicity contribute significantly to the themes of life and death in *Three Junes*. As you were writing this novel did you intend for them to take on such important roles?

GLASS: Yes, I did, because actually the novel originally grew out of a story called "Souvenirs," which I developed into the section of the novel called "Collies." So dogs were obviously important to the story. I don't think it is possible for me to write fiction without animals having some important or at least secondary role, partly because of the way that I grew up.

Animals were very important in my family. I grew up with horses, foxhounds, and cats. My sister was an aspiring veterinarian since the time she was about four; she always had a shoe box with a squirrel with a broken leg or some nest of eggs that she found. And my first published writing was a pet column in *Glamour* magazine. That was back when I was still mainly painting—funny to think that I supported my artwork with writing!—and part of the reason I got the column was that people would always come to me for advice about their pets. So somehow animals always creep into my fiction.

My sister, when she was a veterinarian in Brookline, had a roommate who had an Eclectus parrot. Eclectuses are quite extraordinary. The male is entirely neon-lime-green and the female is fire engine red with a purple breast, and as pairs in the wild they are astonishing. It is not a case where just the male is showy and color; the female is quite remarkable too. She wouldn't say much, but she was a very alluring animal and would sit on your shoulder and groom your ear. And I always remembered that, and when I started writing fiction I knew that I would eventually use her.

ELLIS: I've read that there's a connection between *Three Junes* and the art form known as a triptych. Can you describe what a triptych is and how *Three Junes* relates to it?

GLASS: I was writing along as if I was in a rowboat far out in the ocean, not knowing where I was heading and looking hard for the horizon. I had written "Collies," a story unto itself, and I was about two-thirds of the way through Fenno's section of the book when I began to worry about my direction. Was I writing a two-part novel? Was I going to end up throwing away "Collies"? Was the novel, in the end, going to be totally from Fenno's point of view? I really didn't have an idea. And then I realized how much I like three-part things, and that I'd like to write a three-part novel. So if I kept the father's point of view and moved into the son's, whose point of view would I choose for part three?

The original story that "Collies" was based on, "Souvenirs," was really about Fern. It was about this young woman on a Greek island who has an affair with an English tour guide, the Jack character, and the Scottish widower (who became Paul MacLeod) was a tiny extra in the story; he had perhaps a single line. Somehow I wound up re-writing the piece from the widower's point of view, though I did think I would love to get back and write from Fern's eyes in some other story. So when I went back and decided that I would write the third part, I decided to bring the novel full circle by making it Fern's tale. In the end of the book Fenno is to Fern what she was to his father in the beginning.

I realized the first part was somewhat short, and the second part was getting quite long, I was in the middle of writing it, and then I thought of these beautiful medieval altar pieces that I fell in love with when I audited an art class on medieval Netherlandish painting. In these intense three-panel paintings, there is always a central image of something tragic—a crucification, or a deposition from the cross, a grisly martyrdom—with two flanking panels, narrower, quieter images that often depict a pair of saints, a pair of angels or the donors who gave the money for the altarpiece to be commissioned, and they're usually shown in profile; kneeling and facing the central image. This made me think about the voices I was using in the novel. I knew that Fenno's part was in the first person, Paul's part was in the third person, and I was struggling with Fern's part. Fenno had a frontal relationship to the reader, and his story is to some degree a tragic story, not entirely and not ultimately, but that middle part is quite sad, and so I thought, That's it: This book is a triptych, with Paul and Fern as the flanking panels to Fenno's drama, and I worked hard to keep Fern's section of the book parallel in its brevity. I liked the idea that by telling Paul's and Fern's story in third person I was showing them in profile.

ELLIS: Based on similarities in style and structure, *Three Junes* has also been compared to the work of nineteenth century novelists. Who are your favorites of the nineteenth century and were they inspirations to you when you were involved in the writing of *Three Junes*?

GLASS: Well, my goddess is George Eliot, and I love Jane Austen and Thomas Hardy. I think that I didn't really discover nineteenth century novelists, or most of them, until I'd graduated from college and I was living in New York and painting. I read more at that time in my life than before or since. I read all of E.M. Forster, most of Jane Austen, and I remember reading George Eliot on my ride back and forth to my job at *Cosmopolitan* magazine, which supported my painting for two years. I immersed myself in those books very privately and personally. Basically, I was reading everything I would have, had I been an English major; it was like becoming a fiction writer without going to workshops.

Eventually, I began to feel that I had to write fiction myself, and began to do it at night, which was generally the time I worked on my painting, so I felt very guilty about it. I like to say that *Daniel Deronda* by George Eliot is the book that turned my head back to writing. It is her last novel and not her best, but it is just breathtaking. I remember feeling so excited and even inspired by the way she used language, the compelling characters and the daring structure; I remember saying to myself, "I want to do this." I began to understand the part of my brain that uses language was being neglected and I needed to attend to it.

I have this great thirst now to read more of these writers, and to re-read the books I already love, but suddenly I have so little reading time.

ELLIS: Michael Cunningham stated that *Three Junes* "almost threatens to burst with all the life it contains. Glass's ability to locate the immense within the particular, and to simultaneously illuminate and deepen the mysteries of her characters' lives, would be marvelous in any novelist. In a first-time novelist, it's extraordinary." Are there similarities between your painting and writing, for example, the way in which as a painter you use a palette of color and as a writer you use a metaphoric palette of words?

GLASS: I love words just in and of themselves. My seven-year-old son is very interested in reading and he often asks me what certain words mean, which makes me think about words that I take for granted. In my painting I would say that I gravitated towards using intense greens and reds, and very recently I've actually realized that I love words that have "v's" in them, like "vivid" and "livid" and "vivacious" and "voluptuous." There are words that I sometimes have to edit out of my writing; I use "vivid" all the time.

ELLIS: What do you mean by your statement that writers should allow their characters to set up homes in their heads?

GLASS: Well, I think it's like having imaginary friends as a child. You imagine people in a situation and they begin to talk. Often when I'm walking down the street or doing my shopping or riding on the subway, or waiting in line, which you do often in New York City, or if I sit stuck in traffic, I think of my stories, different people interacting with one another; I don't know where it comes from, it just comes. In the case of Fenno, I was possessed by him as much as I have ever been by any character in my fiction. At the time I created him, I was spending time walking my older son to and from the playground, or to and from his babysitter, and I was imagining Fenno's story, this character and his life; that's how so much of it became set in Greenwich Village.

Spending time alone in my head is very important. That's when most of my ideas come. When I'm sitting at the computer I'm sort of downloading all those files. All the plot twists, and ideas I get about new characters come when I'm just out and about.

ELLIS: E.M. Forster said, "Ends always give me trouble. Characters will run away with you . . ." Did you experience difficulty bringing *Three Junes* to an end?

GLASS: Not really. I knew how I wanted the book to end. Maybe what was hardest was getting to the end from the middle, but I knew where I was going. Writing Fern's part of the book was the hardest for me. I knew I was getting to this moment where she and Fenno were going to be united in a certain way. So, no. It wasn't very hard for me to bring the book to an end.

The novel I'm working on now may be harder to end. But I'm not far enough into it to know. They say you're not really a novelist until you've written more than one novel.

ELLIS: Who are your favorite more recent twentieth century writers?

GLASS: Peter Cameron is a contemporary novelist whose work I admire enormously. I love Faulkner. Andre Dubus the elder—his work was like a bible to me when I thought I was a short story writer; there are very few male writers I know of who write about love, jealousy, the conflicts between faith and lust—all the big questions of the heart—as movingly and intimately as he does. Another writer who stands right up there is Alice Munro. She's mysterious; you can't even begin to try to imitate one of her stories. To me, she writes about how the most seemingly insignificant decisions we make in life change the entire course of our lives. She manages to build, in the space of a short story, a world that you can only imagine would be held in a novel. I love Jim Harrison and Iris Murdoch. I love a short story writer—like me, from Massachusetts—named Ralph Lombreglia who wrote two collections called *Men Under Water* and *Make Me Work*. Another writer, John Dufresne, also from Massachusetts, wrote an incredible novel, *Love Warps the Mind*.

And John Casey. And Michael Cunningham. I'm reading his second novel, *A Home at the End of the World*, which is the first published book I've read in quite a while, and I loved *Flesh and Blood* and, of course, *The Hours*. And I love Richard Russo; *Empire Falls* is a masterpiece.

ELLIS: How did you respond when you were informed that you won the National Book Award, and how has it changed your life?

GLASS: The afternoon of the ceremony the judges for each of the four winning categories are sent off together to make the decision. You don't know you are the winner until it is announced at the ceremony. So that night Bob Shacochis, the fiction chair, described all the fiction finalists and then the winner. It took me a while to realize that book was mine. When he said my name I began to shake and cry, but I bolted up from the table. I think I was afraid he might change his mind. I had never expected to win; in fact, I remember wanting the process of being a finalist to last forever.

And it was so remarkable to be there with all the people who had the faith in my book to publish it. It felt really great to stand up on the stage and say the names of all the individuals who had helped me. Somehow I did it. Steve Martin was standing with me on the biggest stage that I had ever seen, and he made a joke as I was making my acceptance speech. Surreal, to say the least, and terrifying, and glorious.

Thank goodness my agent, Gail Hochman, had called me first thing that morning to check-in and see how I doing. She asked me if I had an acceptance speech written and she reminded me that I could win, though it was unlikely. She suggested that I write the names of people I would thank, so they wouldn't fly out of my head. So I did that, on a tiny piece of paper, along with a few remarks about what books mean to me, and slipped in into my evening purse, and then I went on with my day. It was a beautiful spring-like day in late November, and I went running.

The whole experience was a Cinderella story. But the story's not over by any means. Now I have to go on continuing to be a writer.

ELLIS: What advice do you have for new writers?

GLASS: Certainly I would say you do have to be persistent. I went through having my stories rejected—nicely, encouragingly for a long, long time; many years. But there are people who think you can't get published without connections, and that's not really true. There are people who think that you have to have an MFA; but you don't have to have an MFA. You have to have a lot of self-discipline. Although that is not how I describe myself, the proof is in the pudding. And you can't take all the "rules" of fiction writing seriously. You read a lot of interviews with writers who say there is one certain thing you have to do: the one I hate the most is that you have to write every day. It's not true. To be a good writer you don't have to put words on paper every day. Sometimes, because I had to earn a living while I was writing *Three Junes* I didn't get to write for three weeks; but the characters were alive in my head. Also, I don't believe you have to have a room of your own.

I do think it is tough to get a collection of stories published as your first book. Although people do it, it's harder these days than it used to be. I wrote a novel because I finally realized I wasn't going to get a collection of stories published. It's funny, because I had really thought of myself as a short story writer. It doesn't mean you have to write a novel, but as a fiction writer I think you probably should.

A good agent can make all the difference. I had a great experience. The first agent I queried picked me and I think she happens to be one of the best agents in the business. That was a great fortune for me.

So I think you have to persevere, you have to be able to take rejection, and you have to be patient. And I also think you should apply for every competition you can, big and small, and state fellowships, little short story awards, anything and everything out there, because it helps to accumulate a literary resume. Every month I'd comb through the section of *Poets and Writers* magazine listing grants and contests. And I'd send my stories out to the *Atlantic*, the *New Yorker* and to more obscure quarterlies.

ELLIS: What challenges are you facing as you create a new fictional world for your novel-in-progress, *The Whole World Over*?

GLASS: Well, there certainly are many. *The Whole World Over* takes place in New York City and also in Maine and New Mexico, nowhere you need a passport this time around. One incidental problem, a case of real life intruding on fiction, has to with the fact that when I started writing this book, in the summer of 2001, I decided to set it over two years—2001 and 2002. And then of course September 11th happened. September 11th has changed what it is like to live in New York City now, and what it is like to live in this world, so the novel is digesting this trauma too.

Another challenge is that I'm writing the novel from four different points of view. One is that of a woman who had a serious head trauma that had a lasting effect on her memory and on her ability to function in everyday life. She's disabled. I'm not sure where this character came from, how she emerged from my psyche, but there she is.

Arthur Golden

A Sense of Urgency

Arthur Golden has been interested in writing stories since he was five years old. By the time he was in high school and college his interest in story writing grew and he also started writing newspaper articles. No matter what academic path he followed, including his undergraduate study of art history, his graduate study of Japanese history, his advanced study of Chinese at a university in Beijing, his interest and love of writing and language kept resurfacing. In 1982, after spending a year in Japan working for a Japanese magazine, he realized that he wanted to tell the story of what it was like to live in Japan.

Golden subsequently embarked upon earning a Master's degree in creative writing, and he spent the next ten years writing *Memoirs of a Geisha*. Because he worked on this novel for such a long time his mother and brother worried that he was in a "drop-out phase."

After *Memoirs of a Geisha* was published there was an extraordinary positive public response and it was included on the *New York Times* bestseller list for over a hundred weeks. In 1997 it was selected as a Notable Book by the *New York Times*. In 2005 it was made into a film by Steven Spielberg.

Golden has taught writing at Northwestern University and at the Cambridge Center for Adult Education, but spends the majority of his time writing. He and his wife live in greater Boston. I met with him in the library of their home.

SHERRY ELLIS: The beginning of *Memoirs of a Geisha* is told in a child's voice, that of Chiyo. How difficult was it for you to master the language of childhood?

ARTHUR GOLDEN: Well, I think I can answer best in the larger context of other problems about language. As you know the book is written from the point of view of a woman, but the point of view of a woman who is Japanese. The presumption is that the book is translated to English, which of course it isn't really; it's originally written in English. But there is something very particular that I bore in mind as I was developing the voice of the story, which is that Japanese has a situation that is rather similar to our situation in English. There are good old Anglo-Saxon roots and then there are the Latinate roots, Latinate words. In English language usage for the most part, the kind of language we use is of course Anglo-Saxon language; that you say a car instead of an automobile. People who may not be educated or who may speak in anger will use this more simple language and only educated people tend to speak in more complicated Latinate roots. It turns out that it's similar in Japan with both Japanese and Chinese. Literally, Chinese roots in Japan are just like Latinate roots are in English. And the man traditionally, at least in the olden days, spoke with Chinese pretentious usage words and the woman spoke with the native Japanese words. So right away it was suggested to me that the thing to do was to keep the language of the Anglo-Saxon, so to speak, and not to dress it up with Latinate roots. Right away, that put the voice into the language of simplicity and straightforwardness.

The step from there to a child's voice wasn't anything significant in my mind. I didn't say to myself, "I am now writing in the language of a child." It was more the observation, her experience of the world around her as a child, that I felt was different in the beginning of the book than in the end. That's in part because not only is Chiyo's understanding not as sophisticated, but her experiences are more limited. She has a more limited palate with which to paint when she wants to describe something. She has to draw on ideas about the sea which she experiences, or the pond where she swims; she doesn't really have a lot to go on. When she gets a little older she has cities, electrical lighting, and her world view expands in this way. She is able to draw more and more on more sophisticated things.

ELLIS: How did you leave your male personality and voice behind as Chiyo matured into adulthood?

GOLDEN: Writing from the point of a view of a woman as a man has very little to do with language. I think it has to do more with two things. One is imagining the experience that the character is having, bearing in mind the character's experiences of the world, their attitudes, their hopes and their expectations. I don't think that's any different from what a fiction writer does always. But I do think that when you're writing from the point of view of a woman it's useful to bear in mind that men and women come to experiences in different ways.

There is one more thing though, and that is that when you're sitting down to write from the point of view of a woman and if you ask yourself what it's like to be a woman, what it feels like to be a woman waking up in the morning, that is the wrong question. The issue is *what* woman. You have to be very, very specific about the character. The more specific you can be about your character, their hopes and expectations, the better. You are writing about an innate moment in time, where she's coming from, what has gotten in her way. Then it's not a complicated problem to solve.

ELLIS: Was first person point of view your first choice?

GOLDEN: No, it wasn't. I wrote the novel twice in third person. There were three separate versions of this novel. The first one I wrote after I had begun writing fiction a few years earlier and I wanted to write a novel about Japan. I had been to Japan; I knew the culture and spoke the language. The first draft wasn't about geisha. It was about a woman whose mother was a geisha. I didn't know much and then I found a book by chance about geisha by this woman named Liza Dalby which helped me with background information. After I read it I realized I was writing the wrong thing, because the subculture was so much more interesting than what I had been writing.

So I decided to write a novel about a geisha. Well, at first I wasn't going to write it in the first person because it seemed too scary. What I did was I wrote the novel in third person about an adult geisha focusing on five years in her life. When I got to the end of it—it took me about three years—I got a phone call from a friend saying she had found an actual geisha for me to interview. So I went over to Japan and interviewed her, but I didn't ask her opinion about her experiences, her particular experiences. What I wanted to know from her was what it is like to wake up as a geisha, how you get your hair cut, how much does it cost, what it feels like, how late do you stay up at night, those kinds of things.

Then I realized I had gotten the story wrong and that I had to start over again, but with the same basic premise, this time five years in the life of a geisha. When I finished that draft, now it had been about six years on the project, I passed it around to a few publishers in the industry. There was a lot of interest at first, but after they read it there were a lot of reservations. Everyone found it dry. Of course I wasn't happy about that but I wasn't going to give up the project. What I had to figure out was what I had done wrong. I think what I'd done wrong was that I focused on an adult geisha rather than a child, when so much of the drama was in childhood. And then I had been afraid of impersonating a woman and therefore writing in third person kept a considerable distance from the character. If I was going to get closer and try to really imagine the character's experiences then I might as well do it in first person; and there were very good reasons to do so. I thought about it for a while. I was six years into the project when I took that leap. It wasn't my first choice, in other words.

ELLIS: So you had extreme tenacity. How important a quality do you think tenaciousness is for a writer?

GOLDEN: I think it is *the* quality you have to have as a writer. I think it is more important than talent. Because to be perfectly honest, how talented are writers? Pick your least favorite writer of airplane books. How much talent is in evidence there? Not a whole lot. The person is able to weave "a yarn," but as far as imagining the life of characters and writing reputable prose and the things that we go to literary novels for, it's not there. What the person did was stick with it and put together something that he feels makes an enjoyable read, and other people believe this too. But you can't do that without tenacity.

I actually know one novelist who completed a book on first draft, sent it off to his publisher, and it was purchased; but only one. The other writers I know wrote a manuscript, sent it off, nobody wanted it, and they wrote another manuscript. In my case it's actually three manuscripts. So I think tenacity is very important and an underrated thing.

There's a very sad story I hear from a lot from people. They'll say, "I always wanted to be a writer and after I saved up a little money in my early twenties I went off to a little cabin. I decided to spend a year writing my novel. At the end of the year I read it over and I realized that I had no talent and I went back to my job." That is an extremely sad story because first of all, I don't think it makes any difference if you have talent. If you can write a sentence competently, you can probably write a story that people will want to read. I'm not trying to say that talent is meaningless. I do think it means something and the more talented you are the better you will do when you set out to write, perhaps, but a lot of people have enough talent. What they don't have is that willingness to look at what they produce over the course of a single year, and learn that the lesson is that a year is not enough. The lesson is "I have to do it again." I can see there are things wrong with it, I don't know what I'm doing, and I have to learn. The one thing I love most about writing is that it doesn't matter how long you've been doing it, you're still learning.

ELLIS: Coming back to your use of language, as I read *Memoirs of a Geisha* it seemed as if you were trying to emulate the cadence of the Japanese language. Is this accurate?

GOLDEN: Yes, I think it is. The languages are very different of course, so there's only so much you can do. But within the limitations, I'd say that's right, that was what I was trying to do. I think I was creating an illusion really, because you can't really imitate the cadence of Japanese with English, you just can't do it. When we speak in English we emphasize parts of words, or words, by stressing them, or by raising our tone. Japanese do that in a very, very different way. The Japanese language to most Americans sounds quite flat when it is spoken. What are you going to do in English to reproduce that? But what you can reproduce is the kind of hesitancy, certain indirect qualities with which certain subjects are approached that feels right to Americans, even when they don't know Japanese, that strikes chords with the culture so that they feel some authenticity.

Also, for example, the Japanese don't say the word "you" very often; it is considered too direct. Japanese culture is almost founded on the principle that politeness and being indirect are the same thing. Politeness is paramount. You never want to offend someone. You don't say, "Do you understand?" That's considered extremely rude. First of all, you don't address someone as "you." And secondly, you don't ask them if they understand you because that's presuming that they might not understand. You're supposed to say, "I'm so sorry I expressed myself poorly." It's very different in our culture. Pretty much only outside your house and outside of your circle of friends do you use someone's title or people's names. So Sayuri's always saying, "*Nobu-san,*" this or that, when she's talking. That's another way that the illusion appears in the novel.

ELLIS: What were the challenges of bringing the third version of *Memoirs of a Geisha* to an end?

GOLDEN: Well, there were quite a number of them, and I think of three in particular. It gets a little complicated. One is the challenge that everyone has ending a book. It's hard to give it up. It's hard to end it and you have a certain kind of resistance. That's something that people who never did this kind of work don't necessarily understand. Once you've put so much of yourself into something, it's like sending your child off to college. Very few people give them a kiss and send them off and say they're done with them; it's not like that. So there's that challenge.

The second challenge had to do with somehow finding a way to bring the narrative to a natural conclusion and that was very difficult because I conceived of the book as being about a young girl who has everything in life taken away from her, at the opening of the novel, and struggles forever to find something that will pay her back for her loss. The reason that Sayuri attaches herself to the Chairman, fixates on the Chairman, is because he has been kind to her in a period in her life where there is no one, and he gives her the hope there may yet be kindness in the world, somewhere. She really needs to have the hope, but that is a very different thing than being in love with him. I really don't think this is a love story, that Sayuri's in love with him or that he's in love with her. Not to mention that they don't know really each other the way we know our husbands and wives. He's only ever seen her as a geisha; she's only ever seen him as a customer. That's a characteristic of Japanese society too, this sort of role-playing. The question is, will she end up with the Chairman? Will she end up with Nobu? There were very good arguments in having her end up with Nobu, and I tried it, but I couldn't get it to work. It just felt too artificial. And I'm not going to say there wasn't any artificiality of having her end up with the Chairman. I think bringing a narrative to an end is a bit artificial.

And then there was the third challenge which was the most difficult one of all in some ways. When I had set out to write the book in first person I got to seventy-five pages into the book and developed a cold sweat, because I realized I faced a real problem. When I had written the book in third person the narrator had been at liberty to step away from the narrative whenever we needed him to and fill us in on Japanese culture that we might not have a way of understanding. But the geisha herself, if she was telling the story directly to us, and if she'd lived her whole life in Kyoto, she wouldn't know what we needed to know, what we needed to have annotated, and she wouldn't know how to annotate it; she wouldn't know what was in our mind. That really worried me very much. I realized that if Sayuri spent the last twenty years in the United States and if she told her story looking back through the filter of the American experience, that she would then be in a position to tell the story for us. But the other trick was that she had to tell it to a westerner. If she was talking to a Japanese person or what was presumed to be a Japanese audience the filter would get removed from the camera so to speak and she would be speaking directly. That wouldn't work. So I had to introduce into the narrative, in the beginning, this western-receiving consciousness and that was through the translator. That is the purpose of the translator, is to introduce those things I just explained, so that the reader wouldn't know they were there. So that when she is talking and she says, "You may not know this but in Japan we do it like this and we do it like that," we understand why she is saying it. We understand that she is an older woman and she is talking to a westerner. In the conclusion of the novel I had to find a way to wrap that up. For me, in a way, the narrative ends in Japan, but there is no explanation of how Sayuri got to New York and why. I labored over a hundred and fifty pages for six months trying to find a way to get her to the United States, it was a big elaborate thing with Nobu and a scandal and she had to leave the country. Everything after felt like the engine had died. It just didn't work. So I got rid of all of that and decided to find the simplest possible way in a few pages to find out how she got to the United States, and that ended up being the last chapter. It's a chapter I'm very fond of, as it turned out.

So the answer is it was very difficult. I think it's very difficult to end a book.

ELLIS: Philip Roth once said, "I often have to write a hundred pages or more before there's a paragraph that's alive." Do you agree?

GOLDEN: Sometimes I feel that what I'm writing isn't alive. For me it's usually because I'm not able to project myself into the character's dilemma and to stay engaged. I've found myself writing something that feels a little artificial, a little bit forced. It isn't that it is difficult to remain involved with the character at every moment. In fact most of the time I feel I'm engaged with the character, but having a sense of place and time and specificity are so incredibly important to me. If you don't know what the situation is, if you don't know why you are there, it feels generic. When I read something I've written and I know the smell, for example, if the character is in a lumberyard and I smell the lumber, the sawdust, and the character's gone there for a specific reason, there's something on the character's mind, then I'm engaged. When I take a wrong step it begins to feel hollow, and I get a little lost. Then I have to go back and fix it. I ask myself if this is what the character would really do, if this is what the character would really feel.

ELLIS: Which comes first when you are writing, plot or character?

GOLDEN: Well, I have to tell you the honest truth. I hate the word "plot" and use the word "narrative" instead. The reason why is I think that plot suggests something that is independent of character and is independent of feelings. It's just its own element. I don't think there is such a thing as plot, at least not for me. The incidents that occur in the novel are an expression of something much larger. Here, I'll give you an example of what I mean. If I'm a fictional character at a dinner table and I'm having dinner at someone's house and the host looks at me just a moment longer than he should, that has no meaning. But if the character has had an affair with the man's wife that look means everything, that's a big deal moment in the novel. How the characters are going to react to it depends on everything that has happened before, what kind of character he is. Plot sounds like a pre-configured series of events that you can plug almost anything you want into. It seems to me essential that the next step in your work be determined by everything that is there: what has come before, what are these people trying to do, how do they respond in this moment to this obstacle, how does the character say his words? It's not plot, it's not a construction; it's an integral movement that involves the characters and the meaning of the story. That look did or didn't have meaning based on what happened before, what is in the mind of the character. And so I believe that story is defined by meaning and momentum to events. In isolation the event has no meaning.

So, do I start with character or narrative? Saying all that, I start with character. Then I sit down and try to sort out ways to give expression to these qualities and this dilemma and this life struggle that I've imagined through a sequence of events that constitute in the end the narrative. I do it in a way that is probably different than other writers, that I find very useful. I sit and brainstorm in front of the computer—hundreds of pages. For example, Chiyo by the seashore in the beginning of the novel: What happens if she has a brother? How many family members does she have? I start asking myself these questions. If my aim is to get her taken away from the seashore, what might happen? If her mother dies that might precipitate it, but why wouldn't she remain with her father? Well, one reason might be that her father is very old and he looks like he's on the brink of death too; and when I think of this it has an added benefit. Once she gets to Kyoto she will want to come home, but if her father is very old, she is stuck there. This means she can't have a brother, because in Japan a brother takes over. So her mother has to be sick and her father has to be old and she can't have a brother. These are all expressions of the aim of the narrative and I explore what I want to achieve. When she gets to Kyoto she is suffering over so many wrongs, it's not hard to imagine that the novel would be bleak. But if she has something she wants to do, to find her sister and return to her village, it gives me, the writer, a way to find my way through her struggle. Her desperation to find her sister is an expression of the profundity of her grief without me, the writer, being forced into writing an existential treatise.

ELLIS: How important is the use of metaphors to you?

GOLDEN: Well, to me a metaphor has a very specific purpose to serve. If you get to the end of a passage, maybe a sentence or a paragraph, and you've already expressed what you're trying to, and then you throw in a metaphor, it feels like something that's been stapled on and that is artificial. Metaphors only work when they actually enhance the reader's understanding, and I chose to use them frequently in the book, or some kind of imagery, because I wanted to give expression to an idea about Chiyo, which was that when she was very young she was sold into this world of geisha where cleverness is one of the chief virtues that helps you rise. So cleverness and some sort of liveliness of mind would help her not only to be a successful geisha but would give an explanation of why she gets sold out of her childhood home in the first place. She meets a man who recognizes in her some liveliness of mind and he thinks it would serve her well as a geisha. And for this reason I found it best that Chiyo frequently express herself in images of one kind or another. She has this quality that causes her to express herself in somewhat poetic ways rather than describing things in a way that an engineer might. That's why images and metaphor were really integral to the book.

ELLIS: Why did you call this novel "memoirs" in the plural and not "memoir" in the singular?

GOLDEN: After I wrote it I remember struggling with the title. I remember the act of writing the words "Memoirs of a Geisha" in very large type, and inserting it in the manuscript, and that as I did it I thought I would come up with something better. I thought about it and wondered if it was right or if it should be "memoir." I remember looking at books called *The Memories* and found occasional books called *The Memoir* or *A Memoir* and found that for some reason the phrase "memoirs" is used a lot and so I left it that way.

ELLIS: Katherine Anne Porter once said, "Your style is an emanation from your own being." Do you agree?

GOLDEN: I think it's absolutely, absolutely, entirely true. I have to tell you first that my family was playing a very interesting literary game with friends, a game in which you're given the name and title of a real book and the first line of the book is known by the asker and everyone else has to write a first line. Then everyone has to read their line and you vote on which is the correct line. I had a great time with this game. At one point my daughter, who was then eleven or twelve, said, "I knew that one was yours Dad because it's in your style." I said, "What do you mean? I don't have a style." And she said, "Is it bad to have a style? You have a style, Dad." And I remember feeling kind of terrible, because to me it was critical that my book be an expression of the character, and that the character be the one with the style. I should make myself transparent, the author should hide in there, and so I didn't want to have a style. But it turns out I do have a style that is an expression of who I am. I think the style is just as Katherine Anne Porter says it is—an expression of who I am.

I believe so much in the importance of context, that context determines everything, that I become uncomfortable when reading something and I don't know why the writer is telling me this. There are writers, Rushdie for example, who in the midst of a book will go off on a long tangent about something that is really insignificant to the story. For my purposes I can't do that. I have to say, "Why does this matter?" Not to matter only when you're explaining something that you can't explain otherwise. That's the kind of person I am. I want every sentence to be so clear to the reader that the nuances to be born out of answering the question are clear. You're always helping the reader to know, and for me when that works successfully I feel very pleased with the texture. The reader hardly has to ask the question, because there's already the answer. That's the kind of the book I most enjoy reading, and certainly the kind of book that I struggle to write, and it is an expression of who I am. I recognize this about myself; I have a certain kind of impatience about not understanding.

ELLIS: When you studied art history and Japanese history did you know you wanted to be a writer?

GOLDEN: When I was an undergraduate studying art history I had no idea I was going to be a writer. When I went to graduate school in Japanese history it was with the thought that I was going to be a professor, but it ended up I didn't want to be a professor. I went off to Japan still not wanting to be a writer, and only when I came back did I know that was what I wanted to do. But even then, I didn't know I wanted to be a fiction writer. It sounded too intimidating to me. When I did start gradually working on fiction, I tended to be methodical about things and checked books out about writing. I found I could only get so far. Even better for me as a process of learning was re-reading novels I loved and trying to find out what made them work. And I enrolled in a creative writing program, which to be honest wasn't very helpful. But I loved reading other people's work, work of people who were struggling with the same things that I was struggling with. I'm still friends with a number of the people I met there.

ELLIS: Why wasn't it very helpful?

GOLDEN: It wasn't very helpful for a lot of reasons but one of them was related to the debate as to whether writing can be taught. Can it be taught? Of course it can be taught. The way to teach it is, however, not to say something to the student about going home to write a story about something to do with a pond. And then the student comes back and has written something without guidance.

The way to me to teach it seems to be in a very nuts-and-bolts manner. I've been talking in this interview about problems with narrative, among other things. There are very tangible things that can be said about the very nature of fiction, the roles of characters. Mostly students starting out tend to people their stories with whatever characters they find. It doesn't occur to them the characters are really going to play roles. But when you begin to ask what role is played by this character, and you see that no role is played, it is not difficult to realize that the narrative will be much stronger if you boil it down to the essentials and you take out things that don't work. If you start puffing it up with whatever comes to mind it's not a very powerful novel. You can teach someone how to write by examining the parts. If you can take out a piece, and it still stands up, then take it out. That's what I tell writing students. If you can take it out and the narrative doesn't change then it shouldn't be there in the first place. So can writing be taught? Of course it can be taught. But the way I was taught is how it gets taught most of the time, and that's why it wasn't helpful.

ELLIS: What is your process like when you're writing? For example, do you have a set time that you write, or a set way that you write, or circumstances you need to facilitate your writing?

GOLDEN: A little of all those things, I'd say. I find that if I can't get a good start in the morning I almost always have a bad writing day. And like most writers I don't like being interrupted, but I can recover pretty quickly from interruptions. If by the end of the day I've got four or five hours of really concentrated time I usually can hit my word count goal and for me, right now, that's fifteen hundred words per day. I really don't like to stop before I've gotten that number of words written. But there are days like today, when I'm working over a very difficult passage, or something very complicated is being explained. I'm not only having to make sure it's clear, but realizing there's a better way to do it, and I have to tweak it a bit, and I can see that I'm working hard and I'm not making progress; I give myself a break. Still, I want to write fifteen hundred words a day. That's the first thing. I have to start, really be rolling, by ten or eleven o'clock. If I haven't been at it for an hour by eleven o'clock, I'm in trouble.

I have a couple of funny characteristics. I have to put my feet up. It sort of helps me feel that I'm relaxing and giving myself over to the world of the people I'm writing about. And I have a big screen with a lot of text on it, on one of those mounted arms, sort of hovering over me, and I'm leaning back in the chair with my feet up. That's invariable. If you sit me at a desk, I'm not going to say I couldn't get any writing done, but I wouldn't like it and I wouldn't write very well. I used to think I could catch up on my writing on an airplane, I mean five hours going to L.A., but that's not how it works, if I'm not in that familiar environment with my feet up.

ELLIS: Are there aspects of writing that come more easily to you?

GOLDEN: Well, I don't quite know how to answer that one because I don't know what comes easily to other people. It's a comparative matter. But there are things I don't struggle with. I don't struggle with prose. I find that clarity is something that does not trouble me. I've put a lot of energy and thought into learning it, I suppose, but it's intuitive for me. You write it and the next day you read it over and if it's not absolutely perfect when you read it over, if it does not mean the only thing that you mean to say, then you fix it. There's also a kind of rhythm that you're trying to achieve. You want the reader to know without you saying it that this is important, or that you're leading up to something or this is a conclusion of a scene. These things are achieved by pacing or a rhythm that's intuitive. I don't know how you can teach that to someone. I find myself able to know if it's wrong when I read it over the next day and I try to fix it. So if the next day I read it over again and it's still wrong, by the third day it might read fine and now I know I've got it. It's not always that I get it right; it's that when I read it and I realize I've got it wrong that I go back over and fix it. So does that come easily or not? I don't know.

ELLIS: What do you struggle with?

GOLDEN: What I struggle with the most is a difficult problem that is difficult to explain, which is ensuring that everything in the narrative is there because it belongs there. It has to be there; there's an urgency. That's what I struggle with the most, to give the narrative some kind of urgency. When I say urgency, I don't mean a cheap device to write some kind of page-turner so that I'll be sure to get a lot of readers. It's not something like that. It's because I really believe that when you're reading a novel and you're just turning the pages, that you end up paying attention to just eighty percent, maybe sixty percent. I know those novels well. I read them a lot and my mind is kind of wandering a bit and I pull myself back. That's not a satisfying reading experience and I don't get that much out of reading the book. When I am riveted to the thing, when I am so engaged that I am consuming it almost like a meal when I'm hungry, that's when I put the thing down and say, "That's a good book." So I feel that that quality of urgency is really very meaningful and comes about because there are other things in the book that are working well. That's what I struggle with the most.

ELLIS: When you read *Memoirs of a Geisha* what are your favorite parts?

GOLDEN: You know what happens? It happens to anyone who writes. You write it and forget about it and you go back to it and read it over and you're kind of surprised you wrote it. I think that's fun. I like when that happens. I have not re-read *Memoirs of a Geisha* since it came out. I worked on it so long and even after a decade I'm still not inclined to do it, to read it again. But I have on occasion read passages. Sometimes I'll get a letter that refers to one particular passage and maybe asks a question about it or says it likes the passage particularly well. I'll go back to the passage and read it and find that I say to myself "I like that," and I get a big kick out of something that's tiny, so tiny. I'll get such a charge out of it, because it's important, it's not a throwaway. It's integral to the story, it's embedded in the story and tells a little bit about the character.

ELLIS: How have you dealt with your enormous success?

GOLDEN: Well, it was hugely more successful than I could have ever imagined it being. I think beforehand I hadn't really allowed myself to fantasize what would happen, but there were moments when I observed other writers such as Frank McCourt whose book came out just a while before mine did, he had a big success, and I remembered wondering what would happen. You see, I couldn't really have imagined what would happen. It's been a pretty wild ride. Just the numbers of people I've met, the situations I've found myself in, the people I've met, the invitations I've gotten, the ways in which it has effected interactions with people I don't know, sometimes the people that I know, the way that it's effected my family members; but I don't think it's changed me except that I've been through an experience I wouldn't have been through, and you change as you go through experiences. I think I know more about life now, having seen a new side of it I hadn't seen before. It's very interesting.

But people who know me will say I haven't changed. Some people become prima-donnas. And I'm still the same exact person I was, thank God; I wouldn't want it any other way. It kind of appalls me when people who have success start to believe the reports, who think they're brilliant. There are a lot of writers out there like that and they become convinced that whatever they put out there on the page is great, that whatever they say is worthy and they don't have to worry about how they say it. If I get to that point I'm in big, big trouble, because I believe so much in crafting the novel, in making it work, and it's very difficult. If you just think you are intrinsically able to do it, then what you have on your head is a lousy mushy book that could have been better.

ELLIS: Would you mind sharing what you're reading right now?

GOLDEN: What I'm reading now is a book called *The Unfolding of Language*; it's about the evolution of language. I read about the same amount of fiction and non-fiction. I may not strictly alternate between fiction and non-fiction but I usually do. High on my list of favorite books I would include such things as *The Remains of the Day* or *Middlemarch* or *The Curious Incident of the Dog in the Nighttime*, or *She's Come Undone*, and I'd also throw in *The Making of the Atomic Bomb*, and *City of the Century* about Chicago.

ELLIS: I know some writers are superstitious. Are you willing to talk about what you're currently working on?

GOLDEN: Sure. It's very different than *Memoirs of a Geisha*. It starts off in Amsterdam when the character is about ten; in *Memoirs* the geisha was about nine and the age is pretty close. His grandfather dies and he struggles to develop some sort of a relationship with his father, but it doesn't work out very well. And when he's seventeen he leaves the Netherlands altogether and comes to the United States, settles, in fact, on Cape Cod, and becomes a very successful meat packer in the 1860s. It's also told in the first person, as was *Geisha*. But it's a very different book in some ways; very different in the incidents and characters and circumstances than those in *Memoirs of a Geisha*, but similar in that the emotional journey is not over yet and it's about early hardship and the struggle to recover from it.

Jill McCorkle

Every Town Has Its Stories

Jill McCorkle was raised in Lumberton, North Carolina. The summer after she completed second grade, she transformed her father's wooden work shed into a writing room, and decorated it with dress-up clothing, a tea set and fishing gear.

When McCorkle was twenty-six years old her first two novels, *The Cheerleader* and *July 7th*, were published to critical acclaim. Five additional works of fiction have been published to date: *Tending to Virginia* (1989) *Ferris Beach* (1991), *Crash Diet: Stories* (1992), *Carolina Moon* (1996), *Final Vinyl Days: And Other Stories* (1998), and *Creatures of Habit* (2001). Richard Bausch said of this most recent collection, "*Creatures of Habit* is so rich, so complete an experience... McCorkle paints everything with such clarity, and beauty... With every line, she incites my awe and wonder."

"Billy Goats," the first story in *Creatures of Habit*, was originally published in *Bomb* magazine and is included in *The Best American Short Stories 2002*. McCorkle's other short stories have been widely published in literary journals and commercial magazines including the *Atlantic Monthly*, *Cosmopolitan*, and *Ladies' Home Journal*. Her new story, "Intervention" appears in the fall issue of *Ploughshares*. Five of her works have been selected as *New York Times* Notable Books of the Year. She has received the New England Booksellers Association Award for her body of work in fiction, the Jon Dos Passos Prize for Excellence in Literature, the North Carolina Award for Literature, and in 1996 she was included in *Granta* magazine's celebration of the Best of Young American Novelists.

In 1981 McCorkle earned her Master's degree from Hollins College. She is currently a full-time faculty member at North Carolina State University and has also taught at Bennington College, Harvard University, Brandeis University, Duke University, Tufts University, and the University of North Carolina. She has reviewed books for the *New York Times Book Review*, the *Washington Post* and the *Atlanta Journal-Constitution*.

McCorkle is frequently described as a "Southern writer," despite the fact that she has lived in greater Boston for fourteen years. I met Jill McCorkle in her living room, while her three dogs relaxed nearby. Resting in the corner of the room was a large Victorian dollhouse that she built and decorated.

SHERRY ELLIS: In *Creatures of Habit* you revisit the fictional town of Fulton. What made you decide to return?

JILL MCCORKLE: I think I've always returned there, whatever I've named it. It's certainly my fictional hometown, which is very much like my real hometown, but not the way it looks now, the way it looked when I was a child.

I know we always look back with a nostalgic glance, but I really did have a great sense of freedom and ownership of the town in which I was raised. It was a time when children went out until the street lights came on, and if our parents had known where we were and what we were doing they would have had heart attacks. There was just all this freedom. One of my favorite places to sit was under the bridge of the I-95 overpass.

That time in my hometown marks not just the transition for me into adolescence and adulthood, but I think also represents the transition of the South, into what is now most often referred to as the New South. As I was growing up, I-95 started to pass through my town. As a result, there was a huge growth spurt and suddenly there were billboards and fast food chains. The interstate connected us in a way that I never felt connected before.

ELLIS: The stories in this collection are named after animals and have woven into them the common movements, characteristics, and experiences that animals and humans share. In the story "Cats" you liken an ex-husband to a misplaced cat. Later in the same story, Anne, the ex-wife wonders, "Why else do women so easily settle in with their litters and nests; why do the females in nature blend into the background while the males remain flashy and continue life as sexual predators?" In the story "Dogs" the main character states, "If I were a dog I would have been put down by now." How did you decide to explore this theme?

MCCORKLE: Well, it's funny. I didn't begin this collection with the idea of all the animal connections; it evolved as I was writing. I often think there are natural thematic connections when you have a whole litter of story ideas at the same time; I wasn't just writing one story and putting it down. I had many stored up, and as I was moving from story to story—sketching out what I did know—I started to see the connections. Actually, the opening story, "Billy Goats," was written more as a mood piece than anything. I didn't want the characters directly connected, but I wanted there to be the sense that these people populated the same community. This is where as a writer I realize that it's so valuable for me to take notes of little things I notice in life along the way. Sometimes I hold onto them for years.

The whole idea for "Cats" was inspired by my family losing a favorite cat and actually burying him in Tupperware in my yard (I was afraid he'd explode). So, in real life there was the loss of this cat, which made me think about other cats, particularly one from childhood who was lost for weeks and ultimately found his way home. I was greatly influenced by the likes of *Thomasina* and *The Incredible Journey*, the Walt Disney movie, and I started imagining a situation where a person is attempting a similar journey. It led to the idea of a man with early Alzheimer's, who actually thinks his home is with the first wife instead of the new wife across town. What started out as a more darkly comical theme, about the cat and the Tupperware mausoleum, turned into something much sadder.

ELLIS: In "Tippy's Teeth," an essay you wrote for "The Algonkian"—a promotional pamphlet put out by Algonquin—you state that "human behavior is not so far removed from the most primitive animal behavior as we like to think," for example that "we all crave a sense of the den," and that "a person who is that insecure and fearful is likely—metaphorically to lunge and bite." Can you please comment on this and offer a few examples of how you demonstrate these similarities in your stories?

MCCORKLE: I do believe we all crave the security of home. I think we like to believe that our loyalties are not in vain. And, I think that some of our worst reactions in life are fear-driven. A trapped or frightened animal lashes out in an attempt to survive and humans do the same. Dogs are put down or "sent to the country" as my Tippy was for aggressive behavior.

I was talking to a friend on a particularly stressful day and I said, "If I was a dog I'd have been put down by now." I knew even as I said it that I'd use it for a first line. As I explained in "Tippy's Teeth" I did once accidentally kill a cat by dipping it in a flea dip designed for dogs and I used that incident in my story. For me it was a kind of exorcism as I'd been haunted by the memory for years; I still can't bear to think about it.

ELLIS: The main character in the story "Billy Goats" recalls her life as a seventh grader, when she and her friends prowled through their neighborhood in a pack, "a herd of kids on banana-seat bikes and minibikes," as they discuss their community, the lives and deaths of people they know, and their own vulnerability. How much of this story is based on your own childhood experience?

MCCORKLE: Very much. I felt the opening story and the closing story about the death of the father were my stories, and as close to reality as I'm going to get. The facts aren't necessarily true but the voice and the place are.

I think every town has its stories. I tell my students to write about the character in their community, that person that everybody takes for granted, laughs about, talks about; or to think of the cases of domestic sadness you can reel off in the moment. I mean, here in the town I live in now, there is a house that is referred to as "the divorce house." There's always a divorce house, a suicide house. In my home town there was a house we referred to as the murder-suicide house. When my husband and I were looking for houses I drove the realtor crazy because I kept saying there must be something with a house, if we could afford it. Was there a suicide? Was there a murder? I'm superstitious enough to be bothered by such. I guess there were enough people asking the questions because the realtors have to tell you these things. I think those are the situations and landmarks that really inform childhood; you begin to learn about what's bad and what's not right in the parental world.

ELLIS: Your writing has been referred to as "Southern" and is compared to Eudora Welty's. What does being a Southern writer mean to you?

MCCORKLE: Well, I have no problem being called a Southern writer because clearly as soon as I open my mouth there's the proof. And the South is very much my writing home as well. Even though characters sometimes wind up in different places than where they begin.

There's certainly a wonderful tradition in history that I'm proud to be associated with. I think other characteristics of Southern writing, not that they don't apply to other writers, is that there is a lot of attention to a strong sense of place, and there is also a wonderful tradition of oral story telling. I think that any community or group that, for whatever reason, has been cut off from the rest of the world, usually does have an oral tradition—because it's so important to make sure that the legacy is handed over. And of course in the South, not only was there the war, which of course is what everyone immediately associates with Southern people, but there were other roadblocks as well, literacy being one of the biggest. I mean, my grandmother was very fortunate that she went through the ninth grade; my grandfather only completed the third. So, they could tell stories that they never would have been able to write. There was a lot of power in the spoken word, and it was revered as such, I think. I think a lot of that oral tradition is classic in Southern literature. You can't get from point A to point B easily, you've got to wander off to the side and tell this story. The writer Barry Hannah tells his version of the light bulb joke—how many Southern writers does it take to change a bulb? Two . . . one to unscrew it and the other to talk about what a good old light bulb it was.

ELLIS: When you were in the second grade your motivation as a writer was to get a laugh or a tear. Is this still your goal?

McCORKLE: I think as a child it was wonderful to discover that I had this power to make myself laugh or cry and of course that grew into wanting to have the effect on others. Often what I see or hear in the world strikes me as funny. I start with something that's making me laugh, and yet I'm enough of a realist that I never believe it's that simple; then I start looking for what's under the funny. It's a method I've used often in terms of the stories expanding to a different level. Again, the story "Cats" is a perfect example of this.

ELLIS: Do you think that your childhood and adult hobbies and pastimes, for example fishing and dollhouse decorating, have helped you develop qualities that a writer needs?

McCORKLE: Oh totally, and I always like to credit my Dad with this one. He always said that he loved to sit and look at the ocean, but that if he just sat there and stared and my mother saw, she would start nagging him: "What are you doing just sitting there? Go and do something."

He said, "This is why I fish." And he said the trick is that if they ever start biting too much, you stop baiting the hook. I was his fishing buddy. We rarely caught anything, but it was just that kind of quiet thinking time, and so I did learn a lot as a writer.

It's hard to justify to the world, especially to your family, why you're just going to sit in a chair and stare like a zombie. And so my whole life I've had hobbies that are solitary in nature. You know the saying, "busy hands, busy minds." As an adult I built a dollhouse. The work of putting a house together and then decorating is very similar to writing a novel; you're creating this world and you have a certain level of control over it. Most of my activities are singular. When I think about sports or activities I liked growing up—ballet, gymnastics, swimming—I realize they were actions that didn't require me to interact with others. My mind was free to roam.

ELLIS: Do you believe all writers need "rooms of their own?"

MCCORKLE: Yes, I do, and I think all writers already have a room of their own in terms of within the self. I find when I don't get that quiet time nothing else in life feels quite right; I think it's a constant struggle to find a room of your own. I do have an office in my home, but when there is a lot going on I can't work. Sometimes the room of my own is the car parked in the grocery store parking lot, or wherever I can get it.

ELLIS: The author Willa Cather once said, "There are only two or three human stories, and they go on repeating themselves as fiercely as if they had never happened before." Do you agree?

MCCORKLE: I do. I think we are very limited thematically and that's why we all identify with each other's stories. It's the specific detail and history that we can bring to them, that makes our work or characters' lives unique.

ELLIS: You are quoted as having said, "I have always believed that by the ripe age of adolescence . . . our emotional baggage is packed." In your novel *The Cheerleader*, a story about young women coming of age, Jo challenges stereotypes of popularity. Do you believe that Jo's and Beatrice's "emotional baggage is already packed"?

MCCORKLE: I think the characters have more than enough to think about and unpack and to understand through adulthood. I had a professor say to me when *The Cheerleader* came out, "My God, Jill! Most of us spend all our lives trying to forget all this stuff and you have dedicated yourself to dredging it up." And I thought, well, I guess it's sort of an exorcism. It's such a classic period of life and I am interested in young women because there are so many fears and things that happen in that little space of time, the whole body image, the everything! I hate to say it, but I don't necessarily think we've come too far in taking care of it.

I feel really drawn to that age group and more than any other work, I've gotten more letters about *The Cheerleader*, mainly from seniors in high school and freshmen in college, and one, a letter that I will always treasure, from a grandmother who said that the book had helped her understand her granddaughter, which really meant a lot. I guess of all my books this is the one that most consistently gets the most letters, and they always begin with "Did you read my journal?" And it feels so good, and so right, that this is such a universal phenomenon. We all fit somewhere on that spectrum of Jo and Beatrice. What I had wanted to show in that novel is regardless of stereotype, positive stereotype, negative stereotype, there are real dangers in being labeled by others. I think (I hope) that this book shows that these two girls have more in common than anyone would think.

ELLIS: Do you pre-select the time frame in which your stories and novels will occur?

MCCORKLE: No. The only time I consciously did that was with the novel *July 7th*, when I knew I was going to write about just one day.

ELLIS: You have often written in the first person, as in your novels *Ferris Beach* and sections of *Carolina Moon*. When you write a story or a novel do you know beforehand which point of view you will use?

MCCORKLE: I don't always know, sometimes I flounder back and forth. I feel that usually if I stick with the story and keep revising it, the story dictates which point of view best serves it, the same with tense and genre for that matter. Very often in student work I will see a student set out to write a story in third person, past tense, and it just won't stay there. . . . It won't be in the past. . . . They'll flip into the present, or they'll flip into "I" . . . and so I can always tell when the story is pulled in another direction . . . I think that's something you listen to.

ELLIS: How do you choose your titles, for example *Creatures of Habit*?

MCCORKLE: Titles are often the last thing to come. I was very relieved to be able to look up *Creatures of Habit*. I thought it must have been used zillions of times. I think there was only one novel years ago. It's a phrase I use a lot, to describe myself. The other one that my husband always says in reference to me is "spontaneity has its time and its place," and that's me . . . I have a plan and when I'm without a plan I've sort of lost the concept and I can't see. I'm always saying "I'm a creature of habit." In childhood I went through that obsessive-compulsive thing where you have to go back and make sure the drawer is closed; then I had years of checking the coffee maker. Now I have one that automatically cuts off. I have a system and I am a creature of habit. I had jotted down a lot of title ideas and I was reading Darwin at the time, what I could read of Darwin. I kept tripping on the word "habit."

ELLIS: In the story "Crash Diet" Sandra White Barkley is left by her husband, for a woman who is thinner and years younger than she is, and in the story "Departures," Anna Craven, a widow, spends her free time trying to escape from the emptiness of her home. Do the themes of these stories represent a feminist perspective?

MCCORKLE: Yes, I think so. It's so interesting, I'm glad you're asking this question because people often avoid the feminist question. I have all these young students now who will say, "Well, I'm not a feminist." And I'll say, "Well, of course you are, you should be. That's why you're sitting here taking this class." Somewhere along the line the word got distorted. I don't think all my characters are knowledgeable enough or wise enough that they would necessarily see it that way, but I guess I always feel that they're coming into their own. I love that Rebecca West quote, "I've never been able to find out precisely what feminism is. I only know that people call me a feminist whenever I express sentiments that differentiate me from a doormat." So I do think they are feminists in nature in that they are finding a place in the world and focusing on where they stand and how they affect others, rather than just how they are feeding into the lives of everyone else. It's not always pleasant. I think for someone like Anna, it's like her limbs have been ripped off; Sandra is a bit more open about her independence, I think.

ELLIS: You've been living in greater Boston for many years. Do you think that the sensibilities and styles of the North have influenced you as a writer?

MCCORKLE: Yes. If nothing else, I am always making a mental comparison to the way the experience might play out in the South. More than anything though, what I experience is how much humans—regardless of age, race, religion, geography or any other label you might choose—have in common. As a teacher—both in New England and in the South—I think the bigger differences have to do with urban or rural childhoods.

ELLIS: In the story "Final Vinyl Days" you write from a male perspective for the first time. Can you comment on what this experience was like for you?

McCorkle: That was a stretch. He was a hard character but it was a challenge I needed because I knew that one of my main characters in *Carolina Moon* was going to be a guy. Once I get inside a character and have a sense of who he is, then I don't think it matters that much. I really do think that if you find what is motivating a character emotionally, it allows you to transcend race and age and gender.

Ellis: What are the greatest rewards of writing for you?

McCorkle: It always sounds so selfish when I think about it. For me, the greatest reward in writing is the stability and the pleasure that it brings to me. I love the act of writing. That may be why I have trouble rationalizing to everybody why I do it, because I've never come to a point where I feel like it's work. I feel it is a real luxury. I think it is a fantasy life.

Ellis: What about the hardest parts of writing?

McCorkle: Sometimes it's the frustration of not being able to get there. I've never had just unlimited time to write, so I don't know how I would function that way. I've always taught and had responsibility with kids and family, so it's difficult sometimes to carve out that time. I also think that as much as writers are driven by the desire to be published and read by others, I think there's a kind of love-hate relationship—because I think the whole act of then being published is the antithesis of what your writing life is all about. I mean your writing life is cocooned and safe and then all of a sudden you're stripped and out there, and that's not always easy. I think you have to find ways to keep yourself upright and somehow attached to that center that makes you want to write anyway.

Ellis: In a recent article you wrote for *Food and Wine* magazine, you quote the chef of a restaurant, "I need to know the rules before I break them." Do you believe this adage apply to writers too?

McCorkle: I think it applies to most endeavors. I certainly encourage students who want to write experimentally, that they first go with the more conventional pieces, to show that they can do it. I think there is a lot to be learned within the basics and tradition that will only make it better as you experiment.

ELLIS: In another recent magazine article you wrote, this one for *Real Simple*, you state that comedy and humor help people cope with tragedy. Do you believe that as a writer, you have purposely given your fictional characters humorous situations to help them cope with the traumas in their lives?

MCCORKLE: Absolutely. Or maybe more specifically, I believe there is always humor to be found. Even within the most hideous situations, people continue to say and do quirky things.

ELLIS: Who are the writers that you believe have most influenced your work?

MCCORKLE: That's a very long list. I can certainly say among contemporary writers, my teachers Lee Smith and Louis Rubin and Max Steele, and in terms of just "old faithfuls" and writers I feel I've learned a tremendous amount from reading, the bulk of them being of the old Southern school: Eudora Welty, Harper Lee, Carson McCullers, Truman Capote, Flannery O'Connor, Katherine Anne Porter. I would also have to say Sherwood Anderson; *Winesburg, Ohio* is one of those books that made a huge impact on me as a writer.

ELLIS: Justice Brandeis is quoted as having said, "There is no great writing, only great rewriting." When you have finished revising your work how similar is it to your initial draft?

MCCORKLE: It varies piece to piece, but I would say quite different, I would hope different. I would say that the first draft for me, especially with stories, is like a skeleton and then each run of revision is like transparencies in an anatomy book, you're adding the muscles and the tissues and the organs, and you begin to see how they all connect and work together. That's why I find revision so very exciting and satisfying.

ELLIS: Do you have a sense of knowing when something is done and when it's time to stop revising?

MCCORKLE: Sometimes it's just being so sick of a piece that I can't look at it anymore. But I feel like I know when I'm almost there, and usually that's when I ask for a reader. My editor is very good about responding. She can just zero in on little areas that need a little more or less.

ELLIS: What are you working on now?

MCCORKLE: Well, I've got a novel I've been working on forever, a situation about a group of friends who have come together. Talk about how many stories there are! How many times have you heard that one: women gathering to talk? And then I'm also writing some stories.

ELLIS: How would you describe the changes in your writing over time; for example, the characters you choose, their situations and their voices?

MCCORKLE: I feel they've really changed. I have felt that my work has gotten progressively darker. I think there is still light in there, but I think that I've felt safe enough or confident enough as a writer to push my characters further than I have before. I love to see and express humor in life but I'm always curious about the underbelly of it all.

ELLIS: Do you think you will keep returning to Fulton?

MCCORKLE: Oh, yes. I'll always go back. Actually this new novel takes place very near Fulton. Right now in my mind it's set on Bald Head Island, right off the Carolina coast.

Matthew Sharpe

Novels as Omnivores

The Sleeping Father, the second novel written by Matthew Sharpe, was rejected by twenty major publishers before it was purchased by Soft Skull Press for an advance of one thousand dollars. It tells the story of Bernard Schwartz, who unknowingly mixes two types of antidepressants, loses consciousness, has a stroke, and suffers brain damage—and his teenage children Chris and Cathy, who try to rehabilitate him on their own. After its September 2003 publication *The Sleeping Father* received a full-page review in the *New York Times Book Review* as well as an appearance in the "And Bear in Mind" slot. In February 2004 it was selected by the Today Show Book Club. Also in the same month renowned author Anne Tyler said, in a *New York Times* interview, "my favorite [book] this week is a fresh, funny, quirky book called *The Sleeping Father*, by Matthew Sharpe." In June 2004 Warner Bros. optioned this novel.

According to the *New York Times*, Sharpe's first novel *Nothing Is Terrible* (2000) is "warped and oddly touching, *Nothing Is Terrible* is brain candy for the bright and jaded." This novel tells the story of an orphaned sixth grader named Mary who prefers to be called Paul, who escapes from suburbia and moves to New York with her thirty-seven-year-old teacher/lover.

The stories in Sharpe's short story collection *Stories From the Tube* (1998) open with prologues taken from TV commercials. Anderson Clifton in his CNN.com review wrote that this collection "reads like a *Canterbury Tales* for the modern-day ad age."

In March 2007, *Jamestown*, Sharpe's new novel was published. It's a fantastical account of the Jamestown settlement of 1607 in Virginia.

Sharpe has taught writing in many settings. He is currently an assistant professor of English at Wesleyan College. He previously has taught at Columbia University and at the summer program at Bard College. From 2003 to 2004 he was the writer in residence at the Bronx Academy of Letters, an experimental writing-themed public school in the South Bronx; and as a graduate student at Columbia University he taught creative writing to children with the support of the Teachers and Writer's Collaborative.

Sharpe also has an experience as an author interviewer. Many of his interviews can be read at www.writenet.org.

His short stories and essays have appeared in *Harper's, Zoetrope, BOMB, Southwest Review, Mississippi Mud, Nerve, American Letters and Commentary, Fiction, Witness,* the *KGB Bar Reader, The Alphabet of the Trees: A Guide to Nature Writing, Teachers and Writers* magazine, *Details, Word,* and *Goodbye: The Journal of Contemporary Obituaries.*

Sharpe describes himself as a "sword-swallowing nutritionist and flaneur," about which he says, "First one has to make sure to get one's tongue out of the way—I tend to plant mine firmly in my cheek."

He divides his time between New York and Connecticut. Recently I spoke with him by phone.

SHERRY ELLIS: *The Sleeping Father* begins with a description of circumstance. "Chris Schwartz's father's Prozac dosage must have been incorrect, because he awoke one morning to discover that the right side of his face had gone numb. This was the second discovery on a journey Chris's father sensed would carry him miles from the makeshift heaven of health." Do you believe that circumstance is a particularly effective means of enticing readers?

MATTHEW SHARPE: I don't think I have one particular way of beginning a book that I use repeatedly, or at least I hope I don't. I borrowed that opening from Kafka. *The Trial* and *The Metamorphosis* have similar openings. I wanted that Kafkaesque sense that one's life is about to go out of control, in a terrifying and unknowable and absurd way. That's why I began in this particular story with circumstance. It is after all a kind of accident that causes the mechanics of the plot; that is, the accident of switching the pills.

ELLIS: Your first novel, *Nothing Is Terrible*, begins, "'That girl is not normal, and neither is the boy,' I overheard my uncle say to my aunt late one summer night a month after my parents had been killed in a car accident on the way home from a wedding. My twin brother Paul and I were ten years old at the time and were the children my childless uncle was talking about." With this beginning, you juxtapose words and phrases that give the reader a preliminary sense of the uniqueness of Mary, a seeming hermaphrodite, who at age eleven runs off to New York with her thirty-seven-year-old teacher. At what point during your writing of this novel did you write and/or choose these sentences as the beginning?

SHARPE: I think I had the sentences pretty early on. In that case I was very consciously trying to write a late twentieth century version of the *bildungsroman*, the coming of age novel that had its beginning in the eighteenth century. It was a symbolic form, a way of dealing with a new class of person, the bourgeois subject, who is unheroic and in that sense normal. In my update of the form I wanted to deal with somebody who would be both normal and un-normal, depending on who is looking at her/him and defining her/him. In fact, I wanted to deal with someone who is different from herself, and who will always be two contrary things at once, someone who is both normal and not normal, someone who is a girl and a boy, a criminal and a victim, a nice person and a not-nice person. I wanted to at least signal some of that in the opening sentence.

ELLIS: The narrator of *The Sleeping Father* is wise, knowing and ironic. For example you write, "In the lives of Chris and Cathy Schwartz, hospital and school exchanged roles. Hospital was now the place where they went to be educated and socialized by illness and the resistance to illness; school was the place where they visited their gravely ailing secondary education." How did you determine the personality and level of omniscience you wanted the narrator to have for this novel?

SHARPE: I keep having these very literary answers to your questions and I'll continue in that vein. I figured out the tone of this novel by reading *Middlemarch* by George Eliot. I happened to be reading *Middlemarch* while I was starting *The Sleeping Father*, and for a story whose subject is consciousness, among other things, I wanted to be able to inhabit the consciousness of several of the characters, and I thought that George Eliot tone, which is lightly mocking, always very tender, and sort of maternalistic towards her characters, would be well worth emulating for doing what I wanted to do. I'm glad you picked up on that. Until I know the tone of the voice, I can't really move forward with any of the other aspects of a novel.

ELLIS: In his *Village Voice* review of *The Sleeping Father* Ed Park comments on the "aching absurdities, word salads, inspired semicolon deployment, golden-eared teenage monologues," that you utilize. To highlight a few of your inventive descriptions, Dr. Lisa Danmeyer . . . "smelled of lilacs and competent sweat." "Chris and his mother's sex partner were walking through the woods" is another description. Can you describe how you get into a mindset where you shut out the world and use language so creatively? It seems like it must take a lot of work.

SHARPE: I would say in some ways I shut out the world and in other ways I let the world enter. I mean, thank you for complimenting my linguistic prowess. I have to say that the review by Ed Park is about as good a review an author can ever have hoped to get. If I die before I get another review like that I'll consider myself well-reviewed in my life. I suppose I shut the world out in the sense that I'm not a person who, say, writes with music on. I know there are some people who write to music, who allow the music to infuse the work, but I need a quiet writing space, which is hard to come by in New York City. In terms of letting the world in I'm a real big fan of Mikhail Bakhtin, the Russian theorist. His idea was that any way that speech gets used out there in the world can make its way into a novel, that novels are omnivores of all kinds of speech and writing. So I actually try to let the acoustical and rhetorical properties of all the other forms of language use in the world inform how I write. TV and radio, legal documents and bumper stickers, other people's novels, prayers and apologies, emails and letters, political speeches and medical jargon, I try to welcome them into my novels.

ELLIS: Your language in the short story collection *Stories from the Tube* seems simpler. Do you believe the change in language from this story collection to *The Sleeping Father* has to do more with your evolution as a writer or the topic matter of the work?

SHARPE: It's funny about that. I always thought of myself as a Baroque, fancy, wordy kind of writer, a "putter-inner" as Stanley Elkin called it, instead of a "taker-outer." So I think it must be the topic which dictated the simpler form of most of those stories in *Stories from the Tube*. Again I was dealing with TV as a discourse, and I suppose that the discourse of TV is fairly simple because they're trying to reach as large an audience as possible. But there are a couple of stories in there—"Doctor Mom" and "A Bird Accident"—that I think are probably closer in style to *Nothing Is Terrible* and *The Sleeping Father*.

ELLIS: "The chief characteristic of the annual Day of Dodgeball" in *The Sleeping Father* "was that it was not announced in advance." The goal for the teachers was to "hit every student currently matriculated at Bellwether High School with a ball thrown from not less than six feet's distance within the allotted two-hour time span." Did you intend this game to be metaphoric for Bernard's stroke and coma and its impact on his children or more to stand on its own as part of the cruelty of adolescence?

SHARPE: Probably the latter, not to mention the sometimes institutionalized cruelty of places like schools. That was one of the themes that just happened without too much conscious control from me, and in fact when I began writing that scene I didn't imagine it as a dream. I imagined it as something that would just happen. I don't know if you've ever played dodgeball but it truly is a cruel sport. It's a nasty, Darwinian, *Lord of the Flies* kind of sport and I figured that as long as I was writing about high school, let me pay homage to some of the Kafkaesque aspects. When I was two-thirds through writing that dodgeball scene, I thought I wouldn't be able to put it in the novel or it would wind up being somebody's dream. So it wound up being Chris' dream.

ELLIS: Your characters have what are often considered unorthodox sexual relationships. In *The Sleeping Father*, Lila Schwartz has sex with her gardener and then with her ex-husband's physician's father. A speech therapist has sex with her patient's teenage son. In *Nothing is Terrible* ten-year-old Mary has a sexual relationship with her thirty-six-year-old female teacher. To what extent do you believe this sub-theme of unusual sexual relationships stretches the boundaries of these novels as a whole?

SHARPE: I think I'm discovering that I am a fairly traditional novel writer, at least in the forms I use. I teach in the graduate program at Bard College and if you really want to see experimental writers, check out some of the Bard authors. They are far more adventurous in their storytelling than I am.

I guess in terms of the content of the novel, I think of literature as a civilized space in which to express uncivilized thoughts and feelings. It's not something that I set out to do consciously; it's not that I set out to stretch the form of the novel by having these transgressive sexual acts. One of the ways that narratologists think about stories is that there has to be some violation of the social norm to get the story going. I was walking down the street when such and such happened. I think one of the ways to understand something about whatever phenomenon you're investigating is to imagine an extreme case of it, something that pushes the limits. So to have a transgressive sort of sex act between an adult and a child, or between a doctor/therapist and a patient would be ways of de-familiarizing the phenomenon in question.

ELLIS: By the end of *The Sleeping Father* we have come full circle. Early on there's the notebook entitled "Everything in the World," in which Chris's friend Frank writes his observations of things that he considers meaningless. One section is called "Things that look like things that you already know what they look like." You write "... in the estimation of Frank and Chris, the world was weary of itself—had trod, had trod, had trod or whatever, now ground out shoddy reproduction of stuff it used to take pride in producing. Trees, shrubs, cats, people, clouds, and stars were now 'trees,' 'shrubs,' 'cats,' 'people,' 'clouds,' 'stars.'" By the book's end, when Chris's father is unable to learn the difference between the specific and general, Chris takes him outside and gives unique and personable names to these things. How purposeful was it that you begin and end this novel in a similar place, albeit with many challenges and experiences having been faced by these characters?

SHARPE: I think it was fairly purposeful. Thank you for picking up on that motif, and the way that I introduced it and closed it out. Language is a big topic in this novel. It's how people talk to each other; it's something that the character Bernie loses in his coma. I think there's that sense, especially in Chris and Frank, these two disaffected teenagers at the beginning, that the world has somehow been used up and exhausted by the time they are born into it. That everything feels a bit encroached upon. I was hoping that the scene at the end with Chris and his dad, when they go out and name all the trees, and the blades of grass, and the clouds, and the light in the sky, and the various other things that they name, would be a rebirth of themselves and of the world. It was very much modeled on the scene in Genesis when Adam and God go around naming creatures and things. So, yes, there is meant to be a refreshment of the relationship between words and things that happens when there is a refreshment of the relationship between father and son.

ELLIS: The short stories in *Stories from the Tube* are based on commercials. Can you describe the genesis of this collection?

SHARPE: Well, part of it was very personal. I watch more TV than I feel I ought to. There is a tension in my life between reading and watching TV or movies. You come home from a long day of work and on the one hand you've got Sartre's *Being and Nothingness* on the bookshelf, and you've got *NYPD Blue* on the tube, and it's a whole lot easier to go with *NYPD Blue* on the tube. So, part of the reason for writing the book was to somehow resolve the conflict in my life.

Also, these are ubiquitous narratives in our lives. Americans spend a tremendous amount of time watching TV, and I wanted to try to understand what people were spending their time thinking about in terms of stories. And these are not just any old stories. They are stories that are trying to persuade you to do something. And they're very influential, and I think these particular stories are also a lot about everyday life. Not just a depiction of everyday life, but a suggestion of, a prescription for everyday life. So not only here's this product you should use, Pledge, a furniture polishing spray, but here's the facial expression you should have and the song you should hum when you're using Pledge, and here's the almost holy sunlight that should be streaming into your living room when you're using the Pledge on your furniture. I wanted to understand that phenomenon, the insistence and pervasiveness of that kind of story, which is the commercial. One of my ways of understanding things is to fantasize, to make up stories about them. And in this case I happened to be making up stories about stories and I really allowed myself free reign as to how I would invent the stories; they often quite quickly veered away from the products themselves and into the characters' lives. One of my great inspirations for *Stories From the Tube* was the book *Mythologies* by Roland Barthes, where he examines in essay form very ordinary kinds of cultural phenomena and their significance.

ELLIS: Can you describe your process of revision and which takes longer for you, getting a completed first draft or getting a completed work?

SHARPE: It's probably about the same. There's this long period of fretting that both constitutes and precedes the writing of the first draft. It is all the notetaking and the increasing amount of research—I got into this racket to escape from reality and here I am doing more and more research for each book. Then there's the long period of not knowing I get bogged down in the first draft. But once I write fifty or so pages I'm happy with, I can then carry on with the book without too much impediment. I'm knocking pretty loudly on wood here, hoping that it will continue that way. Once I'm up to around page fifty or so, this is for novels, I seem to say okay, this is what the novel will look like. And here's a list of what I'd like to happen later in the novel. I'd never call it an outline or a plan or a blueprint; that's way too organized for my messy mind.

And then there's revising. I print out everything, and rather than just messing around on the screen, I retype every word in the second draft so that I can reconsider every sentence I have written. It keeps me more creative. And then there's the third draft and the fourth draft and the fifth draft—I stop with the masochistic behavior of retyping each word by the third draft—and then I sort of lose count after a while of how many drafts there are. I'll take the manuscript and re-read it several times and make scribbles and erasures and draw circles and arrows and little people hanging themselves, but that process goes faster than the first draft. Say, six subsequent drafts take the same amount of time as writing that first draft.

ELLIS: Do you think it's important to have a disciplined plan as a writer, for example writing every day, having intentions and goals and reaching them?

SHARPE: Oh, yes. Otherwise I'd die. I think the more you show up at the computer or the writing pad, the more likely it is you will discover the inspiration. There's a nice metaphor which I am going to mangle from Mary Oliver the poet where she talks about this wild part of yourself that doesn't want to be tamed, but if you show up at the same place and same time every day and you offer it your rigor, it will trust you more and it may more likely to show up too.

ELLIS: *The Sleeping Father* was rejected by more than twenty major publishers before it was published by Soft Skull Press. After publication it received a lengthy review in the *New York Times*, it was selected for the *Today Show* Book Club in February, 2004 and that same month in a *New York Times* interview Anne Tyler said, "And my favorite this week is a fresh, funny, quirky book called *The Sleeping Father*." How have you coped with this novel's amazing reversal of fortune?

SHARPE: By enjoying it immensely.

ELLIS: So you've been able to cope with success?

SHARPE: Luckily I'm the same miserable schmuck I was before I had this success. I have a couple of day jobs. I was teaching at Columbia University and at a small experimental public high school in the Bronx called Bronx Academy of Letters. Just having my regular teaching duties made my life not that substantially different than it was before the success happened. And we're just six months into my success and it could all end tomorrow. Sometime this winter I read Marcus Aurelius's *Meditations*. I'm trying to maintain an Aurelian kind of stoicism about the whole thing. The success is not really me. It's just something that's happening to me. It was a hair's breadth away from not happening and it could easily end in the near future. I hope I'll continue doing what I've been doing, which is writing and teaching.

ELLIS: Teenage anxiety is amplified in *The Sleeping Father* for both Chris and his sister Cathy. How much does your experience working with teens inform your writing?

SHARPE: It keeps the teenage experience fresh in my mind. I remember when I was about seventeen my mother said that when she was seventeen she promised herself to always remember what it was like to be seventeen. I asked her how was it going, and she said that she'd really forgotten. To me, as a seventeen-year-old that seemed unimaginable. But now that I'm more than twice that age myself I understand what she meant.

As much as I try to understand my teenagers I don't always. There's a certain amount of mystery that goes on in the mind of a person that age. I will say that being in a room with twenty-five teenagers is not that different from being in a room with drunk people. One minute they're weeping, the next minute they're really angry at you, the next minute they're hugging you, the next minute they're in a depression, and there doesn't seem to have to be a whole lot of external cause for the shift. It's a volatile period. It's also a fascinating period because you're on the cusp of childhood and adulthood. You still have some of the qualities of each. You're trying to grapple with leaving the land of childhood and entering the very scary and complicated land of adulthood without the proper passport.

ELLIS: I'm wondering what happens with age. Can you describe the expressive differences you have observed in the writing of high school students and graduate students?

SHARPE: Well, there's an increasing mastery of the forms that we use to express ourselves, whether it be the essay, or the memoir, or the poem, the short story or the novella. The concerns of the authors get more complicated as they age. There can be a downside to growing up as far as being a writer which is that you become more conservative; that is, the more you know what is expected of you, the fewer risks you are likely to take. Younger writers don't know they are supposed to do something a certain way and that can be wonderful. There is a freedom to try anything, which I find actually inspiring, and I try to remember to always allow myself to screw up really bad.

ELLIS: You've conducted interviews with authors Lydia Davis, Lynne Tillman, Jonathan Lethem, Colson Whitehead, and Linh Dinh. Can you speak about this experience and how you chose to interview these authors?

SHARPE: I chose them because I like them; they're people whose work I have read and admired. I was commissioned to do interviews by the Teachers and Writers Collaborative, an organization I worked with for about twelve years, whose main function is to get writers into the public schools. I got to interview whoever I wanted.

I read for pleasure in my personal life and in my professional life I read to teach other people how to write. But I'd never read to think up questions to ask the author. I don't know how you find it, but it made me pay attention in a whole new way to what I was reading. Then there's that whole social aspect, where you're also having a conversation with that person. It invokes a lot of skills at the same time.

ELLIS: What are you working on now?

SHARPE: You're going to make me break out in hives. I'm working on another novel, a historical novel. It's giving me a major pain in the neck because I'm trying something that's very different for me. My other projects have always been about contemporary American families in one description or another. The people I'm writing about now are not really a family and they're not contemporary. I feel like I'm wandering around in the dark, not knowing what I'm doing. And there's a lot of anxiety in that. As I was saying earlier I think it's important to strike out into new areas.

Mary Yukari Waters

What I Will Follow

Mary Yukari Waters was born in a traditional Kyoto neighborhood where tofu vendors honked their horns each evening, and narrow, crooked lanes led into hidden shrines. This neighborhood is the setting for many of the short stories in her collection *The Laws of Evening*. The book's details about Japanese life and culture come mostly from her childhood memory of the ten years she lived in Japan before her parents moved to the United States (she is half Japanese and half Irish-American). Others are based on memories shared with her by her eighty-five-year-old grandmother, with whom she spends extensive time visiting in the city of Kyoto, where they cook, shop at the open-air market, and go bathing at the public bathhouse.

The Laws of Evening was a Booksense 76 selection and a pick for Barnes and Noble's Discover Great New Writers program, as well as a 2004 Kiriyama Prize Notable Book. *The Laws of Evening* was also chosen by *Newsday* and the *San Francisco Chronicle* as one of the Best Books of 2003. In her review of *The Laws of Evening* for the *New York Times* Mary Park wrote, "Like the spare and prescribed movements of a Japanese tea ceremony, the stories in *The Laws of Evening* . . . present a deceptively smooth and elegant surface. Underneath this unruffled exterior, however, the smallest nuances convey real depth of feeling." *The Independent on Sunday* wrote, "Gorgeous, note-perfect short stories . . . a bittersweet read that transports you into another time."

The eleven stories contained in this collection are chronologically ordered. Nine of them were originally published in *Shenandoah, Glimmer Train Stories, TriQuarterly, Manoa, Black Warrior Review, The Missouri Review, The Indiana Review*, and *Zoetrope: All Story*. Five of these stories have also been included in anthologies: *The 2000 Pushcart Prize Anthology*; *The Pushcart Book of Short Stories: The Best Short Stories from a Quarter-Century of the Pushcart Prize*; *The O. Henry Prize Stories 2002*; *Frances Ford Coppola's Zoetrope Anthology 2*; *Best American Short Stories 2002*; *Best American Short Stories 2003*; and *Best American Short Stories 2004*. Waters' fiction has also aired on NPR's Selected Shorts and BBC. Mary Yukari Waters is the recipient of a 2002 grant from the National Endowment for the Arts.

Waters teaches writing at the low-residency MFA program at Spalding University and at the Writers' Program at UCLA Extension. She previously taught at UC Irvine, where she worked on her MFA. Prior to becoming a writer Waters worked as a public certified accountant for ten years.

At the present time she is working on a novel.

Mary Yukari Waters lives in Los Angeles. Our interview was conducted by phone.

SHERRY ELLIS: Loss, upheaval, estrangement, renewal, and reconciliation are some of the themes of the stories contained in *The Laws of Evening*. When you conceived of this collection did you intend to use these themes as a means of story unification?

MARY YUKARI WATERS: No, not at all. For a long time, I didn't even conceive of a collection, much less plan out the themes I was going to use. Publishing wasn't my concern at first. I started writing because I had a demanding and unfulfilling job in corporate tax accounting that I needed an escape from, and because there had been several deaths in my family. Rilke once told his young poet to write about his belief in anything beautiful. I read that passage years after I'd already started writing, and it was only then that I realized it was exactly what I'd been trying to do, in a clueless kind of way, of course.

The themes in this collection pretty much coalesced on their own. I didn't see them until fairly late in the process, and it was so illuminating and surprising to see the pattern that had slowly emerged in my work. I learned a great deal about my own basic preoccupations. For example, I'd never realized how important the concept of memory was in my overall outlook on life. Also, I'd never been fully aware of my fascination with those certain rare people who can successfully transcend the unfairnesses and misfortunes of life. I think it makes sense, in retrospect, that I found myself drawn to that nebulous period in Japanese history between World War II and modern times. Because what Japan went through on a large, national scale—you know, coming to terms with defeat, reinventing themselves—is exactly what all of us, as individuals, are forced to face at some point in our own lives.

Another thing that was unintentional, at least till near the end, was the chronological pattern of the stories. The first story in the collection takes place right around the beginning of World War II, and the stories progress in time until the last one, which is set in modern times. It would have never occurred to me to plan it out that way, but looking back, it worked really well because that chronological linkage among the stories gave a novelistic feel to the collection as a whole. This is why I don't like to plan too rationally when I start a new project. I think the most exciting part of writing is seeing what pattern emerges from your own subconscious.

ELLIS: The story "Shibusa" begins and ends with the character Goto-san and her relationship with the tea ceremony. When you started writing this story were you aware of the extent to which the tea ceremony would play a symbolic role?

WATERS: Again, no. At first, the tea ceremony was just a minor detail. And like most minor details, they came from the life that I knew. As you know, I was born in Japan and lived there till I was nine. Since then, I've gone back every other year, so a lot of details in my stories come from what I've seen and heard. In this case, my grandmother's sister happens to run a school for tea ceremony and *koto*, so I felt comfortable setting my character in that world. It was only after the shape of the story fully emerged that I saw an opportunity to draw a parallel between the concept of the tea ceremony and the events in Goto-san's life. And at that point, the tea ceremony took on a deeper symbolic importance.

ELLIS: In the story "Seed" you refer to desert flowers, their brief and isolated blooms. How did you choose the title "Seed" for this story?

WATERS: I was interested in the idea of a seed as something small and tenacious that bides its time during bad conditions; that just keeps waiting and waiting until it's safe to bloom. Some seeds survive, but a lot of them don't, especially in the desert. That's the strange thing about life: the random nature of what actually ends up surviving. I think people, too, have seeds inside them, like the main character in the story. You wonder how that brief encounter at the end of the story is going to survive in her mind, and whether it will flower years later in some strange, unexpected way. Or if it will survive at all.

ELLIS: In "Egg-Face," hope is rekindled for thirty-year-old Ritsuko when a matchmaker arranges for her to meet a handsome, eligible young man. "Egg-Face" is rich with symbol and foreboding as manifested through the weather and environment. "The spring air was translucent with smog. All the soot expelled during the day—all the soot expelled during this long depression—was falling back down to earth, the sediment floating in the busy streets. Late-afternoon sunlight slanted through it, creating an amber viscosity in which the traffic below would eventually still." What was the hardest part of developing these images?

WATERS: That's hard to say. For me, they're one of the easier parts of writing. I tend to use physical environment when I'm exploring a particular mood. So they're often loaded with emotion, which gives them a specific reason for existing on the page, as opposed to description that just goes on and on for no apparent reason other than to just put down facts. One thing that helps me is that so many of these scenes are built on places that, for me, are heavy with memory. So, for example, when I describe a tree on the corner of the lane, or the way sunlight comes through a window, those images have years of personal weight behind them. Describing them is almost an act of love, so the words flow without that sense of strain I might feel if I were, say, writing a travel article about a place I wasn't fully invested in. In some ways, it's similar to what we talked about earlier, about details coming from things I've seen and heard. We writers all have so many powerful images just sitting in our memory bank, gathering emotional power over the years. If we could just tap into them, you know—that's the challenge.

ELLIS: In the story "Aftermath" you describe the corn tasting of soy sauce and sugar at the Tanabara Night Festival. Is this taste something your own family experienced or part of a conversation you overheard?

WATERS: Sort of. My mother was Japanese, and after she married my father they moved to America, where she pretty much stayed except for occasional visits back home. Sometimes she'd try to cook Japanese food but it was very difficult, because we lived in a little town where we didn't have access to Japanese foods. I remember one day she tried grilling corn in that soy sauce and sugar mixture, and it didn't come out right. It tasted okay to me, but I guess the method of grilling changed the taste, or maybe the American corn was different or something. Anyway, there was one brief moment when the disappointment and sadness showed on her face. And it was about much more than just the corn, and that look haunted me for a long time. When I was writing this story, I felt this really strong need to make the corn taste just right. I guess it was my way of making it up to her, of taking something that had saddened me in real life and trying to fix it through fiction.

ELLIS: In the story "Seed," radishes serve as a metaphor. You write, "But these radishes had no juicy crunch. They were as rubbery as boiled jellyfish and required rigorous chewing. Shoji didn't seem to notice—he was often exhausted when he came home—and lately Masae fancied that he was absorbing the radishes' essence. Since they had come to Tai-huen, something about him had shrunk in an indefinable way, as if an energy that once shimmered right below the surface of his skin had retreated deep into his body." How did you develop this metaphor?

WATERS: I think it comes down to using details that you're familiar with. I happen to love food in general, so it's always fun to use them as metaphors. Grated radishes are actually a common dish in Japan (you mix them with dried whitebait and a little soy sauce). Fresh radishes have that nice juicy crunch, but old radishes get tough and rubbery because they're trying to conserve what little water they have left. When you're exposed to something all the time, it's much easier to see them as metaphor, to find fresh parallels.

ELLIS: "The Way Love Works" is one of two stories in *The Laws of Evening* told from the first person. It describes a Japanese-American teenager's return to Japan with her mother. I'm wondering why you chose first person point of view for this particular story, and if this story is in any way autobiographical?

WATERS: It's partly autobiographical, actually more so than many of my other stories. You can see clear similarities, like the fact that the main character is half-Japanese, just like me. But it also follows the pattern of the other stories in the collection, where a lot of real-life details are used within a fictional framework. As for first person, there was no compelling reason to use first person in this story. It could just as easily have been third person, I suppose. Most of my other stories are. But then again, I didn't write this story with the idea of a collection in mind, and that's been the case with most of these stories. The most likely answer is that I was tired of third person at the time, and needed a change. Isn't that mundane? But sometimes we do make artistic choices for mundane reasons. When I look back on it now, I find it amazing that this collection hangs together as coherently as it does. I actually think it hangs together better than if I'd tried to plan it out. I think it's because each story piqued a new interest, which led to the writing of another story, which piqued a different interest, and so on. And that process linked the stories in a truly organic way.

ELLIS: Virginia Woolf once said, "Every secret of a writer's soul, every experience of his life, every quality of his mind is written large in his works." How much do you believe your own thoughts, secrets and life have informed your fiction?

WATERS: Oh, very much so. It's crucial to come from an emotionally honest place when you write fiction. And by this, I don't mean sharing your dirty laundry. The world is packed with people who can write well, but the only way a writer is going to stand out is to be completely, emotionally honest in a way that resonates deep down in a reader's mind. You can call it soul, or outlook on life, but whatever it is, it's a certain aura about your writing that's a result of every experience you've ever had, every emotion you've ever felt. And that aura, that insight, is the most important thing you have to offer. In that sense, a work of fiction can be, and should be, every bit as emotionally "real" as a memoir. I think that's partly what Virginia Woolf was talking about. If you ask ten different writers to look at a tree, they'll all see it differently, as if each one was wearing different colored glasses. And that's because each writer sees it through his or her emotional context. I think it goes back to the themes we were talking about earlier. Writing is a way to get these themes out so you can see your own self in a clear light. And in the process of being honest with yourself, you might reach another reader who has similar issues buried deep inside. When that connection happens, it's magical.

ELLIS: Judith Lewis in her *LA Weekly* review of *The Laws of Evening* wrote, "Mary Yukari Waters' characters emerge from her stories like delicate watercolor portraits, detailed enough to be recognizable but never overdrawn. There is no excess in her narratives, no drama, no superfluous preposition or adjective." Your prose is richly descriptive and poetic. What writers and artists inspire you?

WATERS: There are so many writers I greatly admire, but I've never felt that any one person directly affected my writing. I think it's because I started writing so late. I didn't go through that typical process of a young aspiring writer, where you read a lot of writers, pattern your writing after the ones you admire, and finally, after a lot of derivative attempts, find your own voice. When I started writing, I was working as a CPA, so it left me barely enough free time to write, much less read all the writers I was supposed to. I just didn't have that luxury. I was actually a bookworm as a kid, but I didn't do much reading during and after college. The bulk of my "literate" reading came after I had found my own voice. I think this made a big difference in the way I approached other people's writing. Through good luck, or bad luck, I missed out on that stage where I depended on other writers to help me with my own style and technique. Having said that, the writers I admire are Virginia Woolf, Doris Lessing, Edith Wharton, Gail Godwin, among many, many others.

ELLIS: When you are writing a story which usually comes—first plot or character?

WATERS: There's no rule. Each story develops in a different way. Sometimes I'll just start with a feeling. Once I was talking with a poet, and I told her that one of my stories had started with a complex emotion that I had a real need to capture on paper. And then I created an entire story building up to that fleeting moment, so that the reader could experience the exact feeling I had. And the poet said, "Oh, that's exactly the way I write my poetry." That was a really nice bonding moment. Or sometimes a story might begin with a dilemma, and I keep writing to see how it's going to play out. For example, "Egg-Face" is a story that starts with the dilemma of a thirty-year-old woman who's never had a date or a job. I was interested in her predicament, and I wanted to see where it would take me. Or sometimes a story will start with an interesting little detail, one that often ends up being completely insignificant to the story. But you have to start somewhere, and a curious fact or detail can get you into a story. For example, in "Since My House Burned Down," there's a brief section about a girl practicing her silverware skills so she can go to an omelet parlor. This detail came from a story my grandmother told me about her own youth. When she was growing up, the popular girls would be invited by their dates to eat at this tiny store that was open only for lunch. They sold a plain American omelet, served with ketchup from a bottle. It was such a status symbol to go there. I loved that story, because it was so funny and odd. I thought I'd start out with it and see what came of it. The story ending up taking off in a completely different direction, and the omelet never became a significant part. But at least it got me started. There are endless ways you can begin a story. Every time I start a new piece, I feel like I'm reinventing the wheel. And I always have this sense of panic, because I feel just as clueless as I did when wrote my first story. I've never developed a pat system for these things. And I don't ever want to, because then it'll become like a factory, where I'm just cranking out stories from the same basic mold. I like it that each story poses challenges, that you can never rest on your laurels. That keeps it interesting, and rather scary.

ELLIS: Did anyone read your early work and give you feedback?

WATERS: Yes, I was in a workshop for many years with a teacher called Tom Filer. He held it in his home, with the same group of students every year, and that was where I did most of my early writing. It was a real sanctuary. He'd read us letters from Chekhov, or Faulkner's Nobel Prize acceptance speech. We never discussed publishing, or any of the business aspects of writing; it was always about the art. And after the workshop session, we'd snack on wine and appetizers. Tom opened up a whole new world for me. I consider myself very lucky that I stumbled across him.

ELLIS: What has been the hardest thing for you to learn about writing?

WATERS: Without a doubt, the hardest thing is disciplining myself to write every day. I'm ashamed to say I've never gotten the knack of it. It depresses me terribly. It's like being on a diet every single day of your life, in the sense that I'm constantly falling off the wagon. There are periods when I'm so distracted by work or giving readings, etc., that I don't write for days, even weeks. I also find it hard to write when my house is a mess, which is the case much of the time. I do get on a good cycle occasionally, and I try to get my good writing done then, before the cycle peters out. I'm starting to wonder if some people just work better in cycles, rather than in a linear, "write-every-day-without-fail" approach.

When I'm not writing, I'm not consciously thinking about it. I'll immerse myself fully in cooking, or watching TV, or whatever else I happen to be doing. I'm a great believer in not pushing or straining when it comes to creativity, which is probably just an excuse for laziness. But I do think there's some validity to it. Looking back, I think that my best writing has been the kind that just seemed to float up to the surface of my mind on its own schedule, when it was formed and ready.

ELLIS: Truman Capote said, "I believe more in the scissors than I do in the pencil." Can you describe your process of revision in terms of how much cutting and writing you do?

WATERS: I love revision. It's so much more interesting than a first draft, which for me is laborious and exhausting. Early drafts are so discouraging. The quality of the writing is bad, you don't know where you're going with any of this, and you know that most of what you're writing will have to eventually be thrown away. But with revision, you're at the point when language and level of insight and clarity of theme are all at a more accomplished level; you can look at your work without feeling disgusted by it. Revision is where you move away from the subconscious and really scrutinize the architectural way in which a story is put together. You examine the details in relation to theme or mood, you look at the pacing. You have real control, which is a relief and a comfort after that earlier rocky period of navigating the subconscious. Actually, your quote from Truman Capote reminds me of something I once heard in an art appreciation class. Michelangelo was asked how he chiseled sculptures out of stone. How did he know what to chisel out? He said, I visualize the image within the stone, and then free it by getting rid of the parts that don't belong. That's a frustrating comment, isn't it, because what's so difficult is being able to visualize that image in the first place. For me, numerous drafts are crucial in order to get a clear vision of that image within the stone. You can't just look at a blank page and say, "I'll plan it out now, before I get my hands dirty." Well, you can, but in my experience the story is going to come out shallow and flat. You have to give your story enough room to morph in mid-journey, to take on different shapes and different levels of depth. That's what's exciting. Once the story has found itself, it's easy to go back and cut out what doesn't fit, or add what needs to be added. In my writing classes, once my students figure out what it is that their stories are really about, the revisions are often remarkable. The problem with many writers is that they skimp on the revision process. In other words, they're in too big of a hurry to keep writing draft after draft so that their stories can be as deep and rich and insightful as they could be. It takes a really long time to see that image within the stone, in all its clarity. You have to be patient.

ELLIS: So have you ever had a story published, and when you read it after you've had a sense of separation from it you've said, "Oh, why didn't I cut this part out? Why didn't I transform it?"

WATERS: Definitely. It's hard for me to look at a story I've written years ago. I'm always very critical of my technique, always thinking how I would revise it now if I had the chance. It's like watching a videotape of yourself when you were a teenager. You see your own gawkiness, and that's mortifying. But interestingly, I've always felt good about where my heart was when I wrote the story. I've never regretted what the story was about or what it was aiming for—although I do feel I could do it better technical justice now. I suppose that's a good sign, right? It must mean my technique has improved in the meantime. I try to see it that way.

ELLIS: It's rather amazing that you didn't plan on having a career as a writer. How have you dealt with all the recognition and the awards that you've received?

WATERS: It's been very odd. Sometimes I think people assume that since I've gotten the recognition and the awards, I know what the secrets are for a good story. The strange thing is, I still don't fully understand why my stories have received the recognition they have. And I actually don't want to know, or need to know. I feel like pinning it down too securely would be a bad thing. I think it's better if my own writing, or my own voice, remains something of a mystery even to myself. I feel very, very fortunate about what's happened so far. But because I can't pinpoint exactly what it was that "worked," I have no confidence of replicating that success. It's like having won the lottery, then wondering if it can possibly happen a second time.

ELLIS: Have you had many rejections and how do you cope with them?

WATERS: Oh yes, I have had lots of rejections. I still get rejections. Rejections are depressing, there's no getting around it. But for some reason, they're not as traumatizing for me as they are for some people. It's because I don't know the people rejecting me, I'll never have to run into them at the supermarket. And they'd never recognize me even if I did. The sheer impersonality of it takes away most of the sting. But on the other hand, I could never be a telemarketer or a door-to-door salesman. That kind of rejection is too personal, and I don't have the toughness for it.

Ellis: Do you have any advice to offer new writers?

WATERS: I think so many new writers are eager to publish as quickly as possible, to become successful as quickly as possible. I understand that; it's a natural feeling. But I also think that all the focus on outward forms of success prevent them from having the patience to explore within themselves, to find out what really makes them tick. We talked earlier about letting thematic patterns emerge in your work, and about getting a clear view of the image within the stone. All of this takes time and patience. Someone once said that the difference between success and failure was stopping after eleven tries instead of going on to the twelfth. I do think that important developments take place for a writer during that proverbial twelfth try. When new writers shortchange that process, they cheat themselves of discovering what they are truly capable of.

ELLIS: Can you compare your experience of writing short stories to writing the novel you're currently working on?

WATERS: I'm actually enjoying the novel process. I can delve into issues so much more deeply. The novel gives me more latitude to link together scenes and time periods on a much larger canvas, and I'm conscious of having to juggle more balls than I did with my short stories. I feel like I'm able to create something much more layered and complex than I could with the short story form. It's nice having to come up with just one general idea, instead of inventing a brand new topic every few months. The bad thing is that novels take so long to write, and I miss the feeling that I used to have with short stories, that sense of accomplishment whenever I finished a story, or even a draft of one. With short stories, something is always happening: it's being shopped around, maybe rejected, but at least someone's reading it and responding to it. With novels the gestation period is far longer, and you're in a time warp where the final result is delayed for a really long time. Also, the difference in investment is huge. With a short story, you know fairly soon if it's going to work or not. This lets you abandon it without wasting too much time. But with a novel, it takes years to even know whether it'll work or not. I'm nervous about that. But I'm enjoying this process of being able to linger with the characters, to enter their lives and live with them for a while.

ELLIS: Have you written any short stories as a means of taking a break from your novel?

WATERS: I've written one short story, and it's actually helped me with the novel. In the early stages of my novel, my head was whirling with all the ideas I had. I felt utterly overwhelmed, like I'd bitten off too much material to chew. Actually this is normal for me, even with short stories. It's a good sign because if I'm not overwhelmed at the beginning, it usually means I don't have enough to work with. Things always come together if you sit with them long enough. Anyway, it occurred to me that if I took a small, manageable part of that material and made a short story out of it, I'd feel less overwhelmed. The process of writing the story helped me to solidify some ideas, and I found that I was able to understand my novel better when I returned to it.

ELLIS: In your future works do you think you'll continue returning to Japan?

WATERS: I'm not sure. I've really enjoyed writing about Japan, and I'm not sure if I've exhausted it yet. When I first started writing, I naturally turned to Japan because it was the place of my childhood, which is usually the root of self-discovery. Also, I really enjoy the process of translating the sensibility of one culture into that of another. But there's a whole American side of me that I may want to tap into. For now, I'm comfortable not knowing. All I know is, whatever I find myself most fascinated with is what I'm going to follow.

Ron Carlson

Inventory of Ron Carlson

When Ron Carlson was in the sixth grade at the Edison Elementary School in Salt Lake City, Utah, he wrote skits for his friends. His love of words has only continued to grow with time. By 1983, thirteen years into his writing career, he learned to accept not knowing where his stories were heading. He realized that if he let go and paid attention to detail, that both he and the reader would be surprised by the story's end. When Carlson writes stories he creates believable worlds by including what he calls "inventory"—information about the space which his characters inhabit. He also believes that place is an integral character in his stories.

    John Irving said of *The News of the World*, "There is in these stories a certain holiness bestowed on ordinary things, in ordinary lives, that is a powerful reminder of the late John Cheever." *Plan B for the Middle Class* was selected as one of the best books of the year (1987) by the *New York Times*. The *Boston Globe*, in its review of *Plan B for the Middle Class*, wrote, "Carlson's range—from quotidian to surreal, encompassing everything between—is astonishing." *Hotel Eden* was selected by the *New York Times* as a 1992 Notable Book of the Year and it was selected as "one of the best books of the year" by the *Los Angeles Times*. Carlson's fourth short story collection, *At the Jim Bridger*, was published in 2002. It was selected by the *Los Angeles Times* as one of the best books of 2002. Robert Olen Butler said, "If you wish to understand how it is we live in the beginning of the twenty-first century, you must read Ron Carlson." *A Kind of Flying: Selected Short Stories* was published in 2003. It includes selections from Carlson's first three short story collections. In June 2004, this anthology was included on the Vacation Reading list of the *New York Times*. *The Speed of Light*, a coming-of-age novel, was published in 2003 and in 2007 his first adult novel, *Five Skies*, will be published. Also in 2007 a book on writing, *Ron Carlson Writes a Story*, will appear from Graywolf.

    Carlson's short stories have also been included in *The Best American Short Stories*, *The O'Henry Prize Stories*, and *The Norton Anthology of Short Fiction*, and have also been published in the following magazines and journals: the *New Yorker*, *Glimmer Train*, *Harper's*, *Gentleman's Quarterly*, *Esquire*, the *Oxford American*, *Carolina Quarterly*, *Sports Illustrated*, *Missouri Review*, and

Tin House. Carlson has also contributed book reviews to the *New York Times Book Review* and the *Los Angeles Times.*

In 1987, Carlson was awarded a National Endowment for the Arts Fellowship and in 1993, he won the Ploughshares Cohen Prize.

Carlson earned his master's degree at the University of Utah in 1972. From 1983 to 2006, he taught at the creative writing program of Arizona State University. In 2006 he became the director of graduate fiction writing at the University of California at Irvine.

The following interview was conducted by phone.

SHERRY ELLIS: "A Kind of Flying," a story you originally wrote for a National Public Radio assignment, is included in the anthology *A Wedding Cake in the Middle of the Road* and in your collections *Plan B for the Middle Class* and *A Kind of Flying: Selected Short Stories*. It opens with the beginning of a marriage and ends twenty years later, with the husband commenting, "It's marriage. Sometimes it pinches like a bird's mouth but it's definitely flying. It's definitely a kind of flying." You have said that in your stories you often return to where you begin. Can you describe your process?

RON CARLSON: At first it wasn't conscious; I didn't see it happening. Then I noticed that the inventory in the opening of the story had a kind of call for me and, of course the things you invent bend the narrative you're unfolding; towards the end of the story you find yourself being revisited by these things that you weren't consciously expecting.

ELLIS: Many of your stories are inhabited by unconventional characters, some of whom become more self-aware. In "The Towel Season," a story contained in the collection *At the Jim Bridger*, Edison is a brilliant theoretical engineer who is socially inept. He communicates with his wife in an idiosyncratic language that is filled with metaphor. What challenges do you face in developing the peculiarities in your characters?

CARLSON: Well, first, I'm not sure there are any conventional people. I think that if you look at anyone closely enough, you begin to see what we might call quirks. I don't set off to make odd-balls, I set off to distinguish, in whatever way I can, these characters from everybody else. So, the biggest challenge for a writer, I think for any writer, is to bring their attention to the work and to write closely. I don't work from outlines of my characters. I work from small notions of their particularity.

ELLIS: As a college student you spent a summer delivering medical oxygen in Phoenix and its environs. Years later you wrote the story "Oxygen" that was originally contained in the collection *The Hotel Eden*, and is also included in your new collection *A Kind of Flying: Selected Short Stories*. In this story the character David says, "I just drove," at a point when he is particularly displeased with his own behavior and the choices he has made. "Now the sky was ripped apart the way I've learned only a western sky can be, the glacial cloud cover broken, and the shreds gathering against the Superstitious Mountains . . . ." Do you often use geography and weather as metaphors for the feelings and experiences of your characters?

CARLSON: I use place and what I might call inventory of the space, which involves grounding myself. I didn't consciously, in writing the section you just read, look for metaphor.

What I need as a writer is something I can believe in; something that feels real, that I can stand on, that as a writer will help me stay in the current scene for another minute so that I may have the opportunity to find out where I'm going.

ELLIS: To what extent do you believe that living in the west has influenced you as a writer?

CARLSON: I feel a need to live in the west. I like the size of things. I like the way things change. I like being able to get out of town; I mean out of town. And so I would say that living in Utah and Arizona has been a huge influence on me.

ELLIS: "Donner drew a chestful of the sharp air. He'd made a decision last February with the woman whom he could now see dancing inside the painted window. It was made in the frigid early twilight under low clouds . . ." the narrator reveals, in the short story "At the Jim Bridger," in the collection of the same name. In your stories objects and circumstances gather what you have described as "symbolic weight." What do you believe are the most delicate and forceful moments in "At the Jim Bridger" and how did you place them in this story?

CARLSON: Well, that's a nice way to ask that question. What I was trying there, as that story unfolded before me, was really not to design delicate moments, but once I understood what was going on with Donner, and from the minute he sees the dog, I again slowed down, and tried to put in as many real things in that story and to keep it on the ground so they didn't float away in some sweeping gesture about regret.

ELLIS: You have described that several of your stories, such as "Bigfoot," "I Am Bigfoot," "The Time I Died," and "Madame Zelena Finally Comes Clean," that appear in *The News of the World* and *A Kind of Flying*, are "tabloid stories." What do you mean by the phrase "tabloid story" and how are they different from your other work?

CARLSON: Well, I've written probably about a dozen of those pieces. They've appeared, as you said, in *The News of the World* and also *Plan B for the Middle Class*, and they began with the strangest stories. I mean, twenty-five years ago I was in England. That's where they really let tabloids have their way; they make ours look really pale. They are sensational stories about life and death, about other planets, about religion. They're just wonderful and so rich, so challenging to credibility.

What I wanted to do, after I realized I was going to write "Bigfoot Stole My Wife," and these "concept stories," was put human feet under them. One of the stories that isn't in a collection is "I Found Hitler's Golf Clubs." I wrote a piece about spontaneous human combustion, called "Smoke." "The Table Cloth of Turin" is one where the character is really pretty sure that he has the tablecloth from the Last Supper. That one really came to mind recently. As part of a challenge I was reading this bestseller called *The Da Vinci Code*. There's a lot of the Last Supper in that book. So I started to write these monologues from the point of view of these people who had died and come back from the dead, or who were psychics. What I wanted was to ground these strange outcries, try to make them human voices. "Phenomena" is perhaps my favorite; a fellow is pretty convinced he's seen a UFO—and he doesn't want to see a UFO at all.

"Bigfoot Stole My Wife" has been very popular. It's a little bit lighter than the rest. When I come home from work, I'm hoping my wife is here. I mean, if someone came home and learned that his wife was gone and that Bigfoot had stolen her—what would that be like? It would have to be bad! As a writer I'm not afraid to play. I've done it a lot. I'm sure I'll do it again. I'm not a single kind of writer. I mean, a lot of these stories are literary stories, serious attempts to discover what the human heart is like, and others are these more playful ones.

ELLIS: In the story "The Governor's Ball," which originally appeared in the *The News of the World*, and is also contained in *A Kind of Flying: Selected Short Stories*, as the protagonist makes his way to a local dump a mattress flies off his truck, over a ramp, through five stories of air, and falls to the ground. What were the unexpected plot and character revelations that occurred to you as you were writing this story?

CARLSON: "The Governor's Ball" was an important story to me because it was the first time I went far out into territory I did not know, and it was there I met some surprises that helped me finish the story. The biggest single surprise, that really is a metaphor for what happened in my work fifty other times, is when he meets the people on the street, the two homeless people. I was very worried that I had a generic moment going there, and that's when I really slowed down. I did what I call "sit in all the chairs"; I had to be everybody. It was so surprising to me, that when I got around to the homeless man and he says, "Would this mattress fly out of the sky?" I had the thought as a writer that day—"That's right! He got to see it and I didn't." The truth is I did drop a mattress, but I didn't get to see it fall.

Everybody has a right to exist in the story. They're not in the story for me the writer—nor for the protagonist. Those two homeless people are in the story because they don't have any place to go on a cold winter night, and so it was a kind of really small revelation, where when I went around the circle and sat in the homeless guy's chair—he had information I might have no access to—and it helped.

ELLIS: "It was Sunday, and if you want a definition of sterility, try downtown New Haven on the second Sunday in February," the husband says, in "Life Before Science," a story contained in both *The News of the World* and *A Kind of Flying: Selected Short Stories*. He's an artist who loses interest in his craft at the same time he and his wife struggle with their lack of fertility. Was it your intention to juxtapose the lack of ability to procreate with a negative impact on the creative process, or is this an example of your discovery process?

CARLSON: If I'm going to be honest, the answer is that yes, everybody gets a story, everybody needs to have a challenge. What was his? He's a little dried up as a painter, and he stalled. Many times writers write about painters; I think I was writing about a writer when I wrote that story, the same thing when I wrote about the mathematician in "The Towel Season." I mean, there were a few sentences in that story about teaching that were right out of the big book on it. And of course I'd been a teacher for a million years. It is a parallel, I obviously see it as a parallel in terms of the story's theme and motif, but I wanted it, like all things in my story work, to be believable. I mean, a lot of teachers—you turn your energies to your students and it does drain you a little, and universities and schools are where artists disappear primarily. I mean, a lot of writers and artists don't, but it's by sheer stubborn will. I believe both parts of the story were intentional, that the couple's having trouble and that he's having his own difficulties as a painter.

ELLIS: In your story "Milk" which was originally published in *The News of the World* and is also included in *The Best American Short Stories of 1987* and *A Kind of Flying: Selected Short Stories*, a father experiences conflict as to how to deal with his fear for his children's safety. Can you describe the challenges you face in portraying the inner conflicts of your characters?

CARLSON: Sometimes characters, like people, have a fear or a hope, that they don't exactly have words for. And it is the custom of genre fiction to give everybody a word—and help them explain themselves. They're afraid of this or hope for that, and they are fully capable of articulating their agenda; and I don't think that's the case. I think, for example, that all those characters in Ray Carver were people with problems that they couldn't quite put their fingers on, the way that we are, and so in "Milk," here's a guy who's pretty certain he loves his kids with every muscle in his body, but doesn't exactly know what form that should take and is doing everything he can; and meanwhile once he's had children, the world suddenly becomes a very dangerous place, at least it seems to him to be, and so he gets generally vexed. So again, it requires empathy. When I teach, I talk about this empathy; I also talk about sitting in the character's chair with him for a while and try to follow him around, without reducing him to a simple statement, so I try to do that in all my stories. I try to make all my characters resistible to reduction by giving them complicated heads and complicated lives.

ELLIS: "The H Street Sledding Record" is frequently read out loud during the holidays, for example at Symphony Space in New York. The father says, "I have thrown horse manure on our roof for four years now and I plan to do it every Christmas Eve until my arm gives out. It satisfies me as a homeowner to do so . . ." How did you develop the characters and situations for this story?

CARLSON: I had a premise. I knew a guy like that, in fact it was my wife's father, and when she told me about it I knew I'd write a story about it sometime. Of course, a lot of things come together. Many times in fiction you have an amalgam of two or three people as well as a little of yourself. In that story, then, I again did not want it simply to be a joke, I wanted it to be part of a real life. I really went after it a little bit. When I heard you read that phrase I heard you say the word "homeowner" and I'm glad I got that word in there, as he announces his credo for the holidays. So again, you take the idea and try to put human feet under it and you stay with the characters long enough so that they assume a real life underneath the ideas and the story. And the way I do it always with as much inventory as possible, putting in these things that make me believe the story as I'm typing my way through it.

ELLIS: What factors do you consider when deciding whether something you are writing is a short story or a novel?

CARLSON: Well, the only factor I've had for years is that I always knew I was writing a short story. I'd get a notion, and then I'd go in and it was messy. Sometimes it was five or six pages and sometimes, more frequently, it was more like twenty-eight to thirty-two pages. I try to bring stories in at sixteen to twenty-five pages, I guess, between three and five thousand words. I became a story writer, even though I didn't know what was going to happen in a story once I had an idea for it, or a moment or event, which was going to send me into the writing. I sensed it would be a one, two or three week endeavor and I'd emerge somewhere, on some far shore with a story in my hand.

I'm writing a novel now, and it's clear that I'm writing a novel. It's just a very different kind of writing. Daily it's a different kind of writing, and certainly planning is different and a great deal more.

A couple of my stories got long, "Oxygen" and "Blazo." They were very long until I cut them, but even then I just thought these were long stories, I didn't think they were novels. That whole dichotomy and the definitions of the two forms sometimes get blurry. Sometimes a novel is just a long story, but most novels are not. Most novels are layered and much more ambitious than stories, but not all.

I wanted each of my stories to be very convincing little worlds, and I love the short story; I'd write them forever, regardless of the fact that it isn't a particularly sharp career move. Wallace Stegner's agent advised him against writing stories. She told him, "You're burning your principal, if you do that you're using up all those beginnings and endings," and when I read that in the introduction to his collected stories, I was struck by the fact that yes, I've spent a lot of principal; but what would I have saved it for? When you write a story you create a world and then you don't get to use the sets again, it all goes on, and then you have to turn around and get a whole new world up and going in the next story.

ELLIS: How do you decide on point of view?

CARLSON: Well, I almost never schedule that. I write a couple of sentences and then I'm in. I've never really been academic in my choice; would this be better in the first or third person? Of course first person has so many gradations. I write in the first person point of view from a person who is not me. It's either a woman or a monster or a child, and there's also a first person who's a guy kind of like me, who's not in the center of the story, kind of an involved witness. I like that point of view very, very much. But I've been writing in the limited third person more and more, and I think it has as much immediacy and velocity and certainly can be as solid. The story and point of view come up together and we start. I've never finished a story and later changed the point of view. Although we teach point of view and we talk about it all the time, and there are some pitfalls in point of view that newer writers can step into, I've been able as I wrote the monologues or these most recent stories, to get a point of view and just go.

ELLIS: "Plan B for the Middle Class" is a story about a trip to Hawaii, desire, sex, marriage, and children. The protagonist says, "The theme for the spring is sand. It is everywhere," referring to life with his two young sons. Sand is such a powerful image for life sifting through one's hands. How did this metaphor come to you?

CARLSON: There was a period and it was in the 80s when VCRs were new and people were just getting them, and people took care of them and they were talking about the gears, and of course we had kids, and the way I work as a writer is that the metaphor of sand, and what it represents, comes way, way later. I like the idea of sand on the kitchen table, and I really like the idea of sand in a VCR. And now I see, now that you've mentioned it, that there's a lot of sand in that story. Later on in Hawaii there's a lot of sand, there's sand at a beach at the Great Salt Lake.

I'm a writer, who when people ask about theme and motif like this, I'm kind of always a little nervous talking about it because I keep my head down in the things of my stories, and so I was trying for an honest, funny little bit about the VCR repair man who says, "Hey, you've got to keep sand out of here," and I like the sound of sand as it flickered onto the floor, and those are things that I can believe, and I need that credibility to stay in the room to keep working. I try not to rise to idea or not recognize motifs until the draft has survived. Once I've got a full draft I'll go back and say I can polish it. Or I'll say this, as a writer in the second draft, when you finally can see what you've got, if you polish it towards theme, you're almost always pushing it towards a kind of obviousness it doesn't need. It's really interesting; so I try to keep a light touch when I go back and work towards issue about theme.

ELLIS: In the short piece "Disclaimer," contained in *At the Jim Bridger* you write, "If you want the coincidence where some character based on me gets the amazing girl back and has his heart start again after so many years, you're going to have to look in a book." Is this piece meant to let the reader know that, after all, you have been intertwining your life with your fiction?

CARLSON: I wasn't making any message. I was just seeing if I could push that old form, the disclaimer, and it was such a pleasure for me as it unrolled. I was just inventing, finding. And as you're talking about them, I see now, there are a lot of birds. It's so strange, especially in a story you write in a couple of days. I literally discovered that it was going to be about this lost girl. I just love the feeling of thinking, Oh good, that echo from the beginning is coming back. You go out into a piece until you can't touch the bottom, and when you kind of swim back and get sure you're in a place you've been before and it surprises you. That's the best way I can say it. No, I was just thinking, having my little fun with that form, the old disclaimer, and trying to make a story about it. I was surprised by that piece.

ELLIS: Each of your first three short story collections is divided into three sections. How did you decide upon this structure?

CARLSON: I wanted to set apart the comic stuff in the middle of each book. So I was glad to do that. And then I also wanted to bookend each book, to start strong with a story that gets on base; like baseball. You don't need to get a homerun but you need to get someone on first, one way or the other, or second. And then at the end I put some longer and more substantial stories. I'm so used to it now. It's like a record, where when one song ends I know the next story that's coming up. We have some literary stories, then some comic stuff, and come on home. "Life Before Science," "Oxygen," "Plan B for the Middle Class" are longer stories, and I put them all at the back of the book.

I've been so fortunate in these books, because the stories are not homogenous. The texture of these stories is different, from one to another. There are some similar stories in every collection, but as a set they are different from each other, and I've met reviewers who have celebrated my range as opposed to being annoyed that I couldn't settle down. I mean, I'm not going to settle down. I'm always going to use a variety of forms and a variety of textures and a variety of tones. That's what I do. Sometimes things are comedic; sometimes things are serious. Of course I like what one reviewer said—that I could be funny without being unserious. Of course, that's what you want.

ELLIS: *The Speed of Light*, your recent coming-of-age novel, is set in a working-class section of the Salt Lake City of your youth. It focuses on the transitional moments in the lives of three young boys who spend much of their time playing baseball. Is this book based on your own experience?

CARLSON: Yes, I had an amazing boyhood. It was filled with baseball, there was a fine river in it, and a railroad track and all the good stuff: lots of vacant lots, bicycles and a few girls. I just took all that stuff and cubed it, squared it up; I made it logarithmic, I amplified things and as I wrote on the story I began to see ways I could push it into shape. A perfectly normal family began to have troubles under my pen. I pushed and the episodes opened.

You start with these germs that are evocative, these kinds of moments and events, and as I look at that book now, everything is fiction, but everything had its little grains of beginning. My friends were all carefree and happy, but we had our moments.

ELLIS: Mark Twain once said, "I conceive that the right way to write a story for boys is to write so that it will not only interest boys but strongly interest any man who has ever been a boy. That immensely enlarges the audience." Do you agree with Twain's philosophy and do you think *Speed of Light* will also appeal to adults?

CARLSON: That's a great quote, and yes, I do. The chapters themselves were published in the last years and published places like *Carolina Quarterly* and the *Missouri Review* and *Sports Illustrated*. And when we put it together and saw it was about three boys, HarperCollins urged me to submit it as a young adult book, and my first thought was I never met an adult who wasn't young.

And when I read from that book, I read from it the night before last to a group of adults, and I mean everybody was over forty, and it went very, very well. I'm glad you reminded me about that quote. I mean, that is who this book is for. It's evocative of boyhood.

ELLIS: John Irving once said, "Half of my life is an act of revision." How much of your writing life is spent on revision?

CARLSON: Well, now I would say half of my life is revision; ten years ago I would have said about twenty percent is revision. Rewriting and reconsidering and recasting is key to writing. I mean, I want my writing to be right and tight, and you can never get it tight in a draft. You're always happy for a draft. It means you've prevailed up on to the shore and not drowned, but as much as you may be in love with it that day, two to three days will bring the sobering truth that it can be better, it can be tighter.

Usually what happens is almost all my beginnings are changed. Many times I will have written a page or two just to get myself up into the story, and I will have to edit and adjust the first typing. And many times the endings are too dense and concentrated, they need to be slowed down, you need to stop bringing up the soundtrack and stop heading for the barn door and let the story do its work. I do more rewriting, and I read everything out loud and I reconsider every verb; and if you're working steadily there's no hurry. And so, that's what I'm doing. I'm working steadily, there's no hurry, so I try to be careful.

ELLIS: What advice did you receive from established writers when you were a beginning writer?

CARLSON: Just a kind of encouragement. I think that the main thing is that I learned that no one was going to come and give me a stamp and validate me and say, "You're a writer"; I think more and more people know that today, that they're going to have to stamp themselves. I had some wonderful friends and teachers. My wife and I were always involved in teaching and reading. When I was at the University of Utah I met several writers. Hal Moore and David Kranes were professors of mine and they were alertly encouraging in a way that was not saying "Oh, this is good." They actively consulted with me and were diagnostic about my work and just being real about it; it was something we were doing together. I loved that and it affected the kind of teacher I try to be. I mean, I think it's irresponsible to be falsely encouraging. I think it's more important to be a really energetic consultant, an honest describer of what people are doing; I think that's the best help you can give a writer. I mean, the decision to be a writer has to be a personal one. The key is to of course stay in the room and finish your work. No one's going to read your work unless you go ahead and write it.

ELLIS: Do you agree with Charles Baxter who says, "I think most fiction is about desire"?

CARLSON: Well, most fiction definitely has a vector. There is need. Sometimes it's not desire; sometimes it's fear, a desire not to have something happen, a natural dynamic. If there isn't that dynamic, then you have this fiction that's chargeless and neutered. I'm careful with being reductive, I like to rant and rave, but to me saying that most fiction is about desire is like saying there are only two stories: a stranger comes to town and someone leaves on a journey. It may be true, but it doesn't exactly help; but yes, desire is a big part of the equation.

ELLIS: Author Michael Cunningham has said of your work, "Ron Carlson is doing something unique. He's writing the chronicle not only of our losses but of our quirky, unreliable potential for grace. He's creating a fictional world in which freedom and forgiveness hover, sometimes within reach." Ron Carlson, where do you go from here?

CARLSON: Well, I'm working on a novel about work, what people do with the day. I have a couple of stories I can't wait to get to, but I'm being good by not writing them. I'm resisting that temptation which I've always fallen for before. When things got tough, on the other novels I've worked on, I've always gone sideways into the short story door and to good result, but I'm not going to do that. I'm going to finish this novel, and I'm going to finish it this year, and then I can go back to writing these stories. Also, I've been writing a poem a year for twenty years, and that book will be finished in 2009 or 2010. Twenty eleven at the latest. And I'm going to go on with my career as a teacher. I'm very interested in the teaching of writing and I see it as a very active investigation, and there are years when I get real close to knowing what I'm talking about.

Amy Bloom

Characters That Won't Go Away

Amy Bloom started writing when she was thirty-four, after she had already earned a Master's in social work and established herself as a psychotherapist. She is the author of two collections of stories: *Come to Me*, which made the short list for the National Book Award in 1993 and received the *Los Angeles Times* Fiction Award; and *A Blind Man Can See How Much I Love You*, nominated for the National Book Critics Circle Award. Her first novel, *Love Invents Us*, was selected as a *New York Times* Notable Book. Bloom's first book of nonfiction, *Normal: Transsexual CEOs, Crossdressing Cops, and Hermaphrodites with Attitude*, is an exploration of the varieties of gender. *Away*, Bloom's second novel, will be published in August, 2007.

Amy Bloom's success is legendary. Her stories are included in *The Best American Short Stories 1991* and *The Best American Short Stories 2002* and she has won a National Magazine Award. Other stories have appeared in *Prize Stories: The O. Henry Awards*, and numerous other anthologies in the U.S. and abroad. She has written for the *New Yorker*, the *New York Times Magazine*, the *Atlantic Monthly*, *Vogue*, *Slate*, *Salon*, *Bazaar* and *Vogue*.

Bloom teaches at Yale University and lives in Connecticut. I spoke with her by phone.

SHERRY ELLIS: Nadine Gordimer said, "Instead of simply pondering on a question, I will invent a story that encompasses the question and try to see how it is answered by people's reactions and their emotions." How do you create your stories?

AMY BLOOM: Well, that's a great quote from Nadine Gordimer. I think I start with a moment or a character, somebody doing something, something that I can see suddenly, or I hear somebody say something, or I have an image. And then I want to provide information, I want to give my character opportunities to reveal who they are.

ELLIS: About the people you met and interviewed for your book of nonfiction, *Normal: Transsexual CEO's, Crossing Cops and Hermaphrodites with Attitude*, you've written, "Fiction would have failed these people, so I chose the other." How do you choose what medium you'll write in?

BLOOM: Well, I almost always write in fiction, and that's my story writing. And I did actually write a short story that was about a transsexual character and his mother. But I was going more for information or a point of view, something that I wanted to convey, and that led me to use nonfiction. When I'm writing fiction, it's not because I want to show anybody anything. It's because I want to tell a story, not prove a point.

ELLIS: How did you decide to transform your stories, for example "Sleepwalking" into "Night Vision," and "Light into Dark" and "Light Breaks Where No Sun Shines" into the novel *Love Invents Us*?

BLOOM: I think that there are some characters that weren't ready to go away, and I didn't want them to. They kept coming back and I kept being ready for them, and was happy they would come back. I don't want to make it seem as mysterious as it sounds, but I felt I just wasn't done with them and there was more story. And that was something clear to me.

ELLIS: In your novel-in-progress are there links to your prior work?

BLOOM: Only in the way that I write, really, nothing else at all. It's a big novel that covers a lot of geography in a way that my other work doesn't. It's not something that's mostly domestic, meaning internal and about people, marriages in some way; it's very different than all of that. It's very exciting. It has all the things that matter to me. My sons' friend once asked, "What does your mother write about?" and they said, "Sex, love, marriage, death . . . like that." That's fair enough. So, it's still like that.

ELLIS: How long have you been working on it and how will you know when it is done?

BLOOM: God willing it will be done at the end of February, because that's when I'm supposed to turn it in. I have a pretty strong outline that I've been working with closely. But I'll be done when I'll get to the end of the book and I try not to worry too much about it.

ELLIS: How do you do choose your titles? In particular, "Love Is Not a Pie," your short story which begins, "In the middle of the eulogy at my mother's boring and heartbreaking funeral, I began to think about calling off the wedding."

BLOOM: I guess "love is not a pie" is an expression I used to use and it stayed with me. I read a lot of poetry and those are always good places to steal titles from. Titles are very special. Titles are the opportunity to give something to the reader that maybe wasn't there before, so I do spend quite a bit of time on them. You want them to be a little poem, little previews of the work, what you think is important in the work.

ELLIS: In the story "Psychoanalysis Changed My Life" a client, a therapist herself, finds love in a most unusual and unexpected manner, a way which involves breaking traditional therapy boundaries.

BLOOM: Yes, I would say so. I don't practice that way.

ELLIS: In many of your stories rules and taboos are broken and you focus on the need for human connection. Is this a theme you consciously chose or do you believe it is one that you fell upon based on your own life experiences?

BLOOM: Someone said that every writer has only one subject. Mine is love, I think. And I think if you're lucky you like your subject. But whether you like it or not, it's what you're going to write about. I don't think I ever thought I was writing about taboos, only about people who love each other so much, they don't see the firewall.

ELLIS: How did you go from being a therapist to a writer, or was it a writer to a therapist?

BLOOM: No, no, I was a therapist for a long time and loved that work. I just started writing. I was on my way to becoming a psychoanalyst and I took a detour and found myself writing a novel, and I said, "Oh, this must be what I want to do." So that's what I did. I kept on practicing and found myself writing stories and a terrible mystery that I bought back from the publisher.

ELLIS: Do you believe your experience as a therapist gives you the ability to be more empathic and to have more insight into your characters?

BLOOM: What I really think is that if you're lucky and you're a therapist, it is because you are empathic. People who aren't empathic have no business becoming a therapist. I think I'm a pretty empathic person and that's one of the reasons I became a therapist. But therapy is good for teaching you when to keep your mouth shut and let people do what they're going to do, which is not bad training for you as a writer and for your characters.

ELLIS: How important are symbolism, metaphor, and simile in your writing?

BLOOM: I don't write poetry but I do love to read poetry and I'm filled with admiration for how much of a bang for the buck poets are capable of getting. So I think I'm conscious of that, but I think it's mostly about how I like to use language.

ELLIS: When you write are you surprised by what appears on the page?

BLOOM: Sometimes. I'm often actually quite disturbed by what appears on the page, disappointed and stressed. Sometimes I'm pleased, sometimes I'm surprised. Sometimes you just go, "Oh, that's really bad." Or you say, "Not too bad," and that's a good day.

ELLIS: Can you describe your writing habits?

BLOOM: Oh my God! My writing habits are appalling. My writing habits, I think, exist to make other people feel better about theirs. I'm not as disciplined as I should be. I procrastinate and dawdle; all sorts of things. But lately I've been better about getting up and doing what I have to do. I think it's having the deadline. I think Samuel Johnson said, "There's nothing like the prospect of a hanging to concentrate a man's mind." It's the same thing with me and writing. I don't prefer a deadline, but sometimes it helps me.

ELLIS: Do you have any preferences as to where you write?

BLOOM: If I can get my preference I like to have it, which is to write in this little shed in my backyard. But mostly I like to write where it's quiet.

ELLIS: In its review of *A Blind Man Can See How Much I Love You*, the *New Yorker* magazine wrote, "Amy Bloom gets more meaning into individual sentences than most authors manage in whole books." How do you manage to write such powerful sentences?

BLOOM: You have to not be too afraid. Sometimes it will go badly. You have to not be afraid to start over again. You have to not be afraid to rewrite. You can't be in too much of a hurry. It's like anything else. You can have it good or fast. I try to have both.

ELLIS: How do you avoid stereotypes?

BLOOM: I don't find stereotypes very interesting or helpful because I don't find them very compelling; in my real life, in my actual personal life they're not very compelling to me, and certainly not in fiction. So I think if you're a good writer, using stereotypes is really terrible, and I think if you're a bad writer you can't help but be drawn to stereotypes, because that's part of what it is to be a bad writer, and no matter what, it's going to cheapen your writing in a serious way.

ELLIS: How do you choose your narrators?

BLOOM: I think it's the character who, for whatever reason, speaks to you the most, and that can vary.

ELLIS: So in your novel in progress do you have one narrator or several narrators?

BLOOM: It's an omniscient narrator and we travel around; we move from person to person.

ELLIS: How do you make your dialogues work?

BLOOM: I think I listen to other people a lot; I like listening to people. I listen for what people are saying to each other, if there's an undercurrent.

ELLIS: Do you do a lot of teaching?

BLOOM: I do some teaching. I teach in the spring at Yale, which I enjoy, and I do some workshops in different places which I also enjoy.

ELLIS: What are the most important things for students to learn from you?

BLOOM: If they can tell the difference between a good sentence and a bad sentence. If they don't try to persuade themselves that the work is better than it is. If they're interested in serving the story rather than some particular notion of themselves. Also if they're better readers than they were before. I also try to make them better writers.

ELLIS: How can one be a better reader?

BLOOM: I think you can be more attentive. You can stop and pay attention to the flow and the range of the music of the sentences, and I think also what the writer is trying to do, and whether or not he or she succeeds.

ELLIS: Who are some of the writers you've learned the most from?

BLOOM: I think I've learned from everyone. I've learned from their failures as well as their successes. I learned a lot from Robert Davies and *The Deptford Trilogy*, about scope and a certain kind of fearlessness; I learned a lot from Jane Austen about humor and pain and class and the omniscient narrator; I learned a lot from Dickens. I learned from Updike about marital dialogue; from Grace Paley about the rhythm of the voice, I learned from Alice Munro about classic structure and a willingness to bring in variations on that structure. I read a lot of poets all the time: Don Hall's *Without*, Mark Doty's *Atlantis*, Jane Hirshfield; it's a really long list. I read Michael Connelly, I read P.D. James and Elizabeth George and Ed McBain. I don't think there's anybody that I don't learn from.

ELLIS: What are some of the discoveries you are making about yourself as a writer?

BLOOM: Well, that I lied to my students when I told them that short stories were no different than novels, that they covered the same space, just faster. It's not really true.

ELLIS: So what is the truth?

BLOOM: It's a bigger playground and it requires more stamina in a certain way because you have to keep going to a rise, then fall, a rise, and then fall. It's keeping up a brisk pace all the time without losing the voice, without losing the characters, without sacrificing character to plot and plot to character. I think it's the same in that each sentence should be the best sentence you're capable of writing. It's just more in an exciting way.

ELLIS: Can you speak about your experience as a jurist for writing awards and how you make your selections?

BLOOM: I look for what I like and I think everybody does. I'm going to read for the best book of the kind that speaks to me. So if it is a choice between *As I Lay Dying* and *Deptford Trilogy*, I'm probably going to pick *Deptford Trilogy*. I'm going to pick *World of Wonders* or *Fifth Business* rather than *As I Lay Dying*, not necessarily because I think Robertson Davies is a better writer than Faulkner but because one of those books interests me more than the other. You look for the best book and then among those books it will be what speaks to you. You might also want to focus on what's new, what's fresh, depending on the award.

ELLIS: How have you coped with cool or negative reviews?

BLOOM: I tend not to read my reviews, which helps. Every once in a while you learn something from a review, a good one or bad one but mostly I don't feel I learn a lot from them, and there's no reason to get your feelings hurt, if you're not going to learn something. Somebody can say "I don't like the way Amy Bloom writes"; so, I guess they don't like the way I write. And surely that's enough to know.

ELLIS: Do you regret anything you've written, other than the mystery you mentioned?

BLOOM: I didn't have the skills. I was very happy to buy it back from the publisher. That was a gift for me. Have I regretted anything else I've ever written? No, I don't think so.

ELLIS: Going back to your novel in progress, how long have you been working on it?

BLOOM: A year and a half, not quite.

ELLIS: Do you have a title for it, and can you share a little bit more about it as we close?

BLOOM: Sure. It's called *Away*, and it takes place in the mid 1920s and starts in Russia; it ends in Alaska. A young woman's family is massacred in her village, and with the encouragement of some of the survivors, she buries her father and her mother and her husband and her baby, and goes to America. Circumstances require her to return. It's the story of the coming and going, of being home and away.

Lise Haines

Blindfolds, Hypnotism, and Chairs

Lise Haines is the author of two novels, *Small Acts of Sex and Electricity* (a 2006 BookSense Pick) and *In My Sister's Country* (a finalist for the Paterson Fiction Prize), and a chapbook of poetry, *Thin Scars/Purple Leaves*. Her short stories have appeared in literary journals including *Ploughshares*, *Agni* and *Post Road*. Haines has been a finalist for the PEN Nelson Algren Fiction Award. About her first novel, *BookForum* wrote, "Haines is a published poet, and it shows: her language and dreamy images are striking, unexpected, and beautifully controlled . . . a compelling, wonderfully twisted little book . . . very unlike most of the debuts . . . which would argue for it having the unlikeliest of all virtues: originality."

Haines is a Visiting Briggs-Copeland Lecturer at Harvard University and was Writer in Residence at Emerson College for four years. She has also taught at the University of Southern Maine and in the UCLA Extension Writing Program.

Lise Haines spoke with me from her home in greater Boston where she was at work on her third novel, *Intense Prolonged Sequences of Disaster and Peril*.

SHERRY ELLIS: In *In My Sister's Country* you write about twisted love and sisterly jealousy. Did you plan to write about these themes or did they evolve as you were writing?

LISE HAINES: I write on the organic side, grabbing an image or voice which leads to character and then to story. So I didn't sit down to write a book about love gone wrong or a book about jealousy between sisters. It evolved out of falling into the dream state that became *In My Sister's Country*.

ELLIS: Molly, the younger sister, has a precocious maturity. She says, "I'm still convinced people can really change, in a second flat. I've watched it happen to every member of my family. My father, fueled by his corruption of us—and then gone, vanished. My mother, living in new stockings and hopes—then chemically altered, her body suddenly eating itself from the inside out. Even Amanda, running out of her game, altering the course of her life by deciding to marry. I've learned to watch for that moment, catching it midair." How did you decide to make seventeen-year-old Molly the protagonist of this novel?

HAINES: Molly's voice came through loud and clear, and that formed Molly. I saw her older sister, Amanda, soaking in a tub, looking like a crocodile, Molly stealing her sister's cigarettes. That's how it started.

ELLIS: At another point Molly says, "I'm one of those people who believe the Earth will be overtaken by insects someday. Not because I'm a pessimist, and not for personal reasons—like imagining my sister will have her day of reckoning with tarantulas—but I think if anyone does, it's the insects who deserve the place. They seldom complain, and if there's mental anguish among them, I can't really see it." How does this passage work to demonstrate Molly's point of view about her life?

HAINES: Insects exhibit order. The sisters' father created an exacting, cruel structure for the family to live by. Molly wanted to get away from that order. And her acting out sexually was, in part, an effort to avoid her family's pain. She often saw the world in terms of enemies, how to extinguish them, how to fend them off.

ELLIS: You use blindfolds, chairs, and hypnotism as metaphors for control and manipulation. How did you choose them?

HAINES: It's funny, when you write a book you don't always remember everything you've planted, because a lot of what you do is unconscious. Sometimes, as you read through later, you realize, "Ah, that's what I was doing there." So when you mention the chairs I suddenly think about the Three Bears—which goes to status, power, where we feel comfortable, and where we feel fear. The blindfolds hit something more subliminal and I think this should be left to the reader to discover. Hypnotism is about what we allow into our lives, how we allow other people and belief systems to control us.

ELLIS: A quote from author Sven Birkerts appears on the back cover of *In My Sister's Country*, that Molly is "Holden Caulfield rechanneled as a desperado on a wobbly pair of heels." Was *Catcher in the Rye* or any other book with an adolescent protagonist particularly important to you in your development as a writer?

HAINES: *Catcher in the Rye* was a significant book for me when I was fifteen. I was excessively slow in learning to read. *Catcher* overpowered me, so that I forgot about the reading difficulties. I had written most of my life, even before I knew how to hold a pencil, engaged in making up poems and songs, but I struggled with reading.

ELLIS: Last year in a *New York Times Sunday Magazine* article director Sam Mendes indicated that *In My Sister's Country* might be produced by his company Donmar Films. If you were casting the film, whom might you choose to play the central characters?

HAINES: I was in a large supermarket when a friend called on my cell phone and said, "Your life is about to change." She had seen the article with the quote about Mendes and when she told me this, I hit the linoleum. As she read it aloud to me, I sat there sniffing detergents and household cleaners, trying to imagine what this meant and how much one's life can be changed in an instant. Actors? Scarlett Johansson for Molly, Jude Law for Nathaniel, and Charlize Theron for Amanda.

ELLIS: At the end of each chapter of *In My Sister's Country* there are pages that look like photographs of sound waves, or flickering lights, possibly cards from the Rorschach test. Do you plan on using a similar graphic effect in your future works?

HAINES: I didn't select the graphics, though I find them compelling. And I was excessively lucky to get such a sexy, evocative cover, a mysterious cover, but it wasn't my doing. Fred Ramey, my editor, came up with the concepts. The chapter breaks have to do with magic tricks, prestidigitation.

ELLIS: How has your writing been influenced by your childhood experience of growing up in a home with a mother who was a newspaper writer and a father who was a newspaper political editor?

HAINES: Writing and language were always huge, and storytelling. I have many memories of going to the newspaper, watching linotype men at their machines. My mother was always working on large green tablets of paper with fat pencils, my father doing his two-finger method on the old typewriter. When we went out as a family to meet my parents' friends, they were other writers.

ELLIS: How does the experience and process of writing a novel compare to that of writing a short story?

HAINES: A short story gives results faster, if it goes well. Of course, some stories can take two to three years; you keep putting them away and taking them out. At other times you quickly have something in hand to send out and you have a very satisfied feeling about that.

You can't mine character development in a short work the way you can in something longer; you can't go through as many twists and turns of plot, obviously. When I'm writing a novel it's something I'm thinking about work day and night, whether or not I'm sitting at the computer. I've heard of novel writing being akin to creating a nest, how the birds keep adding little bits and pieces, a feather, a rock, and along the way the leaves, twigs, build up the structure. And I've heard it described as a macramé, a weaving in which you keep adding elements: a piece of twine and beads, razor blades. You pull the long threads or chords through, weaving them in your hands until you have a finished piece. I think building a novel is that way; that you keep adding and weaving as you go.

I know it can happen quickly with a book. *As I Lay Dying*, wasn't it written in six weeks? I was very lucky when I wrote *In My Sister's Country*; it came out in almost six months. Later I revised, but it was remarkable to me that it was written so fast.

ELLIS: In the *Chicago Tribune* you are quoted as having said, "For me, writing is a process of vivid daydreaming." Can you give an example of what you mean?

HAINES: For me there's everyday life as I perceive it; REM state which is equally vivid; the place I go to when I sit and meditate; and the vivid dream of living in the world of a novel, whether I'm writing or reading. Maybe that's where the title *In My Sister's Country* comes from, the idea of being in a place so real yet different that it's like being in another country. I see the characters talking, moving, breathing, fighting, making bread, whatever; it's just another part of my mind that's active and alive.

ELLIS: In your short story "Stolen Photo," you write, "I returned in the wedding dress, wig, clown white. I stood up on the coffee table, kicking magazines to the floor. I ignored Tom and tried to fall into a trance. There are times when I'm up on my wooden box and a light breeze picks up the veil of my outfit. I have arranged my gloved hands into a pose; and after a while, they seem like something separate from my body." How do the images you use express particular ideas or themes, for example in the section above?

HAINES: I can tell you where that image came from. I had just moved to the Boston area, and as you know there are a lot of street performers in Boston and in Harvard Square. This particular one was in the Boston Commons and she had drawn quite a crowd. She was a living statue, someone who worked in slow motion. If anyone put money in her urn she would make a gesture to them, and every now and then she would move a body part; mostly she was very still. I was thinking about why people were more attracted to her than a lot of people who do this quiet form of street performance, and I think the fact that she was a bride had something to do with it.

ELLIS: In your short story "A Glue-Related Problem," the FBI visits the home of Karen and Arlene, roommates, while investigating a bank robbery, and by night's end Arlene is dancing with one of the agents. Karen watches them making love. She states, "I kept my door cracked open like I needed light or air, wind velocity. Cyril did things to Karen that I personally found amazing, but I couldn't tell if she realized what his prying meant. After a while, they became abstract like wax apples mistaken for food." As a writer, how do you decide to cast your piece in a realistic genre and when do you find it more helpful to move into a less realistic world?

HAINES: I'm driven by imagery which goes back to having an internalized dream-view. Many of the choices are not conscious ones; they're more about engagement and process, so that I see two girls in their apartment, the FBI agents walking up the drive. . . .

    I did pull things from my own life here. I worked as a bank teller once and I had a roommate who glued wet suits, and at one point when I was working at the bank, someone did steal two thousand dollars and the FBI came out to my house. Yet most of my fiction is fiction and I don't tend to write straight-up reality. My hope is that beyond action and dialogue, I hit thought process, psychology, otherworldliness.

In *In My Sister's Country* there are only a couple of things drawn from direct experience. One is the mother who shows up at the park, having left the hospice as she is slowly dying of cancer, to have a last visit with the daughter. I had a very dear friend who was a writer who had ovarian cancer and did not want me to see her in that state of decline. She actually got in her car and met me at a park and gave me the objects that I described in the book. So that's close to something that occurred. The rest is made up except for the old home, the Wharton Manor.

In her column in the *Chicago Daily News*, my mother tried to save a number of great old homes before they were torn down. She took my real sister (the good sister) and me to these stately homes with ballrooms and buzzers to the upstairs maid, and we played in them. When she knew they were about to go under the wrecking ball, she would have us stealing architectural salvage, and driving off in my father's small Peugeot.

ELLIS: Have you ever wished you could have deleted part of what you've written after it was published?

HAINES: I'm happy with this book and I had the world's best editor. Of course, I think most writers edit a little when they give a reading. It's the process of not being able to quite stop and some of the pencil marks are about making sure the listener will understand context.

ELLIS: How do you decide what to keep in, take out, and/or change when you are revising your work?

HAINES: I know that some writers have to get the story out first, and then, as one writer friend said, he puts in the language. The way I work is to attempt to finish a chapter in its most polished form before going on to the next chapter. I revise, revise, and revise so much that for me, revision is writing. I just don't see any real difference. It's all process. I'm a nervous writer—getting up and down from the desk; now it's email that drives me crazy, going back and forth and checking email. Before I would get up and do the laundry, or read a newspaper, thinking about the book as I did these activities. Then I went back to my computer. I will work for twelve hours if I'm granted the luxury of that kind of time.

ELLIS: How do you know when a novel is done?

HAINES: You have an internalized sense that the book works, that it makes sense, that the words sing so you can read the entire manuscript aloud and not get snagged anywhere. Then you need trusted, talented readers who are willing to give you bottom line feedback.

ELLIS: When you finished writing *In My Sister's Country* did it require extensive revision?

HAINES: The process for me was basically going for that very tight, fine writing, from chapter to chapter, then getting to the end and going back and seeing if there was anything superfluous, or anything I needed to do to deepen the story, or give it added clarity. It didn't sell initially, and a great friend went through it and pointed out problems. Then I went back and fixed those, and it went back out again.

I've never played it, but my guess is that writing a novel is like playing three dimensional chess—you have your mind in many places at once and that's part of the pleasure.

ELLIS: W. Somerset Maugham said, "There are three rules for writing a novel. Unfortunately, no one knows what they are." Do you agree?

HAINES: I buy that statement, despite being a teacher. I acknowledge the mystery of it, and I don't recommend waiting for inspiration to write. For me the inspiration comes out of the act of writing. I think there are a lot of things you can nail down and you can have great conversations about, and then ultimately it's what you can get on the page. When I talk to my students, I tell them you can do just about anything if you can pull it off. I think you have to get to the point where you break rules, that that's how you create something approaching an original voice.

ELLIS: Prior to writing *In My Sister's Country*, you focused on poetry. How does your experience as a poet inform your craft as a novelist and a short story writer?

HAINES: This is a tough one, because forms are often blended now. Creative nonfiction blends with the novel, and the novel blends with poetry. I think of Mary Robison's *Why Did I Ever?*, the way she set up her prose poems, yet it's a novel, it's both. Lauren Slater's *Lying*, it's not fiction and it's fiction. Of course, like so many writers, my work is in part language-driven.

ELLIS: On a day-to-day basis, when you sit down to write, is there a particular way you start?

HAINES: I read a few emails or make tea, then I jump in. I think I learned that skill from my child. She would take long naps, I'd hit the computer, then shut it down when her nap was over. I didn't have the luxury of finding a lot of avoidant behavior. I really had to get to work; and fortunately that stayed with me. And as I said, you're working on the novel when you're not sitting there, so you're riding on the subway, and you're thinking about your characters and what they're doing. It's a pretty fluid, classic process, but the more time I have to write, the more I produce, and when I don't have time I make time. I get up very early in the day and I'm up very late in the evenings. And I write through everything: stress, financial disasters, carrying two jobs, whatever is going on. If you're serious, you're writing. And I'm not talking about spilling emotions on the page, because that becomes self-indulgent and then you aren't standing back enough to create a world of fiction; you're simply getting your stress out. It's all about the work. You work.

ELLIS: How do you begin writing when you are starting a new project?

HAINES: I start with an image, a line, maybe seeing a character's face. Maybe I've read something in mythology or a fairy tale or a newspaper article. It starts with one small thing, and builds from there.

ELLIS: What has been the hardest thing for you to learn as a writer?

HAINES: I feel fortunate because I love the process and the process is filled with constant problems to solve. There's always something I'm trying to sort out. I think about how to approach a passage of dialogue, how to deepen a character. I imagine it's like being a filmmaker. They don't simply watch a movie. They think about lighting, framing, the kind of film in the camera. It becomes impossible to simply read for pleasure, you're always breaking it down. So I can't think of one thing that has been more challenging than another in writing fiction, except that early on, making the shift from poetry to fiction was a leap and I had to stop reading poetry for a while entirely.

ELLIS: Is there any advice you have for beginning writers?

HAINES: A writing career is a tough one. You might go through phases where you don't get a lot of support for what you're doing, and you're constantly making choices to write, which impacts other areas of your life. It can be a difficult financial choice, so you better love what you're doing.

ELLIS: How has writing your new novel, *Small Acts of Sex and Electricity*, been a different experience for you than writing *In My Sister's Country*?

HAINES: I'm still dealing with a triangulated relationship in *Small Acts of Sex and Electricity*. It's about two women, two friends who grew up together, that end up exchanging places. It's a take-off on *The Prince and the Pauper*. One woman seems to have the American dream but is losing her grip on it; her friend has an inability to form lasting attachments but wants to be part of a larger world, a family. In the middle is one, and only one, husband. *Small Acts of Sex and Electricity* is set in a home on Miramar Beach in Santa Barbara, California, a town I lived in for most of my adult life. And now I've begun a new novel, *Intense Prolonged Sequences of Disaster and Peril*, but it might be too early to talk about, in that way that some writers get superstitious. And a few good superstitions are probably a good thing.

Paul Lisicky

Looking for Surprise

Paul Lisicky's books include *Lawnboy* and *Famous Builder*. His shorter work has appeared in *Ploughshares, Short Takes, Open House, Flash Fiction, Prairie Schooner, Boulevard, Creating Nonfiction, Truth in Nonfiction* and in many other anthologies and magazines. A graduate of the Iowa Writers' Workshop, his awards include fellowships from the National Endowment for the Arts, the James Michener/Copernicus Society, the Henfield Foundation, the New Jersey State Council on the Arts, and the Fine Arts Work Center in Provincetown, where he was twice a Winter Fellow. He has taught at Cornell University, New York University, Sarah Lawrence College, Antioch University, and the University of Houston, and is a member of the writing committee of the Fine Arts Work Center in Provincetown. He divides his time between New York City and Fire Island, New York. His new novel, *Lumina Harbor*, is forthcoming.

Recently he spoke with me by phone from his Manhattan apartment.

SHERRY ELLIS: You've written *Lawnboy*, a novel, many short stories, and now *Famous Builder*, a memoir. How does it feel to read about your own life in print?

PAUL LISICKY: Well, that's a tough one. I think of *Famous Builder* as a version of my life, but not my life. Every moment in time is so complex; you learn pretty quickly that it's too complicated to dramatize in every dimension. You try your damnedest to do that, but there's always more to say—and thank God for that. Memoir to me is so much about picking and choosing descriptions and incidents in support of the theme. The final result doesn't feel that much different, at least imaginatively, from a novel or a poem. It's been so worked on the language level that you end up feeling some distance from it. Which is a relief. That distance makes the task of memoir bearable.

ELLIS: In her book *The Situation and the Story*, Vivian Gornick states, "the narrator becomes a persona . . . a tone of voice, its angle of vision, the rhythm of sentences, what it selects to observe and ignore are chosen to serve the subject." How do you think you've created a persona as the result of writing *Famous Builder*?

LISICKY: I've always been drawn to any kind of creative work that wants to do something with the signature of individual character. With *Famous Builder*, I tried my best to enact speech patterns and points of view that I like to think of as unique to me. But there's a bit of distance between who I am at any given moment and who the speaker is. The speaker's tone, the choice of detail—both are informed by the moment in time from which the writer creates. There's no reason to think that I couldn't write about the same material covered in *Famous Builder* at a later date from a different point of view. The actor Dirk Bogarde apparently did that in a series of memoirs he wrote over the course of a lifetime. In one book his mother is kinder than a saint; in another, she's a disaster!

ELLIS: *Famous Builder* begins when you are in elementary school, with you and your fellow classmates changing identities with one another and trying to fool a substitute teacher as to who you are. Why did you choose this beginning?

LISICKY: It seemed false to me to write a book that explored just one thread of my identity. If I were writing a book that focused only on my life as a gay man, I'd have to leave out too much of what I know about myself. Similarly, if I wrote about myself solely as the grandson of Eastern European immigrants, I'd run into the same problem. That's why the opening paragraphs are about the frustration of carrying a single name to the grave. I wanted to write a book that represented the complexity of how we understand ourselves. By foregrounding that classroom scene, the book argues against the notion that anyone is built of a singular identity.

 I also thought it was important to open with a group drama. The boundaries in that classroom loosen, and there's a sense of joyousness about the collective. A certain anarchic spirit emerges again and again in the book, in which the speaker understands himself not as a single being hemmed in by his mortal body, but as a part of something larger. His participation in the collective enables him to participate in eternity, if only for a moment. If you're not pinned to a single name, then you can keep going on and on, right?

Overall, the opening is there to warn the reader that this isn't going to be a conventional memoir in which the speaker comes to some radical self-understanding following a series of crises. The book's work is to ask questions about identity.

ELLIS: From age nine to fourteen you designed your own communities, inspired by Levittown in New York. Do you find that writing is also a way of building communities?

LISICKY: I think any writer is engaged in the work of naming, making shapes, structures, circulation patterns—all the tasks of the city planner. A book is a community, isn't it? Not only between a writer and his readers across time, but on a simpler level, it's brought to life with characters and houses that are entered imaginatively.

ELLIS: How has music inspired your writing?

LISICKY: I hope that music informs every sentence I write. I often think about the relationship between the singer's phrasing and the writer's sentence-making. Virginia Woolf's attention to the musicality of language is one of the reasons why she's important to me. Sometimes when precise description fails me, I type nonsense syllables in order to represent the pitch and contour of the music I hear inside my head. I, of course, go back to rewrite those passages later.

In addition to melody, I think about harmony. A writer can only achieve harmony metaphorically, but certain tensions in the language can lend such an effect. Joy Williams, for example, sometimes uses descriptive elements like "dully gleaming." That yoking of oppositions suggests a kind of happy dissonance.

ELLIS: What is your musical background?

LISICKY: I started playing and writing music at six. I played—still play—both keyboards and guitar. As a kid, I used to come home from Mass and pick out the songs I'd heard on our piano. I started publishing liturgical music at fifteen and recorded an album of these songs at nineteen. But I knew I wasn't destined to go through life as a church musician. That world seemed circumscribed, cut off, even though I enjoyed writing music to be performed by a congregation and amateur musicians. It was a strange time to be involved in music. You could either be a schooled musician or a pop musician who played in bars and coffeehouses, and it seemed a failure of character not to make a choice. I chose the latter, although I wanted to straddle both worlds. I wanted to write accessible music that was harmonically and melodically idiosyncratic. That's why I still love Joni Mitchell and Laura Nyro. Joni's restlessness continues to inspire me. Her experiments sometimes fail, but she's always reinventing herself, which is her great lesson to me.

ELLIS: Eudora Welty remarks in her book *On Writing*, "When Chekhov says there were so many stars and that one could not have put a finger between them, he gives us more than one night, he gives us that one night." Is it easier for you to share specifics about yourself in memoir or to create details in your novels for your characters?

LISICKY: It's hard for me to draw a clear distinction between my work in the two forms. I think the most compelling art lives somewhere on the borders. Most of *Famous Builder* is structurally similar to fiction. Scenes are organized around pivotal moments where the reader is expected to infer meaning from the drama on the page. There's not much in the way of rumination and interpretation. The work's closer in form to Joan Didion's essay "Los Angeles Notebook" than it is to more conventional nonfiction narrative. On the other hand, my novel *Lawnboy* takes the form of an invented memoir of a young man's search for connection. His quest for meaning is the machine that drives the narrative. So in terms of form, I write neither pure fiction nor pure memoir.

ELLIS: In addition to Virginia Woolf, who are some of your favorite writers?

LISICKY: I'm a huge fan of Flannery O'Connor. I love the intersection of the metaphysical and the social in her work, the conflation of humor and dread, the earthly and the otherworldly. Her story "A Good Man is Hard to Find" continues to teach me. The list might change in a year, but these writers have been crucial: Flaubert, Dickens, Salinger, Bernard Cooper, Joy Williams, Elizabeth Bishop, Elizabeth McCracken, Jane Bowles, Anne Carson, Kathryn Davis, Mary Robison, Mary Gaitskill, Sigrid Nunez, Gish Jen, Lorrie Moore, Grace Paley, Mona Simpson, Michael Cunningham, Denis Johnson, Nick Flynn, Richard Powers, Alexander Chee. And of course there's my partner, Mark Doty.

ELLIS: How do you think having a partner who is also a writer has influenced your development as a writer?

LISICKY: We talk about books; we talk about teaching. We talk about ideas that we're grappling with. When Mark's particularly crazy about a work of literature, I make sure to read it—and vice versa. We're each other's first readers. I want to write work that knocks him out. I want to see a whole open embrace on his face. When he's less than thrilled with something, I can see that on his face and know I have more work to do.

ELLIS: Given the many facets of your identity as they are manifested in *Famous Builder*, which of these components do you think you're manifesting in your new novel, *Lumina Harbor*?

LISICKY: I'm interested in thinking about reinvention. *Lumina Harbor* is, in part, about a young woman who's both sustained and depleted by her devotion to a particular place. She's troubled by the fact that the houses in her New Jersey beach town are being replaced with monstrous trophy homes. She's part of an organization that opposes that trend, and the collision between the capitalist turn of her community and her own dedication to cultural preservation overwhelms her. The book wants to think about the value of place and the dark lures of money. I do think the escalation of real estate values we've seen all over the country in recent years has profoundly affected community life, and I want to write a book that explores that situation.

ELLIS: The book is a chorus of voices, two of which belong to women. How did you decide to write from a female point of view?

LISICKY: At the end of last week's workshop, one of my students was worried that her male narrator didn't sound enough like a male. Someone else said, better to excavate the interior life of the character than to pay too much attention to the exterior qualities of gender. That struck me as astute. I think we can get ourselves into trouble when we ascribe stereotypical traits to characters. In *Lumina Harbor*, more often than not, a character doesn't conform to perceived expectations. The central character's brother-in-law is often sensitive to the point of tears, even though he's big and burly, ostensibly heterosexual, the kind of guy who scares people as he walks down the street. I spent a lot of time trying to avoid writing a female narrator, maybe out of the fear that I couldn't pull it off. So the book was in third person for a couple of years. But there was something inert about the point of view. It didn't rise and fall; it didn't breathe. I decided to try a paragraph spoken in her voice, and I had fifty pages in a few weeks.

ELLIS: So it was a breakthrough?

LISICKY: As a writer, I'm looking to be surprised by my own work. I usually have a preconceived notion of what the next book will be before I actually sit down to write it and I tend to plod along trying to inhabit my preconceived notion—until the work gets stubborn. At that point I press my forehead against my desk until I give into what the work wants to do—and then it takes off. I probably have to write one hundred twenty pages in order to get fifteen that I can live with.

ELLIS: The landscape of the New Jersey Shore, Cherry Hill, and Florida play heavily in your work, especially in your memoir. Can you please comment?

LISICKY: I usually start with landscape. I don't know how else to give the reader a precise sense of the protagonist's emotional life except to ground the work in the sensory particulars of place. Without the smell of the trees, for instance, I can't move imaginatively.

ELLIS: What were the challenges for you in shifting to writing your memoir?

LISICKY: After years of making things up, it was a relief to write from the template of a particular memory. You can go anywhere in the creation of a piece of fiction, while memoir is constrained by what happened. Fiction writers seldom admit to this, but sometimes the freedom of fiction can be oppressive. Joni Mitchell has a line about "the crazy you get from too much choice," which makes absolute sense to me. Of course, once the memoirist foregrounds certain details or incidents, the narrative can't help but take on a life of its own—another kind of problem. The memoirist is always being pulled in two directions: he's attempting to honor the truth of memory at the same time he's attempting to honor the internal logic of the story. How to do those two things at once? The task is next to impossible, but the best memoirs are energized by that tension.

What role does fact play in this struggle? Whenever I'm asked about allegiance to fact, I always answer that memoir is less about facts—the realm of journalism—than it is about how the writer feels about the facts. The emotional investigation is the story. A quote from Marilynne Robinson's novel *Housekeeping*: "Fact explains nothing. On the contrary, it is fact that requires explanation."

ELLIS: What about your experiences as a teacher of writing? Do you teach memoir, short fiction, novel writing, and nonfiction?

LISICKY: At Sarah Lawrence I'm teaching a year-long class that's half fiction and half creative nonfiction as well as everything that's in between.

ELLIS: How do you think you build communities in your seminars and classes?

LISICKY: I try to make students feel safe. I bring my own struggles to the table and do everything I can to demolish the hierarchy between teacher and student. I try to foster an atmosphere in which students are supportive of one another, rather than competitive. It's always easier to tear something apart than to name specifically where it's entirely itself. We spend a lot of time working on how to do the latter. Of course the humbling thing about teaching is that you're only partially in control; much of its success depends upon the social chemistry of the group, the building's heating system, the time of day on which the class meets.

ELLIS: Do you think writing memoir has changed you as a teacher?

LISICKY: I often ask my young budding novelists, "How does this character make meaning of her life? How does the narrative enact that?" Those are the central questions of memoir, but they're also relevant to the writer of fiction. By and large, I'm more interested in helping my students envision their characters' inner lives than I was before I started experimenting with nonfiction. I want to help them crack open the life below the surface, the deep private dramas we withhold from one another as we walk through the day, as we go to the supermarket and pay for groceries.

ELLIS: Your mother wearing bell-bottoms: that was a wonderful image. How does she feel about seeing herself as a character in print?

LISICKY: She's read the book three times. She takes it with her to the supermarket. Waiting for my dad to come out of a store, she picks it up and reads a passage out of context. She's admitted to going to bookstores all over Broward County and sneaking the book onto the front tables.

ELLIS: Males, too, have strong presence in *Famous Builder*. You write, "My father is a storm . . . if he were a painting, he'd be a Jackson Pollock . . . all splash and squiggle, no open spaces, no room to breathe." Do you remember how this comparison came to you?

LISICKY: I started writing a list of images and chose what I hoped was most accurate. My process is fairly expansive. When I first sit down to write, so much is gibberish, unformed notes to myself about possible scenes. I try to put everything possible in on the first draft. Then I need to weed the garden.

ELLIS: How did you choose *Famous Builder* as a title?

LISICKY: For a while I called the book *Pygmalion Salon*. That title reflects the central theme of self-reinvention, but it seemed a bit arch. *Famous Builder* is more down to earth; it's closer to the spirit and style of the individual pieces. I thought it was important to use the word famous: from that young boy's perspective, fame signifies transcendence and deliverance; famous people are rewarded for being more fully themselves. That naiveté strikes me as very American.

ELLIS: What scenes were hardest for you to write?

LISICKY: "Naming You" is about my mother's twin brother, Paul, who was killed in a car accident twenty years before I was born. It seemed necessary to think about how his absence was a defining presence in our household, responsible in part for shaping the relationship between my mother and me. The challenge was this: I didn't want to trespass on my mother's pain; I didn't want to "use" it simply to make art out of it. Luckily, the piece is important to her, but I'm not sure what I would have done if it had caused her grief.

ELLIS: Is it possible to have artistic integrity in a case like that?

LISICKY: Writing about real people whom one cares about brings up complex problems. For one, those people probably tell the story of a particular incident entirely differently to themselves. How many of us can imagine our own words and gestures contributing to a pivotal moment in a loved one's imagination? I wouldn't want to be the parent of a child who remembered everything! Fortunately, my family is intuitive enough to know that the book is only one way of telling the tale. And I think they forgive me when I get things wrong, or know that I've conflated two different events in order to make a point. I've tried my best to write them as engaging and dimensional characters. No reader cares about anyone who's idealized or vilified. And it helps if the writer is implicating himself in the dramas explored on the page, if he's willing to express uncertainty, doubt, vulnerability—some gap between what exactly happened and the limitations of language. Once the writer is superior to the characters he's writing about, the whole project becomes suspect.

ELLIS: How long did it take you to write *Famous Builder*?

LISICKY: Four years. The first section was "Luck Be a Lady," which was written in the spring of 1998, just after I'd signed the contract for *Lawnboy*. The pressure to write a new novel was off, and I gave myself permission to write whatever I wanted to. Four pieces emerged within four months—which shocked and invigorated me, because I'm a ridiculously slow writer. A pattern emerged after a while: a period of extreme productivity would be followed by silence. Then I'd start writing again.

ELLIS: When you chose to end the book, what was happening in your own life?

LISICKY: A lot of new material came in the fall of 2001. Many of my artist friends weren't able to work in those weeks after September 11th; at first the notion of sitting at my desk seemed utterly pointless to me as well. But over time I managed to write about fifty pages of new material between late September and the beginning of January. Mark and I had just moved into our new apartment in Chelsea on September 3rd. We didn't have furniture yet or a TV. Writing became a way to channel all that chaos into form.

ELLIS: When you returned to writing your memoir, did you focus on life celebrations or on the catastrophes of life?

LISICKY: In "On Broadway," the final section of the book, the sense of everyday life is much more provisional than in "Luck Be a Lady." "On Broadway" suggests, What's the point in feeling shame if "planes are flying toward us as we speak"? In other words, if everything might end tomorrow. The narrative has a seize-the-day quality that might not have been present in my earlier work. It celebrates and despairs at the same time.

In the wake of September 11th, the world seems so much smaller. Obviously we can't safely distance ourselves from war and terrorism any longer. We can't ignore the consequences of our country's foreign policy or the expansion of global capitalism. Now we're all implicated in it. I remember taking the train to school one morning just after September 11th and looking out over Manhattan and imagining the deserts of Afghanistan imprinted over that landscape. This is the new world, I thought.

But the truth is, tragedy has been in our midst for years: AIDS, poverty, hunger, homelessness, racism, homophobia. Now that we're living in a state of emergency, I feel a greater responsibility to dramatize the pressure of these forces upon the inner life. It's impossible to take everyday life for granted these days.

ELLIS: You have said that one of your goals in *Lawnboy* was to write a book in which no one died of AIDS. Can you comment please?

LISICKY: Large parts of *Lawnboy* were written after protease inhibitors became available. Until 1996, it would have seemed unthinkable to write about AIDS without focusing on the travails of the dying and their caretakers. But things shifted with the advent of new drugs. I wanted to write a narrative that thought about the ways in which the epidemic continues to impact our relationships, our attitudes toward time, attachment, and mortality. How does the possibility of contracting—-or of passing on—a life-threatening illness complicate our sexual lives? How to form an ethic that deals with that extreme situation? And why does the little engine of desire persist in spite of exterior threats?

ELLIS: If you were reviewing *Famous Builder*, what would you focus on?

LISICKY: The interrelationship between the structure and the themes. The repetition of patterns and metaphors. I'd like the reviewer to see that the book dramatizes a particular vision of the world. It's about ideas.

ELLIS: What advice do you have for fiction writers who want to write memoir?

LISICKY: Read, read. Bernard Cooper; Frank Conroy; Mark Doty; Joan Didion; Montaigne; Vivian Gornick; Nick Flynn; Nabokov's *Speak, Memory*; Lucy Grealy's *Autobiography of a Face*. Some fiction writers mistakenly believe that memoir is inferior to fiction, but both forms demand an attention to craft. Any accomplished memoirist uses the same tools as the fiction writer: scene-making, precise language, coherent structure. I think fiction writers can learn a lot about structure from writing memoir, because in memoir, structure is central to its success or failure.

ELLIS: What have you learned about yourself through writing your memoir?

LISICKY: If anything, I've learned what I don't know. *Famous Builder* is less concerned with answers than it is in asking questions. The speaker, searching at the start of the book, is still searching in the end. I don't know what it means to be a body in time or a self in the social world, but I'm obsessed with the investigation of those things. That's what keeps me writing.

Lan Samantha Chang

Memories That Reach Back into Consciousness

Before she could read, Lan Samantha Chang started writing by copying pictures and letters. Since age four, she has known that she wanted to be a writer. She was born and raised in Appleton, Wisconsin, the daughter of Chinese parents who survived the Japanese occupation of China and subsequently migrated to the United States. Her parents didn't share extensive information about their experiences in their homeland, and in writing the novel *Inheritance*, Chang had the opportunity to do research into the world her parents had once inhabited. *Inheritance* tells the story of a splintered Chinese family set against the historical backdrop of the 1920s to 1940s. The schism that divides sisters Junan and Yinan mirrors the fate of China during this time period.

In *Hunger: A Novella and Stories* Chang focuses on Chinese immigrants and their children, who labor for emotional survival. The families in this novella and collection of stories accomplish a fragile balance between remembering and forgetting their past, and starting over on foreign soil. The title novella is narrated after her death by Min, whose husband escaped from China, swimming with his precious violin held high above his head; he is subsequently refused a permanent teaching position at a prestigious New York music school.

In January, 2006, Ms. Chang was appointed Professor of English and Director of the Writers' Workshop at the University of Iowa.

I met with her in her office at Harvard University.

SHERRY ELLIS: "My family story is like a stone," Hong, the narrator of *Inheritance* says. "I often think about its true dimensions, weight, and shape. Many years ago it was pitched into deep water, pulling after it a spout of air, leaving only ripples." Hong worries history will repeat itself, that her family's legacy of unhappiness and betrayal has been passed onto her by her mother and grandmother. Throughout *Inheritance* the reader's senses are powerfully evoked by symbols of nature. How did you choose to contrast nature and betrayal, nature and love, throughout this novel?

LAN SAMANTHA CHANG: I've become very interested in the natural world in the last several years. My husband, Robert Caputo, is a landscape painter and as a result of accompanying him on his air painting expeditions, I have been introduced to the woods of Maine, as well as various lovely parts of New England and the Southwest. Although I wasn't working on nature writing at the time, what I saw and experienced on these expeditions found its way into my novel in figurative language that was able to reach across cultures.

ELLIS: You've said that *Inheritance* is an "imaginary history—an exploration into lives that might have been." Can you describe what you mean by this phrase and the extent to which this novel is an imagined biography, an imagined history of your family?

CHANG: *Inheritance* is about an imaginary family, but in writing I applied some of the same techniques to this imaginary family that have been useful to me in learning my own family history. The narrator, Hong, says that every child is born into the middle of a story she doesn't know. As children, many of us spend an enormous amount of imaginative energy trying to detect or trace out things that happened before we came to be. I think it's natural to a thoughtful person to engage in this activity, and particularly for children of immigrants, like myself, who don't have experience of the old country. The quest to know their parents comes from a place to understand not only the parents, but the culture, the world. There's a part of the world that our parents inhabited and we're trying to seek it out in a very powerful way because we've never experienced it. It's a strange, unknown piece of the past; it's a personal myth.

Hong is a seeker and a detective. She's trying to understand how things came to be. She's struggling to untie this complicated knot of the love affair in her mother's generation because it has such a strong effect on her as a person and on her development as a person, on the person she becomes. In that way, I think that my own need to understand my family and Hong's quest to understand her family are very similar.

My parents were born in China and lived through the turbulent period Hong describes in the book. They left China in 1949, when Mao took over, and moved through Taiwan, then to the United States. In 1949, there was a cut-off between mainland China and much of the world that lasted almost thirty years, and it was during that time when I was born and raised. I grew up with a sense that China was unreachable. I also sensed that the country was enormously central to my parents. And that the loss of leaving China and coming through space and time to Appleton, Wisconsin, was so significant and painful, perhaps, that in order for me to understand my parents at all I had to know what had happened in the past, when they were growing up, in China. I think that's where the idea of the "imagined history" comes from.

ELLIS: I read that you focused on East Asian studies during your undergraduate years. It sounds as though you fed your left brain information about the time period your parents lived through, and then fed your right brain by applying this knowledge to your fictional works.

CHANG: I went through a period in my life where it seemed important to study the facts. I majored in East Asian studies and took a lot of Chinese. But I didn't use any of it, in a practical sense, until I came to write, at which point it was there for my imagination to use. And even so, I wrote one story about China in 1993 and didn't write about China again in an active way until I started *Inheritance*.

ELLIS: *Inheritance* is set during set in the China of the 1930s and 1940s, when the country was being invaded by Japan, when it was plagued by Communist revolutionaries. What opportunities do you think this particular period in history, this backdrop, provided you as a writer and the circumstances you were able to provide to your characters?

CHANG: The circumstances of the book are very dramatic. There's a death by beheading. There's a birth in a bomb shelter. There's a bridge collapsing and hundreds of civilians falling into a chasm on the border of China and Burma. The characters make dramatic moves across country to escape encroaching death. The historical events of China provided amazing material for me as I tried to write my book and they were also quite challenging for me, trained as I was in this contemplative American realism. I had to adapt my language and sensibility to encompass sweeping historic and cataclysmic events.

One of the influences on *Inheritance* that no one has mentioned is the Chinese drama and particularly the television drama that Chinese people and immigrants such as my parents watch all the time. I haven't sat through many of them because they're intensely long, DVD after DVD of these sagas, many of them historical, whose stories sometimes take place over many years and are melodramatic as all get-out. They are historical soap operas for people of Chinese descent. They fictionalize well-known historical characters and dramatize the terrible trials they've gone through. There are always deaths and torture scenes. In writing *Inheritance*, I borrowed from this sensibility.

ELLIS: I understand that as you wrote *Inheritance* you threw away four hundred pages and rewrote it fourteen times. How did you ultimately decide the form of this novel, and what to tell and not to tell?

CHANG: When I began drafting the book, I knew I wanted to have the younger sister and the older sister's husband fall in love, and I knew that I wanted to end the book with a funeral, but all the other scenes in the book were as yet undiscovered to me.

I began by writing short stories, and for many years, I had a problem when I tried to write long work. Instead of moving on I would collect a few pages and obsess over the task of trying to perfect a short passage of prose. I needed to break this pattern in order to write through the arc of a story. I decided to set a goal in 1998 to write ten pages of draft a week. My trick: after every hundred pages I closed the file and did not allow myself to look at what I had written. I knew that if I looked back, I would cease to move forward. That year, I had some interruptions but I did finish four hundred fifty pages of draft—and they were terrible.

Now that I've finished the book, I think of that horrible first draft and find it interesting that it does contain many of the significant scenes that went into the center of the final product. For years, I didn't know how to tell the story to get to these events, and I certainly didn't know what the characters would do after they took place; figuring that out was very challenging. The framing of the central drama was the most difficult for me. Building the narrative arc of the novel was also hard. I had never designed a long narrative and it took a lot of patient effort. I drafted those four hundred fifty pages in a year and spent five more years trying to figure out how to use the best pieces of that draft, and how to fit the pieces together.

I had a fellowship at Princeton and I wrote a hundred and fifty pages that year. It was all about Junan's father's gambling, and that whole generation: how they got into the situation they were in, and who he was and whether he had a mistress; in this draft he did and her name was Swallow and she was a courtesan. I gave the two hundred pages to my editor and to a friend, Elizabeth Rourke, who always reads my work, and they both said the same thing: that the book didn't really get going until about a hundred pages in. I had to take out a hundred and fifty pages, almost everything I had written that year. Doing this,

I had the wonderful sensation a snake must have when it is sloughing off an old, no-longer-necessary skin.

The next year I had another fellowship. I felt so lucky, and because I had shed the unnecessary parts of the first half, I was able to see the story line. I wrote through, got a lot of the first half down to what exists in the final draft. I reached the cave scene and the birth of the son, and then got stuck again. I could not get past the complication of the son being born, and wrote all the way to the end multiple times, at least seven or eight times. In almost every version, Hong, the narrator, had a different fate. It was like a "choose your own adventure" book—whom she married, whether she married, how many children she had. One of the other big changes I had to work through was whether Li Ang would come to the U.S. I couldn't find enough narrative energy to last through the U.S. years of the novel. I cut another one hundred fifty pages, plus the fifty more pages in the middle. I feel good about all this now. I spent so much time working through the alternatives that I'm confident I chose the right one. I just couldn't see the shape of it until I had worked through it so many times.

ELLIS: In the novella *Hunger* you write, "My senses opened; I grew large. I believed I heard in the howling wind a voice of admonition, but in the end I listened to the plunge and whistle of my blood. I put the hat into his beautiful, long-fingered hands." This powerful description is wed to a description of *yuanfen*, a Chinese word that means fate, "that apportionment of love which is destined for you in this world." Min's fate is to have a love unfulfilled. How did you develop her character?

CHANG: Well, that's an interesting story. When I set out to write *Hunger*, I had one goal in mind: to write something that was longer than twenty-five pages; until then I had written only short stories. Some of the short stories were fairly polished; one was in *Best American Short Stories*. But I knew I was incapable of writing a long narrative. I failed in repeated attempts to do this, so I decided on a medium-size narrative; I thought that a novella might be possible.

What I decided to do was take a short story of mine, "The Eve of the Spirit Festival," a story in which there was a dynamic that I trusted: a father and two sisters, one who was favored and one who was not. I knew I understood it. I decided to take this dynamic and put it into something longer. I added more characters, the mother, and the music. I had studied violin as a child, and I had taught it as an adolescent through my twenties for pocket money. With all this in mind, I started with the plan to write from the point of view of one of the daughters. I hammered out some scenes, and I could tell that they were lackluster, but I didn't know why. I was forcing myself to write forward because I knew my tendency to obsess over sentences and paragraphs. So I drafted all these thin, boring scenes. I had set a deadline I had for myself, the end of the summer, and it was already July. Everything felt so desperate and something was wrong, but I didn't know how to fix it.

My mother knew about this project and I told her about this problem. I told her I suspected it was a problem with the point of view. She asked me to describe what "point of view" was, and after I explained it to her, she asked why I didn't tell the novella from the mother's point of view. Now I always smile when I think about this, because of course she would suggest the mother's point of view, but, like many mothers, she was right. After she made this suggestion I redrafted the long scene when Anna is trying to please Tian by playing the Bach Double Concerto and she is failing, and then her younger sister Ruth comes in and ends up being much more talented. I rewrote it from the mother's point of view. I still remember this day. It was early August. I was in the LAIR, the big computer center at Stanford, where I often went to write so I didn't spend my whole day alone in my apartment—I found a certain security in the anonymity writing in that big room, surrounded by students working on their programming assignments. And as I was typing, I could feel the story gather under my hands and take on life. It was as if it literally started to breathe. From that point onward it was much more clear. I finished drafting *Hunger* by the end of September.

ELLIS: In this relatively short time you wove so many manifestations of hunger into the novella, both in terms of description, simile, behavior, metaphor.

CHANG: Sad to say, I don't know how much of it was conscious. I think it's just that if you're writing something that strikes a deep vein, if you find the place from which your story is coming, you find the place where everything is connected. If only you can get to that place. Great artists are the ones who do it on a regular basis. It's not the kind of thinking you can figure out by using your critical faculties.

ELLIS: It seems possible that the circumstances facing Sansan and Ming Hwang in your short story "The Unforgetting" could bear witness to the experience of your own family. In this particular story, a married couple settles in Iowa, the father gives up his dream of being a scientist and becomes a photocopy repairman, the wife cooks using American food and Betty Crocker recipes, they store six rice bowls once used in the emperor's household in their basement. How much of your motivation in writing this and other stories that deal with immigration and loss through assimilation have to do with your own family's experience?

CHANG: That story is in some ways very similar to the story of my family. My parents moved their family out to the Midwest, as pioneers, into a culture nothing like the culture they had come from. There's a sense of great unity and great deprivation in such families. However, in "The Unforgetting" San and Ming try to repudiate their Chinese culture, whereas my family did not. They encouraged us to be proud of the fact that we were Chinese and to maintain our Chinese culture, and yet I could feel it slipping though my fingers the minute I left home to go to kindergarten. I lost my Chinese and began to speak only English. At school I saw ways of looking at and thinking about things that were better for me as an individual. I think all of those issues get woven into the story, but they are distorted. The idea of memories flooding back into consciousness is true of our family, certainly, but I think of that as a human trait, and not only true of my family. The idea of the child leaving home and running away to school, leaving his parents, the great pain of that, is something that took place in my family but in a completely permitted and voluntary way. My parents didn't want us to stay in the Midwest for our whole lives. They wanted us to go out in the world and seek our fortunes, to go the East Coast, and all four of us did. It was an American success story, but that doesn't mean it wasn't painful. I think of this story as about being Asian parents in the Western world.

ELLIS: With the prodigious start of having your second story published in the *Atlantic Monthly*, how much internal pressure did you subsequently experience as a writer to perform and rise up to that level?

CHANG: It was pretty intense, although I didn't understand how much so at the time. Luckily I had other stories I was working on at the time; "San" was more important to me than the story that was in the Atlantic. In fact, "San" is still my favorite story. What happened was I spent two years at Iowa writing short stories, trying very hard to learn to write them. I sent one of them out. One of them was taken by the *Beloit Fiction Journal*, and then I wrote "Pipa's Story" during winter break. I revised it twice and sent it off to the *Atlantic*. They took it in March. Meanwhile, of course, I was leaving the MFA program and I was working on many other things. I was lucky enough to be accepted into the Stegner program at Stanford which gave me more time to find my voice. If I hadn't had that I think it would have been very rough for me. After the story was printed in *Atlantic*, I got a lot of letters from editors asking me if I had a novel, suggesting something about mothers and daughters; it was 1993 and Amy Tan was very popular. I felt an enormous amount of resistance to the idea of writing something under contract at that time. I knew I didn't know what I was doing. I had only two years in an MFA program, and a year before that of trying to write. I also sensed that if too much attention was paid to me, I would become too self-conscious. I was lucky enough to have two years to spend in California, focusing on my writing and building my confidence to write other stories and *Hunger* and then to seek an agent. I didn't want to be called a writer before I was ready.

ELLIS: Pearl S. Buck said, "I don't wait for moods. You accomplish nothing if you do that. Your mind must know it has got to get down to work." Can you speak about your writing practice?

CHANG: Well, when I am trying to work, I try to write every morning first thing for a few hours. That has been the most productive way. Writing whether I feel it is right or whether I have something to say. On the other hand, when I don't feel that I have something to say, that I have something to write, it is very difficult. That was the wonderful thing of writing a novel. I would know every morning when I went to write that it was waiting for me. I knew it was a mess, but it was there. Short stories are much more risky for me; you don't know if the story will still be there or whether it will self-destruct. But that makes it even more important for me to have a routine. Otherwise I just would shy away from it.

ELLIS: What do you like most about your writing?

CHANG: That's a really interesting question. Not all the time, but occasionally when I'm working on something, I get the sense that my characters are telling the truth. It's not necessarily the truth universally acknowledged. It's more of the truth to the circumstances that they are in, that which is usually not said. I suppose that's what I like about my writing, that it's an attempt to see human circumstances in an honest way, without bullshitting or putting on rose-colored glasses.

ELLIS: I'm really struck by your one-word titles, and how much they resonate. At what point in your writing do you choose them?

CHANG: I always choose them at the end. I've never written a book with a title in mind. *Hunger* was the title of the collection, and my editor and I thought it was fine. We came up with all the other titles, though; *The Vermillion Palace* because it's the name of the restaurant Min's husband Tian works. I nixed that because I thought it sounded too exotic and would mislead readers. *Inheritance* is an idea that Jill Bialosky, my editor, had, and I think it's a really good title. I was so up a creek in terms of titling this novel; I was working on it until the last minute. When she called it *Inheritance*, I thought it sounded fine. Ideally I think I would have come up with a title that a Russian novel would have, such as *The Sisters Chang*, but one syllable last names are problematic.

ELLIS: Where does your teaching fit into everything?

CHANG: I'm a very serious teacher. I have had the pleasure of teaching wonderful, brilliant students in almost every school where I've taught. In the last three years I've taught at the Iowa Writers' Workshop, I've taught here at Harvard, and I've taught at the Warren Wilson MFA program for writers. For whatever reason, I've been lucky enough, probably because the institutions are so strong, to come across writers who inspire me, who make me think, and they keep me company and are an enormous pleasure to know. I find that teaching has become very important to me in a way I didn't expect. Of course, I come from a teaching family; maybe I'm just growing into my legacy.

ELLIS: I understand you were once a student of Margot Livesey's. Can you talk about your experience as a student of writing in general, and more particularly as a student of Margot's?

CHANG: I am not a person of great productivity, and so having teachers to guide me, particularly when I was starting out, was very important. They helped me mark time, to set timelines, they helped me see; they were older writers who provided solace, inspiration, and faith. I think Margot is still the writing teacher who inspired me the most along these lines because she taught me to revise. She was always willing to look at my work and read it and tell me how she thought it could be made better, and then look at it again. She did this for a number of stories that are in *Hunger*. Going through this process with her, studying her marks on the page and going to conferences with her,

I learned how to learn. She has been since then an extremely supportive and generous and humane source of support. I can't tell you how grateful I am to have worked with her.

ELLIS: What have you learned to not do as a writer?

CHANG: I suppose I've learned not to spell things out. I try not to focus on what's going to happen. I try not to be too critical of myself when I'm drafting because it will stop me in my draft. I try not to be petty.

ELLIS: As of today, who are your literary models, writers who have most astounded you?

CHANG: As of today, the person who I'm most interested in is William Maxwell. I recently reread his book *So Long, See You Tomorrow*. I read it, my husband read it, we read it to each other, and we talked about it. Maxwell does things in that book that I've never seen before, and in addition the book is so true to itself, it feels as if there's not a false step in it. I'd love to write something like that.

ELLIS: Do you know what you're going to work on next?

CHANG: I have three things I'd like to write. I'd like to write short stories, and a piece that's around a hundred and fifty pages, and a longer novel. Of those projects the only one I know the topic of is a novel. It's going to be about poets. I'd also like to write about Asian Americans living in the Midwest.

Steve Almond

Revealing Your Characters

Steve Almond is the author of two collections of short stories, *The Evil B.B. Chow and Other Stories* and *My Life in Heavy Metal*, and *Candyfreak: A Journey Through the Chocolate Underbelly of America*, a memoirist ode to the origin of the candy bar. Almond writes about passion, sex, and heartbreak and has been dubbed the poet laureate of sex. He believes that having an agent can interfere with the artistic process and sold both *The Evil B.B. Chow and Other Stories* and *Candyfreak: A Journey Through the Chocolate Underbelly of America* on his own.

In *The Evil B.B. Chow and Other Stories*, Almond's new collection, he focuses on the issues of coping with love and loss in our time. *Booklist* compares this collection with his debut, *My Life in Heavy Metal*: "Almond proves himself to be just as irreverent, audacious, and amusing in his new set of stories, but his subjects are more diverse, and he manages to be even more sardonic and affecting." Mark Lindquist, writing for the *Seattle Times*, declared *My Life in Heavy Metal* "the freshest collection of short stories I've read since the 1980s." *Salon.com* noted that readers would be "gasping, gulping, and guffawing from beginning to end."

Almond is a lover of candy and eats at least one piece every day. He wrote the bittersweet and humorous *Candyfreak: A Journey Through the Chocolate Underbelly of America* during a relatively lean period in his fiction writing career. Natalie Danford, in her *Chicago Sun-Times* review states of *Candyfreak* that "Like the bickering couple in the Reese's Peanut Butter Cup commercial, readers may be unable to determine whether Almond has mixed reminiscences into a report on the state of the candy business, or added details about the candy business to a memoir, but no matter: The results are irresistible."

Which Brings Me to You: A Novel in Confessions, which Almond co-wrote with novelist Julianna Baggott, was published in the spring of 2006. *Not That You Asked*, his new collection of essays, will be published in the fall of 2007.

Almond is a prolific short story writer whose stories have been published in literary journals and commercial magazines, including *Playboy*, *Tin House*, *Zoetrope*, *Virginia Quarterly Review*, *McSweeney's*, the *Missouri Review*,

Southern Review, *Ploughshares*, and *Other Voices*. In 2002, he won the Pushcart Prize for "The Pass" and in 2001 he was a National Magazine Finalist.

His fiction has also been included in several anthologies, including *New Stories from the South 2003*, *Best of Zoetrope II*, and *Best American Erotica*. Almond's reviews, essays, and columns have also appeared in such publications as the *Los Angeles Times*, the *Boston Globe*, the *Believer*, and *Boston Magazine*.

Almond teaches creative writing at Boston College and at Grub Street, a private writing program in Boston. He earned his MFA at University of North Carolina at Greensboro. He was raised in Palo Alto, California, and spent seven years as a newspaper reporter in El Paso and Miami.

I interviewed Steve Almond at the kitchen table of his Somerville, Massachusetts apartment. We sat at a brightly adorned table awash with cows, dogs, houses and flowers, painted by an artist named Sam MacMillan. Attached to the living room walls was a large gallery of candy bar wrappers.

SHERRY ELLIS: In Michael Alvear's *Salon.com* review of *My Life In Heavy Metal*, he comments about your ability to "write about sex in a daring, fresh and provocative way, that he [you] writes it within every conceivable context. Some of Almond's most enjoyable descriptions are of tongues, and where they are put . . . " How do you keep making your sex scenes fresh and alive?

STEVE ALMOND: I don't think of myself as writing sex scenes. I don't say, "I'm going to write a sex scene. What parts am I going to describe?" I think much more—oh, here's a place where the characters are going to be laid bare, their emotions are going to be laid bare. It just so happens in a lot of the stories I write that's in a sexual context. It's where people are at the height of their ecstasy, fear, shame, neuroses; it's a highly charged emotional activity. So I'm not really thinking what parts are going to go where, I'm much more thinking what will be revealed about the characters in this context.

ELLIS: In the story "The Evil B.B. Chow" you demonstrate your character's enthusiastic feelings of attraction through expansive description. "We finish off the second bottle of wine and sort of stumble to the couch and now we're really quite close and his skin smells like plums and clay and his eyelashes are so delicate—I've never seen eyelashes so delicate—and I can feel my face get warm and fuzzy as his lips come toward mine." Later in this story, after this character is rejected by B.B. Chow, many sensory details and feelings of loss are shared in just one sentence. As a writer, do you start with an image or a feeling?

ALMOND: I don't know that I can separate those two. When the emotions get intense in the story I linger in that imagined moment. Sometimes I have an image, sometimes I have a feeling, but it's more that I reach a point that's highly charged and I'm trying to slow down. As the action slows down, what happens is the characters have to turn inward and the sensual and psychological details become compressed. That's what's called the lyric register. That's what poetry is, it's highly compressed sensory observation and psychological detail. That's what I'm trying to do in moments like that, when the character is on the threshold of a first kiss with someone they're very excited about. So much is going through your head at those times; it's a little like a sex scene, so many details at once. All I'm trying to do is slow down time so you get more of a thickness of the consciousness in those moments.

ELLIS: In the above passage, how important is sentence length and description relative to the subject matter?

ALMOND: My sentences—this is true of most writers—attempt to reflect consciousness. The sentence is a basic unit of consciousness, just like the paragraph is. So when a character's thoughts and feelings are gallivanting, naturally in my attempt to reflect their feelings, my sentences become long and discursive. At the same time you can't overdo that. One of my central tenets of writing is: Never confuse the reader. Never leave the reader in a state where they're overwhelmed and unable to process the prose. It ceases to become lucid and they'll stop reading or stop absorbing the full measure of what you put on the page. You have to have some variety. In other words, I won't just write long sentence after long sentence after long sentence. The reader needs a short, punctuated, declarative statement. Denis Johnson is brilliant at this. He'll have a long beautiful passage, and then a really short, sharp declarative sentence that nails what the details have been suggesting, usually at the end of a paragraph. So, I think about sentence variety a fair amount, but if things are going well, I'm not conscious of it. It's just a rhythm of expression that I recognize as a reader who is writing. I need a break for myself as a reader.

ELLIS: How do you write such powerful sentences?

ALMOND: Well, one thing that contributes to my economy is that I took a year off from writing prose four or five years ago when I was fairly down in the dumps. I've always been drawn to poetry, so I read a lot. I read C.K. Williams, Yehuda Amichai, poets I think as superstars of the heart. They write brutally true, mostly narrative poems. They get rid of all the bull. Every single word is charged with meaning and oftentimes multiple meanings. The way the words interact gives them an extra jolt. I think writing poems for a year made me aware of that. I have friends who are poets and I read their work, too. I think that helps beat the dead language out of you.

When you try to tell the truth about something that's awkward and painful, the truth lifts the language into beauty. It's not the other way around. You don't say, "I want to write a beautiful sentence"; you don't say, "I want to have great style." You say, "I want to tell the truth, about how this really was, how it really felt for me at this moment," and the intensity of what we feel lifts the language into lyric register. It's an organic thing. If it's not organic then it's just a narcissistic affectation; the reader will not feel what the character is feeling, she will see the author trying too hard, being artificial.

ELLIS: In the beginning of "Larsen's Novel" you write, "Larsen had written a novel, and his best friend Flem Owens had no idea what to do about it. He could, in point of fact, barely lift the thing." How important do you think it is for writers to lay out the parameters of their stories at the start?

ALMOND: I like stories where I know what's happening quickly. And I like stories where a desire or a conflict is established early on. I don't like—and I see this over and over in student work—where the protagonist wakes up and hits the alarm clock or the woman is in the bath tub, and it takes us forever to get to the place where the real source of fear or desire or danger resides. I always want to say, "Quit clearing your throat! What is this story about?" In "Larsen's Novel" I was trying to establish, as quickly as possible, a sense of dread. Who among us has not had a friend who asks us a favor that makes us feel awkward and put-upon and guilty? I like the kind of story where the author trusts the story and says, "Here's what this story is about." Here is what my hero fears or desires. Tell me up front so I can attach myself to that. When people read, they have a certain amount of goodwill to give over to the story, that gets eroded very quickly if they are confused or disoriented.

ELLIS: What effect do you hope to achieve by using a conversational style in writing?

Almond: Well, I think writing is best when the writer is invisible, when the reader feels that they're just hearing someone tell a story. Short stories are the way stories come to us in the world, when you're sitting at a bar or around a dinner table or in a coffee shop. I want to tell the story in as natural a way as possible and the conversational style is just more natural to me.

I guess the other thing is that a conversational style is closer to how I speak. It's easier for me; I don't have to put on a mask. I can just write as I and my friends talk, which is sort of smarty-pants, but vulnerable. I think the reader appreciates not being asked to accept a more stilted or formal narrator. They feel more like they're just listening, one-on-one.

Ellis: How do you make your dialogue sound so real?

Almond: I was a journalist for seven or eight years, so I listened to people talk a lot. One thing to realize is that people don't talk in clean, neat sentences. They double back, they reiterate, they pause; they go off on a tangent. The way that people talk is a reflection of their consciousness in the purest way, and their inner conflicts. So I view dialogue, always, as an attempt to reflect character. It's not there to advance the plot. I'm also a mimic. If I hear someone and how they speak, if someone says something beautiful or exceptional, if someone says something on the radio, or says something at a party, I will automatically file that away. I love the rhythm of people's speech, their inflection, their word choice. I'm just trying to record what I hear with fidelity.

Ellis: When you write, how important is it for you to include gesture and body language?

Almond: You don't want characters to become talking heads, that's the major thing. When you see a whole lot of dialogue with just attributions, "he said, she said," you start to lose a sense of your characters as physical beings. But I don't think people should try to squeeze physical gestures into their attributions. Physical gestures should get their own sentences. There should be a pause, for the reader to process it. My characters need bodies; they can't just be voices.

Ellis: Your story "Summer, as in Love" begins and ends with images of browning hydrangea and tells the story of a summer's love. You begin, "I want say that it was high summer. I want to say the hydrangeas were exploding, and that I was in love. None of these things was true, exactly. It was nearly August and the hydrangeas were tailing off, brown veins seeping in at the edge of the purple clusters." Near the story's end the character says, "Instead, we close our eyes and let our lovers step towards her through the fading hydrangeas, the impenetrable dusk." How important are metaphors in your work?

ALMOND: I think people overuse metaphor and simile. It becomes a way of showing the reader how clever you are. In the case of the hydrangea, I'm not even really sure that's a metaphor. I'm not saying, "Our love was dying off like the purple hydrangeas fading in the dusk." That would be too obvious. I like to just put the object in the story and hope the reader will make the metaphor there themselves, from the psychological association. In the case of the hydrangea, the character noticed it because it was symbolic of a beautiful thing that was decaying. That's how people really move through their world. Their minds snag on significant stuff.

ELLIS: You named one of your shorter pieces "The Idea of Michael Jackson's Dick." Do you think simple is best in title selection?

ALMOND: I have three criteria for titles. The first is the "table of contents test," which is the least important. When I look at the table of contents, do I want to read it? The risk of that is you use histrionic titles. The second test is that title should be a signpost, pointing the reader toward the deepest meaning of the story. And third, the tone of the title should be reflective of the story. "The Idea of Michael Jackson's Dick" is a muttered profane line that is totally in the spirit of the story. I wanted the irony that is beneath it, which is how we deal with fame and self-loathing. "Summer, as in Love" is about a kid who thinks he's in love, but he's totally unprepared to make the commitment that love requires. Sometimes I'll have something like "Larsen's Novel." It's just an object. But Larsen's novel is the transcendental signifier of that story. It is the big lump of guilt and envy that is sitting in the middle of the story. I also want my titles to sound mellifluous. "The Evil B.B. Chow"—the letters "e" and "b" rhyme, and I like that. "How to Love a Republican" has an internal rhyme, too. I love titles that feel particular, as if they could only be the title of that particular story.

ELLIS: In your story "How to Love a Republican" you write, "What Darcy enjoyed most was a good lathering between the thighs. As a lifelong liberal, this was one of my specialties. In some obscure but plausible fashion, I viewed the general neglect of the region as bedrock of conservatism. The female sex was, in political terms, the equivalent of the inner city: a dark and mysterious zone, vilified by the power, derided as incapable of self-improvement entrenched and smelly." Do you ever make yourself blush when you're writing?

ALMOND: No. I'm not a blusher. If the scene is sexy, though, I think you should be aroused. There are things I'm too frightened or ashamed to write about. It's just that sex doesn't happen to be one of them.

ELLIS: Such as?

ALMOND: I think that's what a successful writing career reveals. You take on more and more of what you're ashamed and troubled by. For me, that would be certain kinds of intense failures I feel, guilt and anger about family stuff that I still haven't worked out, that are still very much inside me, and my disappointment and apprehension about failure in the people around me.

ELLIS: In your first short story collection, *My Life in Heavy Metal*, there are three stories that share the same protagonist, David, at different stages in his life. In your new collection are there any links between the stories that I didn't recognize?

ALMOND: No, there aren't; so don't worry. Publishers always want some kind of link with collections, to help with marketing. So I feel extraordinarily lucky that Algonquin agreed to publish a collection that's basically my favorite unpublished stories.

ELLIS: When I interviewed Ron Carlson, he talked about the notion of ideas and worlds getting rapidly used up in short stories. How hard is it for you to keep coming up with new ideas?

ALMOND: The big question for me is not generating ideas, but what to invest my time in. My ideas file is ridiculously long. It's more a matter of what I'll actually be able to execute.

ELLIS: Do you think about the shape or the arc of your stories before you begin?

ALMOND: I tend to think of stories in panels, in terms of the scenes that are going to be important. I don't outline, exactly, but I do write a little flow at the bottom of the story. For the most part, the story tells me how long it will be and what shape it will take. When I write a story such as "I Am What I Am," which deals with the death of a child and the guilt of the boy who accidentally killed him, I know that story is going to be long, that it's going to be five or six thousand words long because of the work it has to do. For the emotions to feel authentic, I know the story needs several committed scenes of struggle. For me to try to write "I Am As I am" in three thousand words, which I probably would have done in graduate school, would have required a leap into sentimentality. I would have had to make assertions about this kid's emotional states rather than leading him and the reader and myself through those emotional states. For a story like "The Soul Molecule," which is more elliptical and symbolic, I really just needed one scene. The whole point when I'm writing stories is to get to the deepest place emotionally in the fewest words.

ELLIS: How do you suggest writers make transitions from scene to scene?

ALMOND: Use a space break, if you have to. Young writers tend to stress too much about transitions. All the reader wants is to be in the "vivid and continuous dream" that John Gardner talks about it. They can be jerked out of that dream by any one of several things. Overt sentiment, being confused, and also the writer calling attention to him or herself by being overly worried about the bureaucracy of the story.

ELLIS: How do you know when your stories are finished?

ALMOND: A lot of the time, I don't. I write past the ending, or don't quite get there. So then you have to look at the story in revision. There's a lot of feeling involved with an ending, especially because I tend to like to go out with a bang.

ELLIS: In *Candyfreak*, you juxtapose your love of candy with candy bars of yesteryear, candy bars of today, information about your own life, your opinion about politics, and a road trip. How did you decide to use this somewhat memoiristic approach for a book that could easily have had a primarily journalistic emphasis?

ALMOND: Well, *Candyfreak* isn't really about candy as much as it's about obsession. I wrote it out of a kind of desperation. I failed at writing a novel into which I'd poured quite a bit of energy, and nobody wanted any more of my short stories. I got quite depressed, and started eating quite a bit of candy and talking about candy all the time. And this returned me to the feeling states I'd had as a kid. So, in a sense, the whole point of the book was to write about the depth of my personal connection to candy, my obsession. All good writing is about obsession. That's what we read for: a sense of the author's passion. Also, once I started visiting factories, I knew I had great material. I could see that candy had a fascinating social and cultural history. As for the writing, I just let it rip. I wasn't trying to create a mongrel book. I knew it might be harder to market a book that was all over the place, but I'm not writing for the purposes of marketing. I'm writing to get the truth of my feelings out on the page.

ELLIS: In *Poets and Writers* you've written about working without an agent. Can you speak about how you came to this decision?

ALMOND: I had an agent and I saw the dynamics between her and me, and I saw the dynamics between all my friends and their agents. Most of the time, agents become this powerful transference figure. They represent the commercial interests of the publishing industry and I really just don't want those voices in my head. To be clear: I think the people who are literary agents are great; they've chosen to advocate for writers. God bless them. I just don't want to worry about anything other than my readers and how I'm going to reach them. As a practical example, by the way, all three of the agents who read *Candyfreak* refused to represent it, because they didn't know how it would be marketed. So my being without an agent is partly a function of the fact that I can't get an agent. As to what it's like not having an agent, it can be difficult. I wind up having to worry about a lot of business stuff that I shouldn't be worrying about. Maybe when I have a novel that's worth sending out into the world I'll get an agent.

ELLIS: What were the benefits and liabilities of co-writing a novel?

ALMOND: The benefit of writing a novel with someone else is that you're not alone; you can show off to someone. It was very galvanizing for both of us. We finished the first draft of this book in a few months. She's a fast writer and when I get going, I am too. The disadvantage is that you're not the only one in charge of the book. You have to deal with feedback. So negotiating that is very difficult, where you feel disappointed in one another's work. It was fascinating what happened with Julianna and me, because the characters in our book are this man and woman who meet at a wedding. They're both unmarried and they start to fool around, but they decide not to have sex, but instead to confess their past relationships to one another. So there's this courtship back and forth and eventually the characters express a lot of disappointment and anger at each other, which is what we, the authors, were doing at a certain point. So if you see what I mean, there was all this intense accusation and vulnerability that was flowing between us as authors and between the characters.

Joan Leegant

The Life Around Them: Animating the Inanimate

In *An Hour in Paradise*, her collection of short stories, Joan Leegant explores themes of Jewish lore, wisdom, and religion. Inanimate objects breathe with life and develop personality traits and behaviors of their own. Characters seize moments of pleasure, moments of joy, when they are least expected. Mystical visitations and experiences speckle the narrative horizons. Some of the stories read like fables; others are more traditional. Louis Bayard in his *New York Times* review of this collection commented on the difficulties a fiction writer faces writing about religion. He said, "Fiction in its ideal form is an open system, suggesting without determining. Religion is at heart a closed system—a ring of certainty. Bridging those two worlds has been the mission of generations of writers, but only a few have kept their footing, their very survival a testament to the dangers they have passed. These are the perils that Joan Leegant in turn skirts, bows to, and transcends in her arresting new short story collection."

The stories in this collection were originally published in *Columbia*, *Crazyhorse*, *Prairie Schooner*, *Nimrod* and other publications. Her essays have appeared in the *Forward*, a Jewish newspaper, and elsewhere.

Critically acclaimed, *An Hour In Paradise* received the Edward Lewis Wallant Award for the best book of Jewish-American fiction and the 2004 L.L. Winship/PEN New England Award for the best book by a New England author; was named a finalist for the 2004 National Jewish Book Award; and was a Fall 2003 selection for the Barnes and Noble Discover Great New Writers Program. Leegant's stories have also won or been finalists for the following literary awards: the Lawrence Foundation Award, the Katherine Anne Porter Prize and the Tobias Wolff Award.

Leegant is at currently at work on her first novel, a story of young Americans living in Jerusalem in the late seventies. Leegant is a recipient of an artist grant from the Massachusetts Cultural Council and fellowships from Yaddo and the MacDowell Colony. She teaches writing at Harvard University. This interview was conducted on Ms. Leegant's backyard deck under the late afternoon sun, amid resplendent greenery. Ms. Leegant lives in Newton, Massachusetts, with her husband and two teenage sons.

SHERRY ELLIS: In the story "How To Comfort The Sick and Dying," Reuven is both a yeshiva student and an individual in recovery from drug addiction and a womanizing lifestyle. He feels guilty about his past and has difficulty comforting a dying man who has AIDS, which prompts a crisis in his faith. How do you develop your characters?

JOAN LEEGANT: I coax them out and then I follow them. When the yeshiva student emerged, for example, all I saw was a young man in the doorway of a hospital room looking at a patient. I was interested in the patient, but I was more interested in the young man. He was in full Hasidic dress—black yarmulke, tzitzit fringes, dark suit—but I knew he wasn't a born Hasid and that there was a story behind his dress. I wrote the story to find out what that was. Within the first few paragraphs, I discovered where he was coming from and why he was dressed that way, but it was through his interactions with the patient, through the rest of the story, that I discovered who he really was and what the story would be about. I didn't know any of it until I wrote it.

ELLIS: In the story "Mezivosky," a Russian Jew and an American Jew are neighbors who seemingly have nothing in common. After Mezivosky begrudgingly feeds a stray dog, he tells his neighbor. Later the neighbor asks himself, "What was a man to do? Ignore the seesaw of right and wrong, the grinding teeth of conscience?" By the story's end the boundaries between the two neighbors are less rigid and a bond has started to develop between them, their conversations about the dog having seemed to bring them together. How do you develop your characters' circumstances and the ways their lives intersect?

LEEGANT: That story began after I finished an MFA program and was giving myself projects, little assignments. I saw an ad for a contest that was looking for culturally Jewish stories with a limit of fifteen pages. Since I usually write long, I told myself it would be a good exercise. I was also in the mood to write something funny. The exercise began by my simply putting down a first line and following it through: "The Russian next door was driving Koenigsman crazy." I liked the tone, the humor, and the built-in antagonism suggested in that first sentence. I wrote the story to find out the kinds of things these two men did to drive each other crazy and to find out what happens when you have that kind of culturally-influenced antagonism.

The dog, by the way, came to me very much at the end of the initial draft. Later, I thought I should move the dog to earlier in the story because it became an important sort of symbol. But ultimately, I concluded that I liked it showing up late in the story. It added a measure of unpredictability, a wildness. Speaking of symbols, readers sometimes think that writers "plant" symbols in their work as some sort of hidden message or puzzle they're supposed to uncover, as if the writer were playing a kind of game. But, really, symbols should arise organically from the material itself. Often they carry weight in a piece that the writer, or reader, isn't fully conscious of.

ELLIS: When you began writing these stories, was it your intention for them to grow into a collection?

LEEGANT: No, I didn't set out to write a collection. In fact, when I first began writing stories, I didn't write anything with Jewish content. I wrote about lots of other things. It took me a while to find the subject matter that moved me the most. Bernard Malamud has a short essay called "On Subject Matter" that appears in a compilation of his speeches and essays called *Talking Horse*, in which he says a writer may need time to find his or her subject matter. In my case, I think I needed to develop more as a writer before I could tackle material that was so close to the bone.

Still, it was quite a while before I thought of having a whole book of such stories. The seed was probably planted when I published my first story—which was about a rabbi in a sort of spiritual crisis—and it won a prize, third place in *Nimrod*'s Katherine Anne Porter Prize. They flew me to Tulsa, Oklahoma, to participate in a writers' conference and receive the prize, and on the plane ride back I was so encouraged, thinking I could tap this vein further, that I began to furiously scribble all over the conference materials possible titles of more Jewish stories. Eventually I wrote some of them, publishing them in literary journals. At one point I saw I had enough to make a book. So that's how the collection came about.

ELLIS: How did you choose the title *An Hour in Paradise*?

LEEGANT: I originally used the title of one of the stories, "Seekers in the Holy Land," for the collection's title, but some of the early readers of the book, including my editor, weren't thrilled with that. Elinor Lipman suggested I look at Yiddish proverbs, which proved to be an excellent source. I read through several thousand proverbs over a weekend and came up with six or seven choices for my editor. She chose *An Hour in Paradise* from the proverb: "Even an hour in paradise is worthwhile," meaning we don't necessarily get a lifetime of happiness, but even an hour makes life worthwhile. I came to love that title and felt it represented the book well thematically.

ELLIS: What about the order of the stories?

LEEGANT: The story order I played with. I tried to alternate the stories in terms of gender, tone, age of the characters, setting—some in Israel, some in the States—and thematic material, so that the experience for the reader would be varied and interesting. I also knew I wanted to ease the reader in with a first story that would help establish the world of these fictions, but not be so dark or hard-hitting as to frighten a reader off. "The Tenth" seemed like a natural choice to start the collection because the world portrayed there is a very Jewish world—a small Orthodox synagogue in Brookline, Massachusetts—with some of the magical or mystical elements explored throughout the collection; but it's also a story with some humor, some lightness in the tone, making it inviting, I hope, to a reader.

ELLIS: How important do you think place is in your stories? For example, in "Seekers in the Holy Land," you write that Neal, an American student, "... has chosen to go to Safad because the Kabbalists came here. The streets are hilly, some of the roads rocky—this is what he wants, what he came for, the ancient feeling, the hard-to-get-there feeling ..." It seems the geography mirrors his internal needs.

LEEGANT: Place is very important to me in my fiction. And, yes, you're right: in that story the geography does mirror the character's drives and needs. All the stories are like that. The ones that occur in the Bronx could only occur, in my mind, in the Bronx, just like the stories set in Florida and Queens and, most especially, Israel, could only be in those settings. I can't write a story and not know where it is anchored, and I find I am unsettled by other people's stories or novels if they don't impart a clear sense of place. I am now writing a novel that's set in Jerusalem.

ELLIS: Do you see your settings as characters?

LEEGANT: Yes, absolutely. In my novel, the city of Jerusalem is as much a character as any of the individuals in the book—it has its own moods and nature and ongoing dynamic story, which actively intersects with the stories of the individuals. In fact, Jerusalem is so prominent in the book—that magnificent and volatile atmosphere, and all that it has evoked for human beings for thousands of years—that I'd venture to say it's the most important character in the whole enterprise, at least to me. Everyone and everything in the book is subtly shaped by the city.

ELLIS: Food and their odors are an integral part of "The Diviners of Desire: A Modern Fable." In this story you draw on whimsy. A young woman has recently changed her diet from strict vegetarianism and eats small portions of meat. She travels to Israel and stumbles upon a matchmaker in hopes of finding a husband. Can you describe the process through which you manifest the different senses in your stories?

LEEGANT: Well, that's an interesting question. I believe one needs to anchor stories in details, in sensual detail that the reader can see and hear and smell and touch. That's how I can get the story from my head into yours, how to convey the "vivid, continuous dream," as John Gardner says. In order to bring these details into the stories, I've learned to stop and take note of things while I'm writing. It's almost a meditative practice. You must be in the moment of your story and notice what is going on around the characters: what they hear, what they smell, what things feel like, what's going on around them. But you can't simply describe these things for the reader; you have to have your character feel it, see it, taste it. Then the reader can experience it, too.

So, for example, in "The Diviners of Desire," the smell of food was so much of the story that, finally, it rose up and sheltered the characters like a wedding canopy—and, along the way, gave me the ending. I actually saw the smells; they became animated, sort of genie-like vapors, almost like in a cartoon, which is something I love to indulge in as a writer, animating the inanimate. I do this in other stories. In "Accounting," there's a digital clock that a character is looking at during a difficult phone conversation. At one point the zero on the clock bobs up and glares at the character, accusing, like a face. Likewise, in "How to Comfort the Sick and Dying," Reuven, the yeshiva student, is carrying a raincoat, to which I ascribe emotions, suggesting, for example, that the raincoat doesn't want to be in the hospital room with him, or that the raincoat is joyful at the end of the story. The raincoat acts something like Reuven's conscience in the story, like his Jiminy Cricket. I love doing this in stories, giving inanimate things emotion, feelings. A terrific essay about this is Charles Baxter's "Talking Forks," which appears in his book of essays on fiction, *Burning Down the House*.

ELLIS: Talmudic sayings augment "How To Comfort the Sick and Dying." For example, you write, "One who leaves the bedside of the dying is worse than a father who denies his own child bread." Other stories in *An Hour in Paradise* also use religious and cultural idioms and terminology. Were you ever concerned your use of Jewish tradition and language might limit your readership?

LEEGANT: I did think early on that my readership might be limited, but I wrote the stories because this was the material that moved me and felt authentic. As I said before, I'd been writing for several years before I delved into the Jewish material, and I knew what it felt like to write honestly and authentically, and what it felt like to write work that was forced. Still, I didn't know where these stories might find a home and was naturally very happy when they were taken by literary magazines and later began to win prizes.

But I'd also learned early on, with that Tulsa trip where I met readers, that there is a universal hunger for work that deals with spiritual issues, a hunger that transcends ethnicity and religion. And I was careful to make sure that readers, whoever they were, could understand the Jewish terminology and cultural idioms from the context.

ELLIS: In "Accounting" the narrator relies upon the language of accounting. Cleaning up after Eliot is an act of penitence for his parents, an attempt to correct the balance sheet of their lives and to minimize the impact of losses. A theme of "Henny's Wedding" is reflected in the words you choose to describe the simple act of cleaning a table. The narrator observes, "Shirley took the sponge and wiped off the table. You didn't spread your shame around the street." Can you describe your process in using these details of language and metaphor as you write, and how you come to them?

LEEGANT: What happened in those stories, in all stories that succeed, is that early on, the writer enters the world of the story, and that world has its own diction, its own tone, what people loosely refer to as voice. I can see this as a teacher, early student stories that are competent but don't have a voice, don't bring a whole world of language with them; often these won't ultimately succeed. When you start writing a story you tap into a world that has its own vocabulary; when things are going well, a story like that will deliver up from your psyche the metaphors and idioms and phrasings that are just right. As a writer you have to let the language and metaphors and images enter the material—you can't artificially create them or force them in there. In my own stories, if within a few paragraphs or maybe a couple of pages this world-of-the-story language isn't there, isn't emerging, then I know something's wrong. Either I don't have a handle on the character or the situation, or I'm in the wrong subject matter, or something.

ELLIS: In "The Tenth" you begin, "After fifty-one years as a rabbi, Samuel Steel had believed until that morning that when it came to the often elusive tenth man needed to complete a *minyan*, he had seen everything. Drag queens, blond farm boys with names like Swenson, Nordstrom. A former monk who sometimes wore his robes." This story begins with humor and whimsy and moves to deeper philosophical and spiritual issues. As a result of an unusual circumstance—Siamese twins who are brought to serve as the tenth man in a *minyan*—the rabbi explores the tenets of Judaism and realizes "that even compassion was a layered thing." Do you use writing as a means of exploring and manifesting your own sense of Judaism?

LEEGANT: Yes, very much so. I came to writing later than some, and didn't tackle Jewish material in my fiction until I was in my forties, so I had by then been wrestling with the question of Jewish practice and identity for a long time. I've lived as a secular Jew and as an Orthodox Jew and as someone in between; I spent three years in Israel in my late twenties and early thirties immersed in Jewish life and study; and I've given a lot of thought to religion and Jewish culture through the raising of two sons. Now, though, I tend to wrestle with these issues more through my writing than through my personal practice. And I'm continually surprised by what I find out.

ELLIS: The story "Lucky in Love" is told in the first person from the perspective of a psychologist who has recently learned the true identity of her father. She begins, "Six people attended my mother's wedding. Her mother Mae, my aunt Rose, who was carrying twins though no one suspected at the time, Rose's husband Lou, my mother's best friend Peshy, who lived upstairs in 6D, Rabbi Wax, and, of course, the groom. My father was not among them." Whereas most of your stories are told in the third person, how did you choose to use a first-person narrator for this particular story?

LEEGANT: It's the only first person story I've ever published and one of a very small handful I've written. I've stayed away from first person for a few reasons. I think when I started writing fiction I learned in third person; it came naturally to me. And I shy away from anything that is autobiographical. The stories

I attempted to write in first person invariably ended up being stories about women and their mothers, which was a recurrent theme, and I couldn't write anything else.

"Lucky in Love" was one of those things where a voice came to me and I couldn't shut it off. I avoided it for three or four days, and every night I would fall asleep memorizing pieces of the story, because it wouldn't let go. So to stop it, I got up to write it down, and found myself engaged, and I couldn't let go. But I did resist it. When you ask, how did I choose? I think stories choose themselves.

ELLIS: Several of your stories have titles with duplicitous meanings, for example, "Accounting" and "Lucky in Love." How do you choose them or, once again, do they choose you?

LEEGANT: I think story titles choose themselves. In fact, I always know when I'm writing that, until I have the title, I don't yet have the story. Once I'm immersed in a story, a title emerges that seems inevitable, and no other title presents itself. Sometimes that can be early on—I've started stories with a title, as I mentioned earlier—or as late as the last few pages. The fact that the titles have double meanings isn't an accident. I like titles to carry meaning and added heft, and sometimes, as in the case of the two you cited, suggest a bit of irony, too.

ELLIS: In two of your stories, "How to Comfort the Sick and Dying" and "Lucky in Love," the protagonists tell stories about themselves. What do you believe these stories within story help the writer to achieve?

LEEGANT: The storytelling in those pieces do double and triple duty. They illuminate character, echo the thematic material that runs through the stories generally, and, as a relief and often surprise to me, provide opportunities for humor. In "How to Comfort the Sick and Dying," Reuven tells horrific pseudo-Hasidic fables to the dying man he's visiting. But unlike real Hasidic fables, these are inappropriate, bizarre, and full of vile behaviors: incest, lying, deceit, feeding people grotesque foods. As a result, they tell us a lot about Reuven who, despite his wish to do right and provide comfort to the patient, can't open his mouth without this awful stuff pouring forth. Thematically, the things that spill out into his stories echo the shameful things he has himself done and for which he is trying to atone: compulsive sex, cheating, feeding bad stuff to others in the form of lethal drug dealing. And, finally, because the stories are so bizarre, they give Ash, the dying man, openings for a few much-needed funny lines, which leaven this otherwise very heavy piece.

In "Lucky in Love," the storytelling accomplishes similar things. Blanche tells stories of what Solly was doing the day each of her children was born, showing us a dreamy side of Blanche we don't otherwise see. Likewise, Solly as not-quite-father in Blanche's reminiscences echoes the story's underlying themes of missed opportunities—Solly was the narrator's father and yet not her father—and of longing to re-create the past. Finally, Blanche's stories give the narrator some openings for funny lines, which, like in the Reuven story, provide needed levity in an otherwise mostly sad tale.

ELLIS: Can you describe your process of revision, and comment on whether it is more reductive or additive?

LEEGANT: I operate a lot by feel, paying attention to what I call the "wince factor": if I find myself wincing somewhere, I make myself stop and take a close look and not allow myself to try to get away with whatever it is. Likewise, if I zone out when rereading something, I'll make myself go back and see if it's boring, or if I'm avoiding something that needs attention, or if there's some other organic reason I'm glazing over.

In terms of adding or reducing, I do both, all the time. Reducing is easier for me; I can usually spot the fluff or garbage in a draft that has to come out. It's harder for me to know what to put in, what's missing. To help with that, I try to overwrite in the first draft, to put in as much as I possibly can, even if it's very unformed, because I can use it later when the draft is cleaned up to help me see what I was initially getting at. This can help me figure out what needs to be expanded.

ELLIS: Can you compare your writing process when writing short stories as compared to your process in writing your novel in progress?

LEEGANT: One of the things I like about writing stories is that I can get into the middle of things quickly, zone in on a particular moment, and be economical. I like that the reader's expectation is that you're going to be succinct and that something is going to happen, or be illuminated, in a short space. I especially like that the thing that's going to happen can be small but significant—because, after all, you're only asking a reader to stay with you for fifteen or twenty pages. The event must have meaning, but it can be small, fleeting, almost a glimmer.

A novel, on the other hand, is more daunting because what happens should, I think, be larger, more monumental—or, cumulatively, there must be enough significant small moments to add up to something pretty substantial; after all, you're asking a reader to hang in there for hundreds of pages. So there's the challenge to make the totality more powerful than in a short story. Yet ironically, in novel writing you don't have the same press for economy that you have in a short story. So I think there's a danger in writing long, of the work becoming too loose or sloppy or baggy, of the narrative losing momentum and edge. This worries me.

On the other hand, the joy of writing a novel is the great space you have for more characters, more story lines, more resonances among the story lines, a greater arc of time. I've loved that aspect of working on a novel. But until this novel is finished, I'll still be worried.

ELLIS: Do you think writers need mentors?

LEEGANT: I think mentors can be incredibly helpful to writers, though of course people can learn to write well without teachers and master's degrees and courses. A good mentor can help steer you in the right direction in terms of your reading and thinking about your own style and subject; they can show you your mistakes and show you how to do things better. Most importantly, they can provide encouragement, because writing is lonely and discouraging, a long road to hoe before you get any recognition. I do think that teachers who are into pronouncing judgment are a big problem—they can do a lot of damage that's hard to undo. Besides, you never know. Someone can be toiling in the wrong subject matter and take years before they find the right material, at which point their writing takes off. I distrust mentors who loudly and overtly discourage. Too often it's an ego trip. What's the point? Someone who doesn't write very well is going to find out sooner or later when they submit their work for publication; they don't need a mentor to nip them in the bud. Meanwhile, you have a lot of damaged souls out there, many of whom write really well, who think they're no good.

ELLIS: Who are the writers whom you particularly enjoy?

LEEGANT: I like a lot of different writers. I'm somewhat promiscuous as a reader, because I sometimes read work and don't remember the author's names. Some of my personal favorites for short stories are Bernard Malamud, Grace Paley, Tobias Wolff, Amy Bloom, Ethan Canin, Lorrie Moore, Steve Stern,

Robert Olen Butler, and the early stories of Philip Roth. Recent novels I've especially enjoyed were J.M. Coetzee's *Disgrace*, Ian McEwan's *Atonement* and Jeffrey Eugenides' *Middlesex*. I read a lot for voice. But I find it hard to read novels while I'm trying to write one, so that puts a crimp into my fiction reading just now.

ELLIS: In "When Invention Paves a Path to Truth," an essay that you wrote that was published in the Jewish newspaper the *Forward*, you write about your experience in writing the story "The Seventh Year" and your own experience of living in Israel during one such "shmitta year." You write, "Stop the striving. Declare your fields and holdings ownerless. Risk starving, and have faith that all will do well anyway. Don't think beyond tomorrow. . . . Take spiritual sustenance." Do you apply these principals in your life as writer?

LEEGANT: I've been thinking a lot about risk-taking in the past few years. So much of writing is about giving up control. One of the first things I discovered as a writer is that characters have their own story, their own path, and one of your jobs as a writer is to follow them and let them go where they have to go. You can't engineer their lives. The plus side is that, in giving up control as a writer, you get to experience true engagement. It's thrilling and wonderful, these moments of discovery and connection that seem out of time, but it's also scary because you don't know what you're doing or what you're going to find. At bottom, I think it's about being willing to embrace failure. It's hard. I'm working on it. I spent some years on a novel that didn't work and eventually gave it up. I'm sure it'll happen again. There's a giving up that everyone has to be willing at points to do. I don't see how there's any way around it.

Kathleen Spivack

Pulling Yourself In

In 1986, Kathleen Spivack was nominated for the Pulitzer Prize in poetry for her fourth book of poetry, *The Beds We Lie In*. While Spivack feels very much a part of the tapestry of current writing, she believes that the most important thing that occurred in her writing career was her long-term study with Robert Lowell, starting when she was age eighteen, and having the opportunity to look at the first drafts of famous authors.

Spivack is the author of *The Honeymoon*, a collection of short stories, and several additional published works of poetry including *The Break-Up Variations, Swimmer in the Spreading Dawn, The Jane Poems,* and *Flying Inland*. She has recently completed both a memoir about her relationship with Robert Lowell and a third novel, *Unspeakable Things*. Her short stories, poems, and essays have been published in numerous magazines and anthologies.

Kathleen Spivack has been a Visiting Professor of American Literature/Creative Writing in France since 1991. She has held posts at the University of Paris VII-VIII, the University of Francois Rabelais/Tours, the University of Versailles, and at the Ecole Superieure (Polytechnique). She was a Fulbright Professor in Creative Writing, France (1993–94). Spivack is also a private writing coach in Boston and Paris.

Spivack has received grants from the National Endowment for the Arts, the Massachusetts Artists Foundation, Discovery, the Bunting Institute and the Massachusetts Council for the Arts and Humanities.

I interviewed Ms. Spivack while sitting at her kitchen table in Watertown, Massachusetts.

SHERRY ELLIS: You've written short stories, novels, a memoir, poetry. What is your favorite genre and why?

KATHLEEN SPIVACK: I think I'm basically a poet; I started out that way. Why? Because poetry is one moment turned over carefully, it is a prism, it's an association of images. But some things have lent themselves to story or to essay or to novels; things that I want to talk about that are more narrative that I can't do in poetry.

ELLIS: What do you mean by thinking in images?

SPIVACK: Poetry is the stone in the lake and it's the ripples; prose is the lake. Poetry is very small and concentrated and intense; a small moment with a lot of reverberations. You might say that a short story is more like a poem, in that it is also one moment. You don't have a lengthy time frame, unless, let's say, you're Alice Munro. Generally you have your characters, you have your setting, and you're looking at a fixed point in things. And in poetry you're very, very small.

ELLIS: Are there similarities in the actual writing of short stories and poems?

SPIVACK: They're not similar. In a short story you're setting up a long walk, and then you expect the walk, and you have to finish the walk. Sometimes the walk is boring, sometimes it's hard, sometimes it's too long, but you're committed to finish the walk. Sometimes there are moments of magic along the walk, which is the poetry in the short story. Or you'll find yourself going toward an end that is totally magical, the ripple. But short story writing is more discursive; it's a journey. A poem is a deep glimpse, a deep reflection, in the meaning in the moment.

ELLIS: How do you think your prose has been informed by your poetry?

SPIVACK: In terms of the use of words it's given me a lot of freedom, a lot of texture, a lot of color; I love language and it's definitely affected my use of language. But you know, I don't consider myself a prose writer even though I've published a lot of prose. If I were pulling out a piece of work to show you it would be a poem or it might be a creative essay; probably not a short story.

ELLIS: How has your process varied between writing short stories and novels? And how have you known if something you're writing is a short story or a novel?

SPIVACK: That's a good question. In the short story it's the moment explored; perhaps there's two people, or a longer moment. There's definitely something that's happened, there's development, there's change that's happened to the person in a short story—the person learns and grows in the short story. You've only got six to fifteen pages to make that happen. When you begin, there's a trajectory with a limited number of pages and you know where the character is going to meet an obstacle or have a conflict and will grow as a result. Maybe there's going to be two people, three people, but you're not going to have a whole crowd. The change is going to be an internal realization in a short story.

This is also true in a novel, but you have a much bigger screen to work on and your novel can easily get out of hand, as we all know. I have at least two novels that seem to have been written just for the desk drawer, they are too crammed and busy.

It's tempting, when one goes from the confines of a poem, to put in too many people, or too many interesting stories. A novel can get out of hand because it doesn't seem in the beginning to have a boundary. If you look at the great novelists, I think you see in their beginnings; let's say *Augie March* by Bellow, you see loads of action because it's possible. He's a virtuoso. In writing a novel, you don't have the barriers or restraints of the short story. But as these great novelists develop, for example if you watch Bellow, he pulled in and became deeper in his later books. Phillip Roth in his early stories seems to have foreshadowed his development; the craft is wonderful. It continues straight through to what he's writing now. Toni Morrison too, all of a piece, her development as a writer. Nadine Gordimer. Or Amos Oz. You just watch their ability to create the characters and keep the focus and concentration and go deeper. Earnest Gaines is perhaps our greatest living American novelist—and in *A Lesson Before Dying* he went into the deepest places. I am very interested in the younger writers, too: Ethan Canin, Jonathan Safran Foer, Anne Patchett, a young Israeli writer, Edeet Ravel and others. They already know so much. Chris Castellani, Jennefer Haigh, Steve Almond—all in the Boston area. The British "postcolonial" writers, from Ishiguro on to successive generations; amazing! Off the scale, that group! And now those wonderful Indian writers—what a proud list!

But I think it's hard when you begin to write a novel, especially if you're a poet; it's hard because you don't quite understand how to pull it in. Our writing is our teacher, really. It helps to write short stories before one writes a novel because you learn to work within limits. There are always the exceptions, of course. I mean, you could write a picaresque novel, there are a lot of good ones, such as the recent one by Terry Tarnoff, but I prefer the concentration, the development, the focus and the subtle changes in a novel such as *Atonement*, for instance.

ELLIS: F. Scott Fitzgerald said, "Find the key emotion; this may be all you need to find your short story." Do you agree?

SPIVACK: Yes, absolutely. But I see the interaction among the protagonists and their development as also being part of a story. I think it's not a bad maxim but a short story is a hard form, it's an American form—perhaps less so now than it was twenty years ago, but it's definitely an American form. There's huge variety in the short story right now, so it's really hard to have a rule for it.

ELLIS: When you begin writing a piece, do you know the point of view?

SPIVACK: Yes. I can't explain it. It's like writing the first stanza of a poem. You flow into it. The problem doesn't come in the beginning. It comes in the middle of the story where the problem is going to be resolved and you don't know how it is going to be resolved; sometimes you have to take a break and think about it. In the beginning I hear the voices before I write it.

ELLIS: Many of your stories in your earlier anthology *Honeymoon* were about the theme of "love gone wrong." What about this theme appeals to you as a writer?

SPIVACK: Well, actually I think the stories are about women and children, women and men, women who have to go it alone and find ways of coping. At the time that I started to write short stories, I was writing poetry, but there were things that I was seeing and living that I didn't feel couldn't be written in a poem; they were more narrative. It was in the early seventies, and women were beginning to find a voice. I was alone with my children and I had a lot of time and I was lonely. I lived on a wildlife reservation as a caretaker, no electricity, no car, a small boat, and two little babies.

I decided I was going to write a story a week, partly to learn the form, I wanted to learn the form, and also because there were things I wanted to say about women's lives that was perhaps too narrative for the kind of poetry that I write: things about my life, my friend's lives, things that I was seeing that were not being validated: a friend with a retarded child who joined a swimming team, a couple where the husband forced the woman to have an abortion, a situation where the woman preferred her child to the husband. These situations were happening. I was seeing them, but they weren't being written about. So I thought that I should spend a year writing about these things I'd seen and maybe at the end of it I would know how to write a short story. I had a year to think about varied situations and to do a story a week. I was very lucky. Some of the stories got published, and then as they got better of course they stopped being published.

I got more into what I really wanted to say. A case in point. I wrote a story about a natural childbirth class from the point of view of the frustrated Lamaze natural childbirth nurse who is trying to be a cheerleader for the people in her classes. *Redbook*, which had taken a lot of my stories at this point, took it, but they asked me to change the ending. In the story the natural childbirth nurse was also pregnant and she had a baby and surprise, it hurt like anything. *Redbook* wrote me and said that it was politically incorrect for childbirth to hurt. Would I, for fifteen hundred dollars, say that the childbirth didn't hurt? Of course it hurt. Those were some of the situations that I saw.

I had another situation where a husband propositions his wife's best friend. In my story the husband sleeps with the best friend, and the wife, who is absolutely devastated, finally pulls herself together and says to her husband, "If I die she'll [referring to her friend] make a great mother for the kids; choose her." Then the husband, who's been denying the whole thing, gets extra furious that the wife is on to him and what's more, has the gall to select her successor. So I wrote a story about that triangle and how unexpected it was. *Redbook* took that one.... That was my domestic period.

Now, however, the stories I write that are being published are quite different because my life has changed. I have this job in France, my kids are grown up. When I went to Europe I was suddenly able to write about the more important things in my life that had to do with exile and displacement and language and refugees.

ELLIS: How old were you when writing started to occupy a prominent place in your life?

SPIVACK: My father was a journalist, among many other things, and by the time I was three I knew I was going to be a writer. That was it, no question. I used to share my bed with refugees coming out of Europe who shared their stories with me, and I used to write poems about their lives, starting when I was six years old. These people's lives were so overwhelming and I would write long poems about their suffering. And I always had stories—I always had stories. One started, "Dead cows tell no tales."

ELLIS: I understand you've written a memoir about your relationship with the poet Robert Lowell. What are the most important things he taught you about writing?

SPIVACK: I started with Lowell after I won a scholarship in college and I stayed with him for twenty years. He was wonderful to me. He gave me letters of introduction to Anne Sexton and Sylvia Plath and later Elizabeth Bishop and Stanley Kunitz; he entirely took me under his wing. He had me come to his house for tutorials in reading the great poets. He taught me to read poetry deeply. We went into the heart of poetry. He shared his poems in process, sometimes he revised a hundred times. He conveyed total dedication. He also conveyed working on the form of the poem, setting out your expectation in the first stanza. Working with Robert Lowell was the formative writing experience of my life.

ELLIS: Do you have specific writing habits?

SPIVACK: I try to write every day. When my children were young I would get up at 4 AM to write before I had to start work. When I go to bed the writing is in my mind, and when I get up I write it. There will be a time when I know I'll be focusing on revising or on a long project. Right now I'm working on a big project of linked essays; I have it in my mind and keep working on it every day.

But I believe there's a real balance between exhausting yourself and getting the work done. A poem is a sprint; a novel is a marathon. With a novel you're there eight hours a day. I've done three novels and it's a very hard process for me because I don't like sitting still. I like to go out and walk and take a break. With a novel you have to be a good marathon runner. Each novel is at least three, maybe five years of your life, and you're going to sit there eight hours a day, maybe ten hours. I'm a sprinter, I'm a poet really.

ELLIS: Have you ever had a dry season?

SPIVACK: Yes. When my first book came out, it was totally terrifying. It received great recognition and prizes and reviews and my teachers liked it, and then suddenly I had a fellowship. I couldn't deal with all the recognition and it was a very difficult time. Also the fellowship—a Bunting Fellowship at Radcliffe—was only for one year and I would go to the Institute and hear all the cheerful women and their cheerful typewriters, and I'd just sit there. Finally one day I heard *The Jane Poems*, my second book, just a few of them, in my head, and that was it. I think when there's been a lot of attention it can be a weight to live up to expectations.

When you've got a big project, when you've finished it, I usually need to rest. Let the well fill up again. I think there's a difference between a dry spell and a rest. You need to be patient with yourself in that replenishment.

ELLIS: How do you help your students be the best writers they can be?

SPIVACK: I'm very lucky because I love writing and I love teaching and I've never had any question about doing both. I have a complete feeling of commitment. I'm good at helping people working through their process; they don't come out sounding like me. Even if I don't understand what they're writing I can help them put it together. I work with all genres: theatre, prose, song, poetry; when I see how well my clients do in all these genres I am amazed; their track record is off the scale!

However, I select the people I work with carefully, even in my groups. I think there's something to the group support—as well as encouragement and pushing. Being protected from uninformed criticism too early is important for writers. At the same time you have to push the writers you work with. You try to keep them from sending out work for publication until they have enough work that a rejection won't destroy them. It's a real balance between letting them be the best and trying to keep the pressure away from them.

ELLIS: I understand that you believe your writing has become more passionate, genuine, and freer over time. Do you have any suggestions as to how a young writer can develop these attributes?

SPIVACK: I think it happens; that as you work you get closer to how you think. In the beginning a poet writes what he or she thinks is poetic, not from their inner voice. One writes to the conventions—right now, with all the MFA programs, there is a big range of what is considered acceptable as poetry. But over time the writer develops his/her voice. Voice is how you think, voice is not the cliché you went to first. You get closer and closer to your true voice. As you work, you are more able to say what you really want to say. I think it happens to every writer during the creative development, if they hang on long enough. As you go on, you become pure spirit.

ELLIS: What do you suggest to a writer working in her/his first stories or a novel?

SPIVACK: Set-up and structure are crucial—the who, what, where, why, when. Sometimes people might work for six months just on getting their first chapter, getting the voice of the narrator. It's very hard to go back and do that once you've gotten through the whole novel. A beautiful set up is James Agee's *A Death in the Family*, which has a fantastic prelude about thinking about summer nights. Agee does this whole set-up of fathers coming home and watering their lawns with the little kids looking at the stars before he focuses on the individual child. Now, that's a brilliant classical set-up.

A short story has to do with both intention and set-up. The set-up can't be too static because you've only got those fifteen pages or so. You can't spend three or four pages describing the inside of a house or a narcissistic woman carefully looking at herself in the oval mirror. Your set-up has to have all the elements of forward motion but not move so fast that you don't understand the story. Hemingway, Fitzgerald, their set-ups are beautiful. They just moved right into it, but they gave you everything. When you think of "The Snows of Kilimanjaro," you have the dialogue, you have the people, you have the emotions right there.

ELLIS: What are some of the discoveries you're still making as a writer?

SPIVACK: I've been working all my life to make a poem shimmer off the page. I think this is what I'm working towards, to become transparent, a window to another world. Pure spirit, as it were. Sometimes you get there, but the shimmering poems are the ones, of course, that are hardest to publish.

There's so much to write, there's so much to inspire me. I have notebooks filled with later drafts of poems, and I want to type them up and get to the hundredth draft and make them perfect.

I'm interested right now in the twilight—colors of longing—and I'm interested in exploring the nuances more. I like nuances; I don't like the vulgar, bright colors.

ELLIS: What are your current projects?

SPIVACK: I'm working on three projects that I'm totally psyched about. First, I should tell you about a new book that I have coming out in the fall, *The Moments of Past Happiness Quilt*, forthcoming by Earthwinds, 2007. It's a collection of poems using the metaphors of handmade things. I'm delighted to be part of their list, as I am working with editorial directors Ifyeani Menkiti and Karyll Klopp. We've worked together on many other projects in the past, and so when they proposed doing the book I practically wept, it seemed so right to work with them!

In terms of my other current projects, right now I'm working on a book of poems called *Their Tranquil Lives*; it's about painting and history, and it's a miracle of self-discovery for me. I have a new collection of short stories, *Refugee Love*, and I'm working on a collection of essays called *The Alphabet of Lost Letters* which is about displacement. It's being translated into French and will be published in France as well as in the U.S., I hope. Many of the poems, stories and essays have already appeared in individual magazines. So perhaps my work is coming into fashion again. We're all part of this tapestry. Anyhow, I have more projects than I know what to do with—a lifetime of writing to look forward to.

Chris Abani

Coming to Elvis

When Chris Abani's 2004 novel *GraceLand* begins, the protagonist, Elvis Oke, is trying to earn a living on a beach in Lagos, Nigeria. He puts on a wig, a thick layer of talcum powder, and does impersonations of Elvis Presley. However, unlike his hero, he is impoverished and lives in a slum, a world without opportunity, where he is introduced to a world of vicious crime. Towards the end of *GraceLand*, Elvis Oke is in prison, hanging by his wrists from metal bars in a cell. Justice doesn't seem to exist. Abani's personal history is reflected in these painful scenes.

Author Percival Everett said of *GraceLand*, "To say that this is a Nigerian or African novel is to miss the point. This absolutely beautiful work of fiction is about complex and strained political structures, the irony of the West being a measure of civilization, and the tricky business of being a son. Abani's language is beautiful and his story is important." Anderson Tepper, in his *Village Voice* review describes *GraceLand* as an "irresistible, kaleidoscopic novel, the shantytowns around Lagos are full of wonders—and festering dangers." *GraceLand* was named one of the 2004 best books of the year by the *Los Angeles Times*, was included on the *New York Times* Vacation Reading List in June 2004 and was a Today Show Pick in January 2005.

Chris Abani wrote his first novel, *Masters of the Board*, when he was sixteen years old and a resident of Nigeria. Two years later, in 1985, he was arrested and imprisoned for six months; the Nigerian government believed that *Masters of the Board* served as a blueprint for a failed coup. In 1987, Abani was arrested a second time and incarcerated for a year at a Kiri Kiri, a maximum security prison, for his performance in plays that were critical of the leadership of his country, as well as for a second novel that was never published. In 1990, he was incarcerated under treason charges after a play he authored, *Song of a Broken Flute*, was performed at his school, Imo State University.

Abani has written four collections of poetry: *Dog Woman*, *Kalakuta Republic*, *Daphne's Lot*, and *Hands Washing Water*. His essays and shorter fiction have been widely published in journals and anthologies. A man of multiple talents, Abani also plays the saxophone, primarily to accompany his readings.

Abani's 2006 novella *Becoming Abigail* was a *New York Times* Editor's Choice, a *Chicago Reader* Critic's Choice, a selection of the *Essence* Magazine Book Club and a selection of the *Black Expressions* Book Club. In January 2007, his second novel, *The Virgin of Flames* was published; the *New Yorker* likened Abani to Pirandello. A new novella, *Song For Night*, will be published in August 2007.

Abani has taught literature and creative writing at the University of Southern California. He has received many awards, including the Lannan Literary Fellowship in Poetry and the PEN USA West Freedom-to-Write Award.

I spoke with him by phone after the publication of *GraceLand*.

SHERRY ELLIS: There is an early passage in *GraceLand* when Elvis, the protagonist, goes into his bedroom and puts on the song "Heartbreak Hotel." He then takes out a makeup kit and transforms himself from black skin to white. You write, "He walked back to the table and pulled the wig on, bending to look in the mirror. Elvis has entered the building, he thought, as he admired himself." Can you speak about Elvis's hopes?

CHRIS ABANI: Elvis's hope is to find a way out of his situation, which is one of poverty, one of brutality, in terms of the family and in terms of the state; and to be able to transmute it all into something beautiful; to realize his dreams; to make his art, in this case art as a dancer, as an Elvis impersonator. But we realize the parallel of the real Elvis's attempt to make something in America, the making of Graceland, which becomes an exaggerated Xanadu as it were. It becomes a parallel of the character Elvis's attempt to find redemption, to make a Graceland of his own, a place where all his hopes can come together.

ELLIS: Throughout *GraceLand*, Elvis reckons with the forces of good and evil. During the 1970s when he was living in Afikpo, his mother and grandmother imparted to him a strong sense of family values, whereas the more recent influences in his life have been in Lagos, in the form of the characters King of Beggars and Redemption. How did you develop the character of Elvis and select the characters and circumstances that inform his life?

ABANI: Well, the novel itself is a coming of age story, a *bildungsroman*, and in any situation like that you want to come to terms with the major things that form the character. Having once been a sixteen-year-old boy who wrote a novel, who had a similar artistic pursuit, it was easy to look back into my life and the lives of the friends who were around me to find a way to explore the character in a relevant way. Also, I'm always curious about the question, the whole notion of redemption, not in a Christian sense, but how to find a personal resolution; to come to terms with the self. In some ways, I was pushing this character to the limits or the extremities of every situation, so that he was bounding back and forth, and trying to explain something that is very hard to explain, which happens to all teenagers. This core, it's not innocence in the strictest terms, it's a naivete that we need to save ourselves and every teenager has it. Teenagers go from being a monster one minute to a sweet character the next. It was all these things that were built into the formation of the character. When you create fiction, you have to up the stakes all the time. That's how I came to Elvis.

ELLIS: Does Elvis do things that surprise you?

ABANI: As I was writing the book, yes, always. One of the examples is, even as Elvis has seen all the things he has seen, and after they had been trying to export these kids to be harvested, illegally, for human organ transplants, on the way back with Redemption, the fact that even with all that exposure he was still so wrapped up in himself and what he desired. That kind of selfishness completely threw me, but I thought, this is what really happens, especially for teenagers. But also what surprised me and was also beautiful was that in the face of all that, in order for his character to remain true, he was always shocked by it. So there were some pleasant surprises.

ELLIS: In the latter portion of *GraceLand* there are scenes of Elvis being tortured in prison. You write, "Sweat was rolling off him in bucketfuls; his arms went numb and his fingers began to swell like loaves of bread. The rest of his body was torn by a searing hot pain and he stretched himself downward, trying to bring his feet into contact with the ground." How difficult was it for you to write these scenes given your own experience in Nigeria prisons?

ABANI: Extremely difficult, even though I experienced it directly. Just the act of creating the space in the imagination is always difficult. And even when one has experienced it, memory is a very tricky thing, and so at a distance and with time, again even though one has experienced it, bringing integrity to the moment is always more important and it's difficult to realize. There's the normal difficulty of it and the long-term artistic difficulty of realizing it with a sense of integrity.

ELLIS: Anne Dillard said that "Every book has an intrinsic impossibility, which its writer discovers as soon as his first excitement dwindles." Do you agree with this quote, and if so, what was the impossibility of *GraceLand*?

ABANI: Well, the impossibility really is that Graceland as a novel is trying to do a lot of things that other novels and stories don't have to do. It's carrying the weight of trying to be an epic representation of a culture, to provide in many ways all the short-handed history one outside the culture will need to read it, and at the same time allow access to all this while creating what is essentially a very intimate portrait. You realize that the impossibility is one of ever truly realizing cohesiveness. But that is what then becomes beautiful about the book. Every time it seems to be tightening up, it continues to unravel. I realized that the reason that this was happening was because of the intrinsic question that drives the whole novel: "Is redemption possible?" and if it is, what are the required situations to achieve it? You realize as you begin to write that there is no way to answer the basic philosophical impulse that drives the novel. The structure reflects that impossibility.

ELLIS: Can you discuss the role Percival Everett played in helping you develop and shape this novel?

ABANI: Certainly. It wasn't so much that I came to work with Percival, but once I arrived here (in the U.S.) I realized perfect synchronicity, the universe had positioned me perfectly in his path, which became, if anything, the most important thing to have happened.

I started off writing action thrillers and then I started to try to write literary novels. I was playing mostly in a field of ideas, and I had completely left what would traditionally drive a story-based novel. I was writing these things that were either loose, rambling ideas or stories that were too tightly wound and they didn't allow space for anything. What Percival did, essentially, was to marry the two aspects of the craft together for me; he simply pointed out how I could tie in the notion of idea and philosophy and still have a tightly wound story and plot driving these things through. What I did was to start to work with him over a nine-month period because he had nine months before he left on sabbatical, and he basically drove me hard to finish the book. I think there were eleven rewrites over a nine month period, and he read everything I had ever written, not just the last two novels, but my poetry, any short stories, so he could come to understand the moments in which I was strongest. Having found those he pointed me in that direction. In many ways he was the midwife of my craft.

ELLIS: Do you believe writers need mentors?

ABANI: It's impossible to write without mentors. Whether it's a mentor you need to know, at a university program, as I was lucky to, I'm not sure. I've had many mentors before then, because you have silent or non-mentors. Baldwin was my mentor, Dostoevsky; the books you read, the craft you try to emulate. You can't make art without direction; unless you're some kind of prodigy, which I've never met. So you need the experience of someone, like any master craftsperson would in a guild, the best container for that particular moment. I think that's what it is. I think it's essential for every writer, and I can't think of any writer who hasn't had one.

ELLIS: How has your life changed since *GraceLand* has moved into the literary limelight, for example being included on the *New York Times* summer list of recommended fiction?

ABANI: It's one of those curious things, isn't it? To me it hasn't intrinsically changed, say, my output, because I'm a driven writer. I write endlessly and I usually have one book coming out a year. I am so caught up in the moment of a new book or a project that the past project doesn't hold that sort of glamour for me. It surprises me, because I didn't think the book would garner the kind of attention it did garner critically. It's a book set in West Africa, it's not even set in America, and it's a first-time novel here. To have that sort of attention can become frightening because your next book has to outdo this one in so many ways. I was talking to a writer friend the other day, Tayari Jones, who interviewed me for the *Believer*, she's also a novelist, and she said, "Look, get over it. There is no need for second novel angst. If you didn't get any attention and you didn't do well then you'd be terrified and the impetus would be to have this one make it. If you got enough attention on the first one, you worry that your next one will bomb." Just hearing another writer say that can bring the walls of a block tumbling down. So, yes, it has changed in that I've begun to take the critic's perspective into the creative process, which I never did before.

ELLIS: "Daphne's Lot," the title poem of your second poetry collection of the same name, tells the story of your mother's courage and of your family's migration from Nigeria. It is sixty-three pages long and weaves back and forth over time. Can you describe your process in writing this poem and if in fact you consider it a poem or an epic given its length?

ABANI: Well, it is a single poem, in a sense, but I considered it an epic. I had been reading Derek Walcott and I had been intrigued by the book he had written, and by all the epics I had been reading. I noticed and was impressed by how women were never focused on and that they were used in many of the epics as foils; that love was never the driving impulse. It was war and heroic deeds. So I set out to craft the story of my mother, which itself was interesting. Here is this white woman who married into an African home in the fifties, lived in Nigeria. Then a civil war occurred in the sixties and she had to gather these five children, who, upon her return to England, no one associates as her blood; they think she has adopted them. She has to make her way her way through Africa, through Nigeria, to get out of this war. I decided to set an epic poem around that and to situate a woman as the hero of this epic, and to set love as the driving force. So even though it has the traditional sense of an epic, in that it has the traditional length of it, and is set against the war, it subverts in a way traditional ideas about courage. What are highlighted are not the traditional things of the epic, but the gestures of people. In order to do this and represent the war I had to write another section of the book, the second section, which is short, contains almost photographic moments of the war that capture the true horror of it so that it was not glossed over. That's what's behind it and how it came out.

ELLIS: What impact do you believe your collaboration with Adrian Dutton, the painter, had on the poems contained in your second poetry collection, *Kalakuta Republic*?

ABANI: Well, what's interesting is that Adrian, who is a friend of mine, is a painter in London. I went to his studio one day and saw these paintings, which were incredibly dark and incredibly beautiful. I had never really discussed my circumstances with him or anybody, and that night, sitting in his studio, the whole story came out. He said, "Why don't I paint twelve paintings and you write twelve poems about the experience and we'll have an exhibition?" I thought it was such a generous offer and I had unlocked something that I had suppressed for such a long time. It allowed me to release it without damaging my mental health. I was so grateful to him for that. We did this work together.

It taught me the ways in which the rigor of one art form, in this case a visual art, can influence the rigor of another craft, which is poetry. So he ended up making the paintings, and what you have are simply almost picture frames, portraiture, that allow you to step into an experience without trying to direct you in any way, which might not have happened if I hadn't come about it through that collaboration. That collaboration, in a sense, was important in determining the form and sequence of parts.

ELLIS: Can you describe more specifically how this collaboration made you feel safer emotionally?

ABANI: I said, this was a difficult subject matter, a difficult experience, that I had repressed for at least four or five years at the time, and to bring that experience to the surface without any parameters of safety or rigor, which is basically the rigor of art, I had no idea where it would have taken me to. I can tell you it was a very difficult process, even within that context. There is something about the rigor of collaboration. When you collaborate with someone else, you realize that this is not just about you, it is about their work, their art, their reputation, their integrity, so what happens is that you are able to dialogue not only with yourself but with this exterior art which in itself is so self-contained. It allows you to contain the experience and to render it in a way that becomes beautiful and not bitter, and which means that you don't completely go off the edge of darkness.

ELLIS: When you start a poem do you start with a subject and then find the form? Or does the subject come intuitively?

ABANI: Well, the thing about me is that I have never written a book of poems in the sense of writing poems and collecting them. I approach my books as books and they start off as books pretty much like a novel does. So I come with an idea, sometimes more just a title, and I'll come with an idea of what I want to do and I'll sort of map out the shape, and then I'll start poems to fit the different movements, almost like a composition, and so each poem can stand apart in each of those books. One comes out at the end of September called *Dog Woman*, and again all the poems are dialoguing with each other in these orchestral movements. I'm trying to work on a new book that will just be about poems coming together in that thematic sense. But much more frequently my books are driven by a clear idea, an arc, are almost plot-driven like the novel in a way.

ELLIS: On a day-to-day basis, how do you make the transformation from one literary form to another, for example fiction to poetry to plays, and does your work in one creative form inform the other?

ABANI: Well, as to the first part of the question, I never work on one book at a time. I work on at least two or sometimes three projects at a time. I work on a piece of fiction, a collection of poetry, and either a novella or a play. What happens for me is that when I work in one genre, it gets to a point where I reach a wall, so I simply put that project down and begin another, which will be a book of poetry. You sit with that a for a week and your brain makes the transition to a different form, and you find that the work you've done is suddenly fresh and new; you push forward and you hit the wall, and you go back to the next project, but when you go back from poetry to fiction, for example, you bring all this precision of language and beauty of imagery straight into your fiction and you're able to shape moments and have more of an economy and have the work be sparer and richer. So, they each inform the other. The narrative arc of the novel informs the narrative arc of the poems, the precision of language and economy of the poems informs that in a novel. It is a constant dialogue between them but for me it is a continuum. I'm an academic as well, and so for me that's another form of writing. I've always been open to any kind of writing since early on, so I ride up and down the scale with ease.

ELLIS: Do you agree with Nigerian playwright Wole Soyinka who said, "Theater is more than text. Theater is the most revolutionary art form"?

ABANI: I suppose there is something too that isn't there. Because even music, in the context of it in a performance, it is theater in a way. You think of opera, even your pop performance, even if you're Britney Spears on tour, there are the whole theatrics and histrionics of the back lights and the smoke effects. All that stuff that goes into making theater are brought into that, and it goes into the making of the videos on MTV which inform the sales more than the music alone.

Even with the poetry, when you do a reading, it is a performance. Most of the books are sold at that moment rather than in bookstores, so I think that there is something to that. I really do, I think that it is revolutionary, and part of the revolutionary ability I think is that in as much as it can be a removed and elitist form, as Ngugi wa Thiong'o, an African writer, has shown, it can be a way in which average, everyday, disempowered people can gather their ideas around politics and enact the change they want their life to become. So yes, I think he's really onto something there.

ELLIS: What artistic medium do you enjoy the most?

ABANI: It's probably the one that I'm the worst at, which is music. I play the saxophone and I enjoy that in a way because there's spontaneity as I do a lot of improvised performances. I don't really worry about anything, because I'm not very good at it and I don't think there's the same demand on my craft and so I probably enjoy it the most. But then that's probably why I'm not good.

ELLIS: What are your struggles as a writer?

ABANI: Well, for me, I'm always driven by complex, philosophical moments that are connected to human experience; and my work has to dialogue in all these different kinds of ways in terms of archetypal, in terms of mythology, in terms of philosophy, in terms of what would be considered everyday banal, in the notion of the transformative and the political as well. The thing is, when you start a work you can see it so beautifully, and then you're like "Oh!" [sound of disappointment]. The trick is to try to bridge the gap. It's not an unconscious thing, it's an informed moment when you can see what it is you're trying to make, so that you can bridge the abyss until it becomes a little gap that you can hardly insert a piece of paper into. If you can bridge it that much, that's the real challenge, because your work needs to be so specific and so universal all at the same time. To bridge the gap between what you're imagining and what you're making so that it it's not an abyss, only a small narrow space. That's the struggle.

ELLIS: When you revise your work, is your process primarily additive or reductive?

ABANI: It depends on the stage in the revision. Since I just finished the first draft of a new novel, I'll talk about it. I had written maybe a hundred and fifty pages and went off to Texas for a month. I stripped it back to seventy pages or less, and then grew it back up to two hundred fifty pages, and when I went through that I went back and edited for grammar and then I went back and started checking for continuity. There are different levels and aspects that the editing process takes on for me. Instead of trying to do the whole at once I try to do what filmmakers do even in the creating process. I try to write the scenes and then connect them. Sometimes I'll have to take things out and replace whole sections, and make sure the cigar he was holding in the left hand here is the cigar he is still holding in his left hand there. It can be very reductive, it can be very specific as to just checking punctuation. But I do numerous, numerous drafts. Even though I'm saying it's the first finished draft it is draft number seven; the novel has gone through seven reincarnations to get to its first finished draft. It took me about a year to come up it. Between now and when I send it to an editor or an agent, it will go through another three or four and then they will have their suggestions, so you're looking at maybe between ten and fifteen drafts. It's different with every project and every moment.

ELLIS: What suggestions do you have for writers working on their first stories or novel?

ABANI: There are two things, really. One is staying power. I think the people who you see the most in this form are not necessarily the most talented people in their form. It's the people who can hack it long enough to sort of have the industry finally wake up to what they're doing. Two, it takes time for you to have the depth of perception it takes for you to shape your craft. The thing really is craft, craft, craft, when you write. Keep challenging every sentence, every phrase, every word, if it's the right word, why "rock" and not "stone," or "stone" and not "rock," what are the sounds. It's an endless obsession, and even when it does get published you'll probably be two years ahead of it, and you'll read it and you'll think, What was I thinking when I wrote this? So you also have to go easy on yourself, in a way, and realize it's always evolving. You're never going to write the perfect book, and if you do, either your art is questionable or you're putting yourself out of business.

ELLIS: Where did you initially learn about writing?

ABANI: Well, what I did was I started reading when I was very young. My mother taught me when I was three or four. I had already read Baldwin by nine. So I was a precocious child in that way. I wrote my first story when I was ten. I didn't learn about it. I was one of those people who knew since they were seven what they were going to do.

ELLIS: In your essay "The Lottery" that appeared in the *New York Times*, you describe a scene when as a ten-year-old child you went to the market, and the horror that you witnessed. You write, "My aunt spat. I looked away, hand held over my nose at the smell of burning flesh, horrified that it reminded me of kebobs. 'Spit,' she snapped, rapping me on the head with her knuckles. I spat." Do you think that the act of self-exposure and weakness of the self in writing is a form of bravery itself?

ABANI: I am not sure about that word, "bravery." I don't know that it has much place in the making of art, partly because it is so hard to quantify and becomes a means of obfuscating the deeper obligations of art. I do think that the most successful art finds a way to expose some of the artist's vulnerability. This allows the audience to not only locate themselves in the work, but to feel safe to explore that in themselves. That is how connections are made. Was it brave of Monet to paint even though he had cataracts and his work was out of focus? I don't know. Did it reveal his vulnerability? Yes, and that's why we connect with it, even if we don't articulate it quite like that. James Baldwin once said that your suffering and pain, in art, mean nothing unless they serve to allow others to connect to their own suffering and pain—or words to that effect. Poor Uncle Jimmy, he has been so misquoted!

ELLIS: Are you willing to share some information about the subject matter of your novel in progress?

ABANI: Only that it is set in Los Angeles and that it is a thematic sequel to *GraceLand*. Which is an entirely different enterprise from a direct sequel, you know? Always trying to mix it up. It will be out soon. Watch for it.

Elizabeth Searle

Mistress of Ceremonies

Elizabeth Searle writes about gender-bending, actresses and actors, mentally challenged and autistic individuals, women, and their bodies. Several of the characters in her most recent book, *Celebrities in Disgrace*, are obsessed with fame and being watched. Her most recent work is the libretto for *Tonya & Nancy: The Opera*, an original opera based on the infamous Harding/Kerrigan ice skating scandal. The opera premiered in the American Repertory Theater's Zero Arrow series in 2006 and drew coverage from the Associated Press, ESPN Hollywood, MSNBC, *Sports Illustrated* and National Public Radio. In her novel, *A Four Sided Bed*, Searle explores the shifting boundaries in a marriage and a ménage à trois. Searle is currently at work on a novel about grassroots politics and erotic filmmaking. She is also interested in working on an anthology of erotic writings by current literary writers. *Celebrities in Disgrace* was a finalist for the Paterson Fiction Prize; *A Four Sided Bed* was nominated for an American Library Association Award; and her first short story collection, *My Body to You*, won the Iowa Short Fiction Award. Searle's work has also been published in *Michigan Quarterly*, *Agni*, *Kenyon Review*, *Redbook*, *Five Points*, *Scene*, and *Genre* magazine.

For the past six years Searle has served as the mistress of ceremonies for "The Erotic Pen: Passion, Eros and Naked Lust," PEN/New England's Valentine's Day Eve literary reading in Boston.

Searle teaches writing at the Stonecoast MFA program and has taught at Emerson College.

She lives in greater Boston with her husband and son. I met with her at her home. We sat at her dining room table surrounded by photos of her family and pictures drawn by her son.

SHERRY ELLIS: In *Celebrities in Disgrace*, many of the female characters are preoccupied with fame and a hunger for attention—being seen and being watched. What are the challenges of writing about this theme?

ELIZABETH SEARLE: Ambition and women are subjects I had not written about in any realistic, sympathetic, in-depth way before, and they're easy to satirize. One reason for the theme of *Celebrities in Disgrace* is what I have observed to be the obsessive need for attention. I taught special education for a while and noticed that this is the common denominator of all people. The phrase is used, "they're trying to get attention," and it seems that so often the motives of people centers on the need for attention. I'm writing a novel now, in which the siblings struggle for notice. I think the challenges are that it is one of those things that people don't want to talk about, and also portraying the characters so they are somewhat sympathetic.

I have a phrase in my mind, "the witch of ambition," and I think there is this sort of dark force inside of people and any of those dark forces are hard to write about but they're the ones you want to write about. It seems like such a driving force of our time. *Celebrities in Disgrace* is a book where I started with the title; it came to me during the time of Nancy and Tanya. It is hard to make the characters sympathetic when they are that ambitious, and it is hard to get past that and not make them shallow caricatures.

ELLIS: *Celebrities in Disgrace* is both the title of your book and your novella. In the novella, a struggling actress, who is elated to believe that her career is about to take off, becomes vulnerable and "the accused." How did you juxtapose the events in this novella for maximum impact?

SEARLE: Oh, that novella was so much fun to write; it was the most fun writing experience I've ever had. During the era of Nancy and Tonya, I was obsessed by it. It was this "girl thing," the pretty skirts, and I remember there was a quote in the *Boston Globe* that got me thinking about it that I use in the novella: "America's full of Tonyas who want to be Nancys."

During the scandal my friends would clip articles and send them to me. I didn't know what I was going to do with them; I just knew I wanted a lot of information. That's what always happens; you have one thing you're thinking about and then another totally different thing happens and you band them together and something happens. I had the title in my mind even before the "Nancy/Tonya thing," and it all connected with Lowell, Massachusetts. I had some connection with people doing Repertory Theater there, and I had done some theater in high school and at Arizona State where I went to college, and I wanted to write about it. Then I heard that while the "Nancy/Tonya thing" was still happening, producers were already casting a movie, even before it resolved itself. That stuck in my mind and triggered the novella. I thought, what if I wanted to write about a struggling actress, and wondered how could I make it happen during the week of the scandal.

ELLIS: The novella *Celebrities in Disgrace* begins, "He stapled his face over hers. In the subzero dawn of Skate-Off Day—7 AM in Lowell, 1 PM in Lillehammer—the staples shot back at him, the kiosk's corkboard as ungiving as ice." Through this image the reader can almost feel the cold, can almost feel the staples. Do you frequently use metaphor to evoke a physical response on the part of the reader?

SEARLE: Sense memories are important, I think; you can convince the reader of almost anything if you connect it to their sense memories and I always think in terms of how the reader is feeling. I always try to get physical immediately, to evoke physical sensations, to be very concrete and very sensual. I feel things when I'm reading, so that's very important to me.

I used to read for the blind and I used hearing the typing machines in a story, printing the Braille, it's a terrifying sound; the whole story is in that repeated rhythm. I always try to put sounds in my stories.

ELLIS: In the poem "The Road Not Taken," Robert Frost wrote, "Two roads diverged in a yellow wood / And sorry I could not travel both . . ." Your short story "101" is about a young woman who contemplates dramatic changes in her life as she approaches an intersection. "I approached an intersection, poised my foot over my brake, thinking the way my dad had taught me, Stop, stop, stop, then as the light stayed yellow and I floored the gas, Go no matter what." Do you frequently use metaphor to evoke an emotional response?

SEARLE: Oh, yes, definitely. I think it's very hard to write about emotions in the abstract. I'm always telling my students to find some physical thing that their characters can be doing. I remember having a breakthrough with my editor at Graywolf, when she was trying to get me to show emotions. I had just been abstractly describing it, and we figured out that a character was mad at her husband—he was gone, and she decided she was going to sleep on the couch; she tried to unfold the bed and then she couldn't, she started hitting it, and then she tried to fold it back up but she couldn't. That was so much better than what I had written before.

I use the theme of the road diverting often. In my novel I have girl "A" and girl "B." I love doubles in fiction, two characters that are similar but follow their diverging paths. In this story, "101," the use of the intersection seemed to be a good way to say the character is plunging forward no matter what.

ELLIS: In *The Joy of Writing about Sex*, Elizabeth Benedict states, "A well-written sex scene engages us on many levels: erotic, aesthetic, psychological, metaphorical, even philosophical." Do you agree with these criteria?

SEARLE: I agree with it completely. I used Benedict's book for my master's-level seminar at Stonecoast, called "The Erotic Pen." So-called erotic writing does not work for me if it is not connected to real characters and does not contain emotional content.

I'm in the early stages of trying to put together an anthology, and one possible slant we might take is to call it *Not Erotica*. The word "erotica" seems to be used to describe work that is written just to put a sex scene together, that isn't connected to the larger work.

ELLIS: "101" ends with the primary character holding an ostrich egg shard as she drives back to Phoenix. The next story in the collection *Celebrities In Disgrace*, "Celebration," begins with the sentence, "Cracking an egg for her husband's birthday cake, Sarah spread her thumb and index finger so the white stretched." In "Round Objects" from your collection *My Body to You*, you write, "She lies still as an egg. A heavy egg hidden in a hole." As a writer, how do you find symbols for your characters, or do the symbols become apparent to you from the stories themselves?

SEARLE: I love eggs and I'm fascinated by visceral and primal things, and I'm always putting them in my stories. It seems that you don't choose the symbols; they just keep coming up over and over again. I believe that the things that stick out in your mind and you're not sure why, are the perfect fiction material. There are often babies, missing babies, and things having to do with the female body in my work; my story "White Eggplant" is another example.

I give an exercise to my students to help them free-associate about objects or animals in their stories that they think are important or charged. I always use as an example something that was really helpful to me in writing the short story "My Body to You"—free-associating about the whippet. I knew I needed a dog in this story, but at first I didn't know why I made it a whippet. I thought, okay, the whippet has a greyhound shape, it's like a woman's body, but it's all hard, it's not at all soft. Just thinking that—suddenly the whippet made sense to me, and I thought, This is why I have the description on the subway where everyone's flesh is jiggling—the character hates that and she's sort of starving herself. I also free-associated about a friend, whose sister was "going berserk," who called and came over to our house, and when she got in her car the only thing she grabbed was her dog. That became a big scene in "My Body to You," when the character escapes from her house and takes only the dog with her. The other thing I got out of thinking about the whippet was my last line, where the character is looking at the bodies of the airplanes, that are so sleek, and she thinks that they are like whippets waiting to run—and she is about to take off too; it makes her feel for a minute that flying is a perfectly natural act.

ELLIS: "My novel was also inspired by the singer k.d. lang, who says that she sets out to 'seduce' her whole audience," you said about *A Four Sided Bed*. When you wrote this novel, how did you attempt to achieve this goal?

SEARLE: Oh, I had that very specifically in mind. I was fascinated by k.d. lang during the writing of this book and she was such an inspiration. In *A Four Sided Bed* there are three-person love scenes, there's a homoerotic element, there's a heteroerotic element, there's sort of something for everything. I thought there was a chance to write sex scenes that could turn on practically anyone, hook them in. You set yourself a challenge that is really interesting to you. I saw k.d. lang as a lesbian performer who was very welcoming, not only singing to "her" group. In other ways I felt very nervous, treading on this territory, but I loved having a challenge in writing the sex scenes. Yes, that was a real overt goal of mine.

ELLIS: Are there things that you would be afraid of writing about?

SEARLE: My husband sometimes quotes a line from the movie *Tootsie* where Dustin Hoffman is thinking of something awful or shocking he can do on camera to get out of his soap opera and someone says to him, "I can't think of anything sick and disgusting you haven't done already."

I haven't tackled the theme of violence too extensively, although there is a scene of violence in my new book; and I don't do strictly autobiographical material, as I would be afraid of hurting people too much. I do take a lot of autobiographical material and use it as a springboard.

ELLIS: How does your process vary in writing a story or a novel?

SEARLE: It's a whole different thing. For me, a novel involves thinking about a story for a couple of years before actually writing it. I take characters and try them out. Then there is a whole first draft, and rewriting, which I have to do a lot of, because I tend to write dense and long. I cut things down an incredible amount, so it is just such a huge undertaking, whereas with short stories everything is reduced. I might think of it for months in advance, and work on it for months, although if you added it all together it might be years that I've worked on the same story. I take something like a big six-month run at it, then time passes and I look at it again. Short stories are more manageable. They're fun in that you can know a few important things about your character and have a story, whereas in a novel you have to do so much more character work. A novel is a long, long trance; it takes over your whole life. You have to push though and keep the threads going. Short stories are so instinctive; it's more like putting a poem together; in some ways, I don't like them ending so soon. A novella is a fun mix of the two. You can get immersed but it's not so unyielding.

ELLIS: You use the title "The Young and the Rest of Us" both for a short story in *Celebrities in Disgrace* and as the title for a chapter in *A Four Sided Bed*. How difficult is it to return to familiar territory and yet change the meaning of the material?

SEARLE: *The Young and the Restless* was so much a part of my childhood. I could not do anything without that show. I hate typing, and for the past twenty years I have taped it and then listened to it while I transcribe my longhand to typed form. Maybe I'm fooling myself, but as an otherwise "literary writer," I believe that I have learned a lot from that show about plot. I picture it like a stove, something simmering here, different plots, and I imagine which one was on the front burner, the back burner, on boil, which is a helpful technique when you're writing a novel and you are trying to develop different plots and have them converge. In each scene, *The Young and the Restless* puts in a hook, and the rhythms of the plot get into your brain.

ELLIS: For the past three years you have served as mistress of ceremonies at a Valentine's Day Eve festivity in Boston, where writers read their work, "The Erotic Pen: Passion, Eros and Naked Lust," hosted by PEN/New England. How did you conceive of this literary celebration and how has it been received?

SEARLE: I came up with the idea of this event as a board member of PEN/New England; serving on this board is such an honor and a privilege. I wondered what would be the dream event that I would want to see, and I love high quality writing about sex. We got Jayne Anne Phillips and Maria Flook our first year, who are literally two of my favorite writers—and I read that first time too, a loss of virginity piece; and Andre Dubus III for the second year. It is a literary event but it also has this fun, sexy element that people love and people who don't ordinarily go to readings can enjoy.

ELLIS: Carl Jung said, "The meeting of two personalities is like the contact of two chemical substances, if there is any reaction, both are transformed." How does the interaction between characters in your stories and novel result in transformation?

SEARLE: I always think in terms of ramming two characters together and seeing what happens. I think what helped me with my novel *A Four Sided Bed*, and what my editor at Graywolf showed me, is that there had to be a spark of transformation for Alice, the wife character, what happens to her; I already had an understanding of what happened when J.J., Kin, and Bird, when they came together. I always seem to have two female characters; I have two sisters in the novel I'm working on now, and girl "A" and girl "B" in *A Four Sided Bed*. I like to have characters come up to each other and come to know each other in different ways.

ELLIS: What advice do you have for new writers?

SEARLE: The standard: Read, read and read! If you don't find yourself to be someone who loves to read, and to be excited by what you read, you might be barking up the wrong tree for a form of expression. You have to enjoy the process itself. Of course, we know that the publishing life is very difficult; writing has to be satisfying in itself. I would advise new writers to seek out workshops. You have to have other people looking at your work to move forward. When I was a theater major I remember a teacher saying, if there is something else you guys can do, do it. This is only for you if you can't live without it, and I thought about acting and wondered, whereas I did feel this way about writing—that I couldn't not do it. Writing can be very satisfying if you are a serious reader, to explore it, give it a serious shot. It is somewhat like a religion; it can give you tremendous spiritual satisfaction.

ELLIS: Which writers have most influenced your work?

SEARLE: Virginia Woolf, I was really struck by her in college; *Them* by Joyce Carol Oates when I was a teenager, I cannot imagine not having read her; Alice Munro; James Salter, who by coincidence wound up being the judge of the Iowa competition; Don Delillo; David Foster Wallace, who I think is hilarious; Rick Moody; so many contemporary writers: Mary Gaitskill; Maria Flook; there are really sensual female writers, they are my favorite kinds of writers.

ELLIS: What are some of the common problems you find in your students' work?

SEARLE: I agree with something David Huddle said in his book *The Writing Habit*; in fact, I'm doing my seminar at Stonecoast this semester based on seventy-seven autobiographical questions he gives his students that are designed to illicit concrete memories. He says that sometimes students' work is so unconnected to their real lives that they are not invested in it—there's a kind of slinging things around and shooting people left and right. Huddle says that they are writing from their false selves. You have to find a natural voice for yourself. Huddle suggests that when you help students start with the real material from their lives, they care about it more. Often when people start writing they get stilted or self-conscious. It is hard to find a way to tell a story in a voice that is natural to you.

ELLIS: In a recent *Poets and Writers* article in which Jeffrey Skinner discussed revision, he said, "writing is revision and yet each time I suggest revisions to a student or a friend, each time I face what remains to be done in my own writing, I feel the specter of resistance rising anew." Do you resist the process of revision?

SEARLE: I don't resist it anymore. I did when I was younger, which I regret; I could have done so much better. I agree with something Janet Burroway said, that revision is "more dreaded than dreadful." Now I see that I know how to get my prose under control, it tends to be very dense at first, the drafts I would not show to anyone but my husband, you have to hack through them with a knife practically; I actually like doing revision. I boiled the five hundred pages that I had for *A Four Sided Bed* down to three hundred, not cutting a single whole scene, just taking words out. It takes a long time to get a sense of how to edit yourself. Students who really balk at it and refuse to do revision won't reach a publishable level; the ones that are willing to give in, go over and over it again, that's what it takes.

ELLIS: E.M. Forster said, "Some reviews give pain. That is regrettable, but no author has the right to whine. He invited publicity and he must take the publicity that comes along." When you read reviews of your work, how do you cope with negativity?

SEARLE: I agree about not having the right to whine. Especially in this age, you are so lucky to be published. I think it is a privilege to have these problems. But at the same time I think that every review I've read takes a year off my life. To have that helpless feeling of knowing that this is the way it is going to be presented to the world. But even the bad reviews I've gotten have had good things in them. It's a very emotional experience to have people react to your work in print. Of course it can hurt, but sometimes you look back at it later and see that there's some truth in it.

ELLIS: What are you working on now?

SEARLE: A novel about an aspiring actress who half-accidentally lost her virginity on camera, which comes back to haunt her in different ways. The political family that she has come from has given her competitive drive. Something violent is triggered by an autistic character, who is obsessed with John Hinkley, Jr., almost an assassination attempt. I've just got to figure it out.

Margot Livesey

A Little in Common

Banishing Verona, Margot Livesey's most recent and fifth novel, tells the story of Zeke Cafarelli and Verona MacIntyre, who share a passionate one-night affair in London. Zeke is a handyman who has Asperger's Syndrome and a host of related symptoms. Verona is already seven months pregnant, a confident, quick-tempered, moderately successful radio show host. After their evening of intimacy, Verona leaves for Boston and Zeke feels he has no choice but to pursue her.

In Livesey's captivating fourth novel, *Eva Moves the Furniture*, Eva McEwen is visited by two other-worldly companions; the reader is never sure if the companions are there to protect or harm her. "This is a novel that enters the reader's life in much the same way that the companions come to Eva," wrote Valerie Martin in her the *New York Times* review. "It looks harmless enough, like a child's fantasy, inhabiting a fairy tale in which powerful, otherworldly forces are at work, but reader beware." *Eva Moves the Furniture* was a finalist for the L.L. Winship/PEN/New England Award, a *New York Times* Notable Book, and an *Atlantic Monthly* Best Book of the Year.

Livesey is the author of three other novels: *The Missing World*, *Criminals*, and *Homework*. Among her first published works of fiction were short stories that are in the collection *Learning By Heart*. She also co-authored *Writing About Literature: An Anthology for Reading and Writing*.

Livesey has been received fellowships from the Guggenheim Foundation, MacDowell Colony, Yaddo, the Massachusetts Artists' Foundation, the National Endowment for the Arts, and the Canada Council for the Arts. Since 1996 she has been a Writer in Residence at Emerson College and since 1990 she has been a Visiting Professor at the Warren Wilson MFA Program. She was previously a Visiting Professor at Brandeis University, at Boston University, at the Iowa Writers' Workshop and at Williams College; an Assistant Professor at Carnegie-Mellon University; a Writer in Residence at Cleveland State University; and a lecturer at Tufts University. She has also taught writing at the Bennington Summer Workshop, the Napa Valley Conference, the Sewanee Writers' Conference and the Bread Loaf Writers Conference.

Her essays and short stories have been published in the *Atlantic Monthly*, *Five Points* magazine, the *AWP Chronicle*, the *New Yorker*, *Story* magazine, and the *Kenyon Review* as well as many other magazines and anthologies. She frequently writes book reviews for the *New York Times Book Review* and the *Boston Globe*.

Livesey grew up in Scotland on the edge of the Highlands. She and her husband divide their time between the U.S. and Britain. I met with her at her dining room table on the second floor of her three-story townhouse in Cambridge, Massachusetts.

SHERRY ELLIS: When *Banishing Verona* begins, Zeke, the protagonist, is changing light bulbs. Unbeknownst to him his life is about to change as well. In this novel electrical surges and electricity itself are motifs that carry the novel forward. How did you develop this powerful symbol?

MARGOT LIVESEY: Zeke was a character whom I'd long wanted to write about. He was hovering in the margins of several other novels, never making it onto the page. But specifically, about electricity, I had this image of a man working in an empty house, in particular Zeke working there and light bulb after light bulb popping into darkness. I don't know if you remember Nabokov's story "Signs and Symbols." It's about this elderly couple whose only son is in an institution because he thinks everything in the world—the wallpaper, the clouds, the trees—is sending him messages. The parents go to visit him, and they too keep reading everything as a sign, including a series of phone calls which turn out to be wrong numbers, until, perhaps, the last one. It's a very short and beautiful story about the way we both over- and under-interpret the world. In Zeke's case he largely forgets about the light bulbs but maybe readers will think that they did mean something; that they heralded the approach of this electrically magical person, Verona.

ELLIS: On the surface, lovers Zeke and Verona have very little in common. Zeke is a man who can't lie; limited by Asperger's Syndrome, he is an open book. Verona is a woman who rarely tells the truth and whose attitudes and beliefs often take the form of questions. Yet these characters share behaviors and problems in common. For example, difficulties with their families, a propensity for making lists when they are trying to solve problems. How did you develop the relationship between them?

LIVESEY: I think it's just right that you ask about developing them in relationship to each other, because that's such an important aspect of how character works in fiction. It is very rare in fiction for a character to really operate in isolation. Zeke and Verona, although they had very different childhoods, did grow up on the page together.

Besides having a longstanding desire to write about Zeke, I wanted to write about a woman who was stronger, more definite, and more forceful than my other female characters had been. I felt I'd written, for one reason or another, about a number of troubled women. Molly, in *Criminals*, who ends up hanging onto a baby because she believes her affection gives her a right to motherhood, and Hazel, in *The Missing World*, who is kept semi-captive by her boyfriend after she loses part of her memory in an accident. But it doesn't fit with the way I see women in the world that my women characters should be too fragile. I very much wanted to write about a woman who, at least at some level, is more in charge of her life and who, even if she makes mistakes, makes them in a more forceful way.

It has been my good fortune over the years to be interviewed on a number of radio shows and I've been very struck by these people who do ten or twelve hours a week of live radio. They can chat until the cows come home. They know a little about a great deal and they're great at thinking on their feet. So, trying to invent a more forceful woman who would appeal to Zeke, I decided to make Verona a radio show host. He relishes her capacity for both listening and telling stories and he also finds it very appealing that she's pregnant; he can have a baby that won't be genetically connected to him, that won't be in danger of inheriting his faults.

As for Verona, she finds Zeke very beautiful, and she also appreciates his lack of guile. The end of the novel, which I obviously don't want to give away, plays very much to that side of his character.

ELLIS: Just a moment ago I described Verona as a liar. However, there's a moment early on in *Banishing Verona* when Verona is helping Zeke sand a wall and she's "surprised to find herself longing to tell the truth." Just as the little extra bumps and grit are sanded away, she, Verona, wants to speak the truth. Do you recall how you developed this metaphor?

LIVESEY: In the early nineties I had the good fortune to teach at the Iowa Writers' Workshop with the wonderful writer Deborah Eisenberg and I remember her saying to me at one point that part of the trouble with writing fiction is that so much of life takes place around a table, and as a result so many conversations in fiction are conducted over meals. So I thought one of the ways I could allow Zeke and Verona to become closer was to follow Aristotle's dictum and give the characters an action to do together other than simply eating, although they do that too.

I have a decrepit house in London, and over the years I've watched numerous people work on it. Elderly British houses are basically held up by wallpaper, and when you take it down you never know what will happen. That seemed a wonderful metaphor for the surprises of intimacy and the way in which, when we reveal ourselves to another person, we don't quite know what will come of those revelations. Even when we do manage to tell the truth, the truth may not be heard. So there is something about the way Zeke and Verona gradually make the room bare and perfect that becomes an image for their romance.

This also connects with how Zeke imagines his brain, as a house with all these different rooms that he has to take care of, and he's always rushing from one to the other.

ELLIS: When Zeke travels to Boston, he is surprised by the appearance of hydrants. You write, "He was outside a bookshop when he spotted a metal effigy like the ones he had spotted from the taxi the day before. He bent down to examine the silver body and faded orange helmet with its snout and two stocky arms, even on closer inspection it seemed to have no obvious use." At the same time that this scene reinforces Zeke's foreignness in America, it also emphasizes Zeke's lack of understanding, his need for concreteness. Do you think it is important for writers to provide their characters with repeated circumstances that reinforce their traits?

LIVESEY: I knew from very early on that I wanted to bring Zeke to America, and I hoped that bringing him here would offer particular opportunities for reexamining his difficulty with reading the world, how hard it is for him to figure out everyday things that most of us take for granted. Partly, too, this was an opportunity to remark on some of the surprising differences between America and Britain. As many people have commented, the seemingly common language does mask considerable differences in the culture. As I've spent much of the past twenty years here, I had to think myself into the head not just of someone with Asperger's but of someone arriving in Boston for the first time.

As for whether it's important to see a character acting out their traits in different circumstances, I do think this is one of the things that gives a novel depth. Think of Jane Eyre, for instance. First she is selected by Rochester in spite of her looks, and then by St. John Rivers, the cold missionary cousin, because of them; one of the things that is repellent to Jane and to the reader is that St. John doesn't overlook her plainness. Throughout the novel we keep being told Jane is plain and we get to see how that plainness works in different ways. We see how it affects her life as a school girl, as a governess, as a woman, as a refugee.

ELLIS: In *Eva Moves the Furniture* you make the otherworldly "companions" seem real through scenes and character descriptions. The narrator says, "The older ghost appears first on a day that she is preparing to make currant pie with her aunt. A woman was peering through the branches. Everything about her shone as if she had been dipped in silver. Her hair was white as the swans I saw when David took me fishing, and she wore a white dress with little blue checks." How did you imagine the ghosts so clearly?

LIVESEY: Perhaps you know I began *Eva Moves the Furniture* in 1987. It was a novel that went through many drafts that were substantially different from each other. One of the biggest challenges was figuring out my rules for the apparitions. How were the companions going to be presented? I wasn't sure even about the simplest things. For example, were they going to change their clothes? It would be too weird in Scotland in winter not to have a raincoat or coat. So, it took me a while to find out if they should leave a room by the door or walk through walls to demonstrate their powers.

Finally, everybody kept telling me to, I reread *Turn of the Screw* but it took me quite a while to figure out what James was showing me: namely that all the people in the novel are real, even the ghosts. They're not just vague beings in white sheets being scary. When I finally got my head around that it was very helpful and the companions began to come alive. I began to think of them as just like characters, but with different characteristics.

ELLIS: When Eva was a child her father constantly talked to her about her mother. Eva says, "In my imagination the gravestone became a door. It swung open and there was Barbara, going about her daily business, polishing brasses, wearing her spectacles. She was nearby but inaccessible—rather like Aunt Violent, who lived in Edinburgh." What were the challenges and importance of making this deceased mother so real, such a strong presence, and so central to the story?

LIVESEY: Another of the challenges for me with *Eva Moves the Furniture* was the information I had about my mother's relationship with the supernatural, which was unfortunately limited to a very small number of anecdotes. So rather than thinking like a fiction writer and asking what kind of person would have a relationships with the supernatural, I had the character and this very surprising characteristic but no sense of how the two went together. Readers of early drafts kept asking why Eva sought the companions, and "because she's my mother" wasn't a viable answer. I had to start thinking about what kind of person has this sort of inner life? The role of Eva's own dead mother seemed one way of making her relationship with the companions more plausible.

During some of the years I was writing the book, my goddaughter, who lives in a seventeenth century house outside of Oxford in England, had five ghosts living in her house. Year after year she drew me pictures of them and they all looked the same. And then when she was eight or nine, and started to have more friends and activities, they disappeared. I thought one way to make Eva's situation more convincing was to make her somewhat lonely and isolated, so the companions could get a stronger a hold on her. I was also struck by the way adults make silly little jokes to children when they talk about imaginary things and how confusing that could be if a child took it literally. So, for instance, I made Eva's aunt ask if the companion likes two spoons of sugar in her tea, or one.

ELLIS: Eva has very ambivalent feelings about her relationship with her ethereal companions. She feels a weight in having them in her life and yet she appreciates that they are gentle to her when she is sick. She wishes someone else saw them, she likes that they advise and protect her. She dislikes that they keep her from intimacy. From a literary standpoint, why did you make her relationship with them so complicated and what opportunities did these complexities provide you as a writer?

LIVESEY: This too was something I was slow to come to terms with. In the early versions of the novel, the relationship between Eva and the companions was a simple friendship and the interactions struck the same note over and over. But when I reread it, I felt bored. It wasn't interesting to have them so straightforward in their desires. One of the things I often say to my students is that one way to make your story better is by thinking about it from the non-point-of-view character. I don't mean writing from their point of view but if, say, it's a mother-daughter story, told from the point of view of the mother, just go through the story thinking of the point of view of the daughter. What is her motivation for her side of the story? What is she thinking and feeling? I realized I needed to do this myself with the companions. Once I figured out their motivation, after only a decade or so, I realized how to write the book, where the ending was going, how that relationships play out.

The question about the companions, whether they're real or not, isn't finally an important question. What is important is the revelation that Eva has chosen them as much as they have chosen her. Of course, she doesn't feel she's had a choice, which I think is true to the way we often feel about the more important aspects of our lives: they don't feel chosen.

ELLIS: Can you describe the challenges of writing a novel that was very much about your mother?

LIVESEY: The challenges were huge. When I started writing the novel I'd just read a wonderful biography of W. H. Auden and another of Katherine Mansfield. I was impressed by how much was known about these people. My initial thought when I turned my attention to my mother, whom I had not previously devoted much thought to, was oh, I'll be able to find out lots about her. What I soon came to realize was that it's very hard to find out about a person who didn't leave written evidence and who wasn't famous. Perhaps if I had run advertisements in newspapers and been more aggressive, I would have been able to find out more, but as it was, after considerable effort, I still had only a handful of stories. My idea of writing a novel that would reflect her life as she actually lived it was foiled. If I had been writing a novel in a normal way, at this point I might have said this is not a good subject for me, but because of my strong attachment to the material, the fact that I couldn't find out anything about my mother, made me want to write about her even more. Her life had vanished and this was a chance to have her back in the world in some way.

But I couldn't presume that my mother would be important to other people, that readers would say "Oh, I have to stop everything to read about Margot's dead mother." It was finding a way to get around my personal attachment to the material, and make that attachment publicly interesting and relevant that was my biggest obstacle.

ELLIS: How did you go about doing that?

LIVESEY: One significant step was compressing the life so it didn't feel sunk in daily tedium. Another was finding an angle from which to write about the massive event which was the Second World War. A third was figuring out what story I was trying to tell. When I realized what the revelation at the end of the book was going to be, then I knew how to go back and organize the novel, so that when you got to the ending it would seem satisfying and somewhat inevitable.

ELLIS: On page seven you lay out the story and scope of this novel. Do you think it is important for writers to guide their readers early on, to map out the journey they're about to begin?

LIVESEY: This was a very late decision, one of two in the novel. The other was to tell the novel in the first person. Because of the plot, this was not the most natural voice to choose. I also had to overcome considerable resistance to writing in the voice of my mother; it seemed a kind of heresy. Once I had the novel in the first person I still wondered if this really implausible story could work. I decided to tell the reader up front: this is very far-fetched. Either the reader could stop reading or suspend their disbelief and continue. In earlier versions of the novel I'd kept the existence of the companions and their nature secret but that really didn't work. People thought they were reading a conventional, realistic novel and when they found out that some of the characters weren't real in the way they imagined, they were cross. So I decided to lay everything out at the start and to tell the story both backwards and forward, which I think increases the effect that this is a memoir. All the events really happened, and Eva is just picking and choosing the order in which to tell them.

ELLIS: You've said that the title of a novel is your "first ambassador." Can you describe what you mean, and perhaps share what you hoped to achieve with the title *Banishing Verona*?

LIVESEY: It seems very important to me to give a gentle signal to the reader of what kind of world they're about to enter. I think the role of the good ambassador is to smooth the path of the person who is coming, so I think the title is the ambassador of the book. For me, titles usually come early and easy or late and hard. Whenever I'm really stuck with one I think of what the father of a friend told me: a good title is the title of a good book. If I can just write, say, three hundred good pages then the title doesn't matter so much.

In the case of *Banishing Verona*, the title was very late. I had various other working titles, including *The Third Chance*. My editor was actually the one who picked the phrase *Banishing Verona* out of the novel and suggested it. I liked the lyricism and the mystery. I also liked the Shakespearian overtones. Verona is called after the Italian city where Romeo and Juliet lived and loved and came to not-so-great an end, so that too appealed to me. I hoped it would seem an invitation rather than a prediction of what would happen.

ELLIS: As a writer, how do you strive to keep readers turning the page?

LIVESEY: Oh, I do strive, very much so. Like most writers I admire I'm working with the three great elements of fiction, namely plot, character, and language. I hope to write sentences that are inviting and exciting, but not too intrusive. As a young writer I received many rejections that said, "This is beautifully written, but . . ." It took me a while to understand what was good writing in the service of the novel.

As for character and plot, I grew up reading the great Victorian novels but it never occurred to me that they were literary. I didn't think when I read, for example, *Jane Eyre* or *Wuthering Heights* or *Great Expectations* that these were great books. I thought they were thrilling and interesting and more vivid than my own life. They made me keep wanting to read; I thought of the characters as neighbors and friends, and what happened to them next was desperately important. Those books remain among my most important role models and their perfect marriage of character and plot is part of what I aspire to as a writer.

ELLIS: How much do you know when you begin?

LIVESEY: It varies a lot from book to book. I wrote my novel *Criminals* at a time when there were a lot of articles in the paper about the struggles between biological and adoptive and natural parents. I was fascinated by those struggles and by how hard it was to figure out one's own reactions in these complex situations. When I had the idea for *Criminals*, about writing about someone who finds a baby at the bus station, I simultaneously knew that I was heading towards a judgment of Solomon where two mothers would struggle over a baby. I had a beginning and end. But there were many wrong turns on the journey.

I think I usually do have a destination. I knew in *Banishing Verona* that the novel would begin in and end in an empty room. What would happen in between those empty rooms I was less certain about. I wish I were one of those writers like Henry James who could rehearse these things in notebooks and then write them out beautifully as he does, but I've never quite managed that.

ELLIS: Is there anything you've written that you've regretted?

LIVESEY: Interesting question. I think there are things I regret publishing, because if I hadn't published them I could have come back to them and written a better version.

ELLIS: Norman Mailer once said, "Being a real writer means being able to do the work on a bad day." Do you agree?

LIVESEY: I think writing fiction has become my job in the world. I was very reluctant for that to be the case. It took me a long time to not think it would be better to work for something more obviously useful, like Amnesty International. But I've come to the conclusion that this is what I can do, and the way in which I'm useful in the world—other than donating money to worthwhile causes—has to do with writing novels and helping other writers. There is a lot of stubbornness in being a writer, a lot of just showing up at your desk, persisting in the face of one's own mediocrity.

ELLIS: I understand that Alice Sebold was one of your former students in L.A. First of all, how does it feel to have a student of yours go on to become so famous, and secondly, have any of your other students gone on to receive such public acclaim?

LIVESEY: It's an amazing feeling, yes. She was actually my student at University of California at Irvine. And I have had quite a number of students publish wonderful novels. Alice Sebold's husband Glen David Gold published a beautiful book, *Carter Beats the Devil* that came out a year or two before *The Lovely Bones*, and got wonderful reviews and a lot of acclaim. Locally, Lan Samantha Chang is one of my former students, and I love her work. It's been thrilling to see her publish *Hunger* and more recently the splendid *Inheritance*; I think she is an amazingly gifted writer. Another very gifted student who published recently is John Dalton. His novel, *Heaven Lake*, is about a young American man who goes as a missionary to Taiwan and ends up making an epic journey to mainland China. Whitney Terrell published a terrific novel called *The Huntsman*, Elizabeth Stuckey French published a really good collection of short stories, Susan Powell published a wonderful novel called *The Grass Dancer*. I'm probably forgetting quite a few.

ELLIS: Are these books you helped them work on?

LIVESEY: I was involved to some degree in many of the first books. Obviously, by time she wrote *Inheritance*, Lan Samantha Chang was long past needing me.

My father was a teacher and, by the time I was conscious of his profession, he was in his fifties and not a very good one. I always vowed that I wouldn't enter a classroom as a teacher. When I did at the age of about thirty, I discovered I really liked it. I like being in the company of young writers, and the energy they bring to their work. I like the challenge of helping them discover what their material is and how to shape it. I feel lucky.

ELLIS: Do you have any suggestions for new writers about how they can focus on their writing or improve their craft?

LIVESEY: Well, we do live in a rather overcrowded and hurried age. So, it is important, at some point, to be able to answer the question, why should someone read this, and to be able to do so as articulately as possible. The answer can't be, as it was in the early stages of *Eva Moves the Furniture*, because this is my mother. We have to be able to make a persuasive case about what we're offering that isn't being offered in another story or book. I think this comes relatively late in the creative process for most writers, but I do think it is an important stage in that process.

I think it is important to write in a way that doesn't squander the reader's attention. Years ago Richard Ford told me that he read all his work aloud. Since then I've tried to do this myself. It is often absolute torture but I do find it an invaluable tool for detecting those places where I'm rambling on, wasting the reader's time. If a sentence isn't interesting to me, or I can't read it without wincing, then that's a pretty clear sign to me that there's a problem. When I first started writing novels, I thought, oh, there's so much space in the novel, I can put in nearly anything. It took me a long time to understand what the Anglo-Irish novelist Elizabeth Bowen meant when she said the biggest sin in a novel is irrelevance. Now I really feel that, if pressed, I should be able to justify every sentence.

I think most young writers aren't sufficiently ruthless. When they reread their work they think, as I did, oh, this isn't very interesting to me but that's because I wrote it; if I were reading it for the very first time it would be brilliant. We actually do know when our work is tedious, or repetitive, but we are often slow to admit it.

I guess I think the way we get around this myopia, other than by reading aloud, is to get good readers for our work. Early on my first readers were people whom I knew as friends and what really helped me to progress as a writer was finding readers who knew me as a writer first and who didn't bring too many expectations, didn't fill in the gaps in the generous way that my friends did.

ELLIS: Are you superstitious about talking about a work in process?

LIVESEY: If I were working on something I might be able to answer that question. I have to confess since I finished the galleys of *Banishing Verona* in July I haven't written anything other than a book review and a postcard, and a few comments on my students' work. I'm really looking forward to the Christmas holidays so I can sit down and write.

Fred Leebron

Growing the Story

Fred Leebron's novels include *Out West*, *Six Figures*, and *In the Middle of All This*. His stories have appeared in the *Gettysburg Review*, *Ploughshares*, *Grand Street*, the *North American Review*, the *Quarterly*, the *Threepenny Review*, the *Iowa Review*, *TriQuarterly*, and *Double Take*, and are included in the anthologies *The New Generation*, *Flash Fiction*, and *The Exiled*. His essays are included in *The Eleventh Draft* and *Bastard on the Couch*. He is the co-author of *Creating Fiction: A Writer's Companion*, and a co-editor of *Postmodern American Fiction: A Norton Anthology*.

In 2005, the Canadian production of *Six Figures* premiered at the Toronto Film Festival and was nominated for the Canadian equivalent of an Oscar for best adapted screenplay. *Six Figures* was also shown at Cannes, at the Museum of Modern Art in New York, and distributed throughout Canada.

In 1996 Fred Leebron was recognized by Discover Great New Writers for his book *Out West*. In 2000 he won the Pushcart Prize and the *New York Times* recognized his novel *Six Figures* as a Notable Book, and in 2001 he received an O. Henry Award. Leebron also received a Fulbright Scholarship in 1983, the Henfield Foundation Award in 1986, a Wallace Stegner Fellowship in 1989, the James Michener Award in 1990 and the Cohen Award in 1994.

Leebron completed his undergraduate studies at Princeton, and he earned an MA in writing at John Hopkins University and an MFA at the Iowa Writers' Workshop. From 1993 to 1994 he was a fellow at the Provincetown Fine Arts Center. From 1994 to 1995 he served as the director of the Provincetown Fine Art Center, where he proposed and helped to develop the summer program. Leebron is an associate professor of English at Gettysburg College and he is also the program director of the Queens University of Charlotte MFA program. He has also taught at John Hopkins University, the University of Iowa, Stanford University, and the University of North Carolina at Charlotte. He has served on the advisory board of Provincetown Arts since 1996. Leebron, his wife, and three children live in Gettysburg, Pennsylvania.

SHERRY ELLIS: *In the Middle of All This* takes place in Gettysburg, near the graveyards of war. It is a novel that deals with death and loss. "It felt like one long endless slide, as if they'd rolled the wrong number and found themselves tumbling down into a place so far behind that it wasn't a question of catching up anymore, they were just trying to stay on board." How important do you think the choice of setting is in fiction?

FRED LEEBRON: I think it's everything. It's not only where the story happens, but it provides the impulse for the story. If you really live in the setting, I obviously literally live in Gettysburg, you can grow the story and you can expand, because the setting's opportunities are limitless. But you can never, ever fully know any one place. There are always pockets of energy waiting for you.

ELLIS: In both the short-short story "Water" and the novel *Out West* you develop the premise of a character turning on a gas stove to kill a cheating lover. Which work came first and what made you decide to revisit the situation?

LEEBRON: "Water" came first by three years. I've written several short-short stories and I think they're really fun to write, and they allow for the opportunity to experiment and to really cut to the chase and be as deft as you can be. Sometimes you produce work that you want to re-explore; there's a lot more opportunity than you thought. So, I went back to "Water" because I thought there was more there to dig out and to learn. I went back and pursued it and it was a really good experience to re-inhabit the situation.

ELLIS: Charles Baxter once said, "Try to get your characters into interesting trouble. Allow your characters to misbehave. Let them stay out after eleven." In *Out West* you involve the characters Ben and Amber in a shared, sordid history early on in the book. How did you as a writer develop the dramatic relationship of these characters?

LEEBRON: Benjamin West was sort of the alter-ego for Nathaniel West. I wanted to rewrite the migration of Nathaniel West for the West Coast in a contemporary way. I started with him first and I didn't know that I would come to Amber. I wrote until I had nothing left to say in that very first part. I had the idea of "Water" in the back of my head, and I went and transposed the genders of the characters. I tried to figure out what it would be like to be this particular woman having done something like that character in "Water," and I saw a connection between the two in terms of guilt. They're both guilty from the get-go. I really spent a lot of time in guilt, being Jewish, and I became interested in occupying their guilt. I felt like I had a connection and empathy to both of them because of their literal guilt which had grown so much.

ELLIS: At the end of *Six Figures* the reader is left wondering if Warner is negative enough to have attacked Megan. How important do you think it is to leave readers with a sense of mystery?

LEEBRON: I think mystery is very important because it creates resonance. If you resolve all the questions that you pose, then you seal the thing up tight and there's nothing left to wonder or speculate about. Paula Fox once said that a good story begins with a small question mark and ends with a big question mark, and I think that is something I've learned from. To really create that resonance, at least ambiguity is essential, and obviously ambiguity and resonance are closely linked. I once had an editor who suggested that I cut a last sentence from a story she was going to publish of mine and I wrote her back and asked, are you sure you want to do that? She said that a writer always wants to be a little ambiguous and that a little ambiguity never hurt anybody. I think there's a lot of truth to that.

ELLIS: In the beginning of *In the Middle of All This* Warner Lutz has two mishaps in one day. "There was so much worse, he told himself, than two flat tires and a lost week of groceries. So much worse that it was all practically unspeakable." Can you describe the route you took in relating these seemingly minor upsets to the larger theme of this book?

LEEBRON: So much of the daily struggle is to find context and balance. A minor irritation can grow into rage, and that anger is just one step from danger.

To find a way back from that, to have characters that are real and trying to live with perspective, really working with a character that is desperate for perspective, led me to inhabiting his point of view. That was the rationalization the character was in. I really enjoyed working with that because I think the struggle of working for perspective is a universal one.

ELLIS: In *Six Figures* you write of fatherhood, "The little wobble head was already imprinting an island of drool above Warner's heart. He felt the familiar surge in his throat of gratitude and awe at the unearthly ripeness of the boy's cheeks, the tender narrowness of his neck." How much do you think a writer needs to know about the subject matter they write about, and how much has your own experience of being a father helped you in writing such a sensitive scene?

LEEBRON: I don't think a writer needs to know everything about subject matter, per se. I just think that a writer has to have enough empathy to inhabit a character's point of view.

Obviously for me I wrote the majority of *Out West* and all of the books after we had kids, and I think having children and being a parent has meant everything to my writing. To grow my own sense of the world and that perspective, to have that sense of the larger world is very important to me, and my children have given that to me.

ELLIS: In *In the Middle of All This*, you write of Elizabeth, "I am keeping a journal so that no one will have to hear how afraid I am, how being afraid of death is not good enough, how you can't give in to it and let it rule you, how exhausting it is, how careful you have to be in everything you ever do." How did you get inside Elizabeth's psyche?

LEEBRON: Well, inhabiting a point of view is the main way I get the energy to write. When I was living in Charlotte, I was teaching an evening class, and on the night of these classes I would walk to my car and look in the face of everyone I passed and try to imagine what their story was, try to find what they were capable of in terms of empathy, in terms of other emotions and feelings, to feel who they were, and that's something I haven't been able to stop doing. It's a curiosity and hope that everyone is capable of empathy. On the flip side, my own sister did die of cancer some years ago. That obviously informed my writing. But the woman in this book is not my sister.

ELLIS: Do you think it's harder to write from a male or female point of view?

LEEBRON: Well, I think for me it's much easier to write from anyone who's not me because then the invention begins with the first word and you can get out of your skin. Being in your skin for a writer can be pretty nasty and confining. I'm much happier being with characters other than myself. So the female point of view, being further away from me than the male point of view, is easier for me to write from.

ELLIS: Peter Ho Davies said, "One of the things I enjoy about fiction is its slyness. The ability to slip things in... It spurs my imagination. I tend to find that I'll come up with two or three facts and then I'll be inspired to join the dots between them with my fictional imagination." What do you think of this approach?

LEEBRON: Everyone has different approaches, and I think everyone has different temperaments and different aesthetics. My own approach is to inhabit a situation, inhabit points of view, and see where it takes me—so to start with a single point and to grow it. In general, I think it would be harder for me to go from two different situational or factual points and grow them, although in *Out West* I started with two. In *Six Figures* and *In the Middle of All This* I started with the one and tried to grow the one into many.

ELLIS: The *Library Journal Review* said of *In the Middle of All This*, "Leebron's new work is being compared to works by Richard Ford and Raymond Carver, though he may be more reminiscent of the former than the latter. His third novel . . . focuses on a man caught in strong, eddying currents who wants to control them but cannot and must either make a separate peace or be drawn under." Do you think there are similarities in your work?

LEEBRON: I'm not sure. I mean, I obviously learned a lot from both of them; when I was in graduate school I read a lot of Richard Ford, I read a lot of Carver, I read a lot of Chekov, a lot of Proust, a lot of Kafka, a lot of Joyce. For me, Carver's earlier work took language and distilled it into its essence, which was his primary accomplishment, and in his later work he was getting sloppier and more mysterious and I think I like that work better. Ford's work has a kind of vulnerable humility to it in that's he's never too afraid to come out and say, "This is what I'm going after here, this is what I'm trying to do here in terms of the characters." I admire that boldness but I don't really think we have that much in common. I'm not really sure.

ELLIS: Nelson Algren said, "A certain ruthlessness and a sense of alienation from society is as essential to creative writing as it is to armed robbery." In your essay "I Am Man, Hear Me Bleat" which appears in *Bastard on the Couch* you write, "I'm like a dog with a bone, and I can't let it go, and if the bone is more truly metaphoric—if the bone is something as intangible as one side of an argument—then I really cannot let it drop." What were the challenges of revealing your tenacious side in the writing of this essay?

LEEBRON: Well, they wanted me to reveal my tenacious side. I obviously concur wholeheartedly with what Algren is saying. I feel exactly what he says.

There was no problem with revealing it, in that I'm not easily embarrassed and it's very hard to offend me and I'm not really worried too much about what other people think about me, so I'm just going to say whatever the hell I want to say and see what happens with the prose. If it works in the piece—it works in the piece. That was what the piece was all about. Asking and trying to answer the question, why is someone so argumentative? What are the virtues of being short-tempered?

ELLIS: How do you choose the point of view you use in your writing?

LEEBRON: I believe it to be Darwinian—survival of the fittest or the struggle to survive on a moment-to-moment basis in the pieces that I write. Whoever wants it most, gets it. And when that person's desire for language ceases, then someone else takes it over.

ELLIS: How do you choose time span? For example, your novel *Out West* takes place over the course of a week.

LEEBRON: Yes, and I realized it wasn't ambitious enough so I tried to grow the time span in *Six Figures* and *In the Middle of All This*.

I don't think I choose time span so much as time span chooses me, in that every piece demands its own scope of time that it wants to take on. As you begin the pacing, you begin to look at the situation and you begin to exhaust the characters. How long will the character speak to you? At the end of *The Color Purple* Alice Walker says, "I'd like to thank all my characters for coming," and in a way I view my role similarly as a medium through which characters speak and they begin to take on lives of their own. How much time are they demanding? The characters in the last two books wanted to demand more time. They wanted to own it and they wanted to own me for a longer time in terms of the narrative time, and so they did.

ELLIS: Frank Conroy once said of the writer's life that "a certain amount of uncomfortableness simply comes with the territory" and that "it is a hard life because one is dependent on forces that are not fully understood and usually impossible to control." What are your thoughts on the writer's life?

LEEBRON: You write with the hope and the faith that you'll get better, and the hope and faith that what it is you're writing will eventually have an order and an artfulness. At the same time, for me, I don't know where the next word is going to be, let alone the next paragraph or chapter. There's a certain desperate quality to it. It's so hard because you're just stepping on air, in a sense, and that has its own discomfort. The imbalance of not knowing. I like it. I like being uneasy. I don't recommend it to everyone, but I like a certain tension. It's okay.

ELLIS: What have your biggest challenges been?

LEEBRON: I think it's the everyday challenge. Just getting in there and trying to make something out of nothing—that's the hardest thing to do. Then going from there. It's all in the process. If you buy into the idea that you can write from the not-knowing state and you're writing to discover something, then that pressure you put on yourself to be someplace you've never been before and find something out about it, it certainly can be very challenging.

ELLIS: How important is it to for you to have a community or fellowship with other writers?

LEEBRON: I think it's important to have a small group of people you can show your work to who will be honest with you and help you make it better, and I think it's important to work in service of opportunities for other writers, for all writers, because we're all in the same boat together. It's important to find a community without pretentiousness and without the heavy breathing that can happen among a group of writers—the false anxiety and self-congratulation. That, for me, is what I need, and it all works well, if you hang out with people who are pragmatic and thoughtful and honest and vulnerable. It can be a very enriching experience and it helps me.

ELLIS: Who are the writers who have most influenced your work?

LEEBRON: I like Tim O'Brien because I like how he phrases ambiguity, and I like the lyricism and episodic quality of Denis Johnson's work and I like the relentlessness of Flannery O'Connor's work, and I obviously love Kafka and Joyce and Chekov—and I learned the most from them.

ELLIS: How does your experience as a teacher influence your writing?

LEEBRON: I learn something new every day when I'm in the classroom. I like to work very closely with students and I view it as a partnership, where the utility in conferences and actual real dialogue of workshops helps bring you to a new level of understanding of the work and hopefully maybe a new level of understanding of what it is people can do or are trying to do in their writing. So I'm still learning something from teaching and I imagine I always will be.

ELLIS: Richard Ford revises his work by reading it out loud to his wife, to reinvigorate himself in being interested in his stories. Can you describe your revision process?

LEEBRON: Well, I write on very small pages of paper in a stenographer's notebook, so that I'm not anxious about filling a large page. Then when I type it up I do some revising. Before I type it up, every day I have to read what I wrote the day before. So, I'm line editing it then. There are two sorts of line edit phases, in the rereading of it and then in the typing of it.

Once that is done, it's sort of an endless process of getting to know the work and trying to shape it so that you can stand to look yourself in the mirror and say it doesn't suck.

I do this thing at the end which I call the "random page reading test"—I have the whole big manuscript and I'll just do one page after another randomly, and never in sequence, just read a page at a time and see if it can stand up. That's a really nasty experience. It's usually the last step.

Otherwise it's giving the thing shape and seeing where the gaps are, where the opportunities are, the overlaps are, and trying to make it a "leaner, cleaner" machine.

ELLIS: What do you think of Edna St. Vincent Millay's comment, "A person who publishes a book appears willfully in public with his pants down"?

LEEBRON: I think there's a certain sense of shame that comes with publishing a book and the realizing of one's limitations. There's no such thing as a perfect work of art. I think she's utterly on target on that. There's a certain kind of vulnerability that comes with trying to be completely honest on the page, and that's another way in which one's pants are down. There's a level of exposure, and that all helps to make the writing life even more uncomfortable than it already is.

ELLIS: What advice do you have for new writers?

LEEBRON: The easy advice obviously is to keep reading and to write every day. It's a craft and it has to be practiced every day. Just keep writing until it gets better and until you're learning something new. These are the reasons to write.

ELLIS: If someone were writing a blurb about your writing career how would you hope it might be described?

LEEBRON: I would prefer not to read it, so I'm not going to have any thought on how it would be described.

Yiyun Li

Tell, Don't Show

In *A Thousand Years of Good Prayers*, Yiyun Li's short story collection, China's twentieth century history is always close to the surface.

Li was born and raised in China. She was a high school student in Peking when student protests occurred in Tiananmen Square. Two years later, when she was eighteen years old and planning on attending Peking University, she was conscripted into the army for political re-education. Later, after completing a year at Peking University, Li was accepted into the doctorate of immunology program at the University of Iowa. She chose to participate in an adult education program in writing as an adjunct to her scientific studies and fell in love with writing. Her next writing course was taught by James Alan McPherson, winner of the Pulitzer Prize. In this class Mr. McPherson emphasized the difference between the writing of the Western world and countries of the East. He stated that writing from the orient emphasized the voice of the community, whereas Western writing focused on the individual. A short while later Li presented her story "Immortality" to Mr. McPherson, which begins, "This story, as the story of every one of us, started long before we were born."

Li went on to earn both a master's in fiction at the Iowa Writers' Workshop and a master's in creative non-fiction at the University of Iowa. Prior to completion of these degrees, she sold "Immortality" to the *Paris Review*, "Extra" to the *New Yorker*, and Random House had awarded her a $200,000 two-book contract.

Li's awards include the Frank O'Connor International Short Story Award, the PEN/Hemingway Award, the California Book Award for first fiction and the *Guardian* First Book Award. In 2007 she was selected one of *Granta*'s best young American novelists.

Li has lived in the United States since 1996. In February 2006 her petition for permanent residency on the grounds of "extraordinary ability in the arts" was denied on appeal. In March 2006 a new petition was submitted.

Ms. Li teaches at Mills College in Oakland, California. I spoke with her by phone.

SHERRY ELLIS: In the story "Extra," Granny Lin is an old spinster who has been fired from the state-run factory where she worked. She finds a job at a boarding school where Lin finds love in the form of a young boy. You write, "Granny Lin tucks him in and watches for a long time, the unfamiliar warmth swelling inside her. She wonders if this is what people call falling in love, the desire to be with someone for every minute of the rest of her life that sometimes she is frightened of herself." Can you describe some of the techniques you use to reveal your characters?

YIYUN LI: That's interesting. I never thought about it. Often when we learn to write we are told to show not tell, but actually I'm a strong believer in telling. I guess that the passage you read is just generalization and telling and that I do a lot of exposition. I think it is a useful tool for the writer, an efficient way of getting into the character.

ELLIS: How do you choose your titles? For example "Extra," the story referred to above?

LI: For the first draft of "Extra" there was one more part to this story, about Granny and her father. She was not married and she was a big disappointment to her father. In the part that I did not have in the final draft, Granny had this nickname "Extra" from early on because she had enough brothers and sisters. The story evolved and the name "Extra" carried on. The name fit her well, I think. She's an extra in her own story.

ELLIS: Do titles come easily to you?

LI: No, I'm very bad at titles. "Extra" came to me easily, but most of the times I think I struggle with titles a little.

ELLIS: What was the hardest title for you to come up with in this collection?

LI: I think "Love in the Marketplace" was really hard for me to title; that story was also the hardest story for me to write. Usually stories come to me in the first draft, but that story, I changed many drafts. The title was not obvious to me. The story was not obvious to me.

ELLIS: In your story "After A Life" you write, "Mrs. Su studies Beibei and imagines how she looks to a stranger; a mountain of flesh that has never seen sunshine, white like porcelain. Age has left no marks on Beibei's body and face; she is still a newborn, soft and tender wrapped up in an oversized pink robe." How difficult was it for you to make the transition to writing in English from your native language of Chinese?

LI: It was not very difficult because I had not written in Chinese. I started writing in English, so English is my first language in writing. I think I have this richness in my head. Once I am writing, I switch into English. It is actually very hard for me to write in Chinese now. I had to translate some dialogue recently and it was hard for me to do.

ELLIS: How old were you when you learned English?

LI: I was twelve or thirteen. I was in junior high school, middle school when I started to learn English.

ELLIS: So you must have a pretty good command of the English language?

LI: Well, not really. I have a pretty good knowledge of grammar. In Chinese we learned about six years of grammar, from age twelve to eighteen. That's how they teach English. Grammar. The first book I read was in college. We didn't really have English classes in college. We were on our own by then.

ELLIS: In "Love in the Marketplace," an English teacher in China is known to her pupils as "Miss Casablanca" because she makes them watch the movie *Casablanca* so often. You write, "*Casablanca* says all she wants to teach her students about life." Can you describe why you chose such a well-known American movie as such an important symbol in this story which takes place in China?

LI: Because in a way Sansan is my age, is of my generation, and the first English movie that I watched was *Casablanca*. I was in college, first year, in a really crowded classroom with two hundred people with two tiny television sets hung on the wall. I couldn't understand one word because I couldn't hear anything. I could just see the characters' faces and I was very moved, even though I didn't understand what they were talking about. I think that movie mattered to me.

It also fits Sansan's character. The woman, Ingrid Bergman, after she went back to her husband, there was this contract, a promise thing, that stood out in her character. I think that if this movie were made now, the Ingrid Bergman character wouldn't go back to her husband. The movie reflects an early age in America, and the world really echoed with the Sansan's point of view.

ELLIS: In your story "A Thousand Years of Good Prayers" Mr. Shi advises his divorced daughter, "Women in their marriageable twenties and early thirties are like lychees that have been picked from the tree . . . Each passing day makes them less fresh and less desirable, and only too soon will they lose their value, and have to be gotten rid of at a sale price." He finds it impossible to talk to his daughter who has embraced American values and language. In "Son," a successful software engineer who is gay, now living in America, visits his widowed mother in China but feels disconnected from her given her newfound faith in Christianity. Family disconnectedness after migration appears to be a theme of some of the stories in your collection. What about this topic intrigues you?

LI: Well, it reflects how I look at China or the China I knew in the past twenty years. There is the migration of the younger generation to the West, either physically or in their mental state even if they are in China; they are attracted to the western world and the western values. Then the older generations in my book, the parents, they are not communists, but in a way they still represent the communist values, the traditional values. I think I am very interested in that it reflects what China is at this moment and the pain in changing.

ELLIS: In many of your stories you emphasize the intersection of your characters' individual choices and China's recent turbulent political history. Do you consider yourself to be a political writer?

LI: I do not, actually. Let me just backtrack. I should say that I always make social comments on the politics or the events or situations in China, but I don't think that's my goal, to be a political writer. I am writing about China, and in the past fifty years not one single person in China has been living outside of the political situation. When I write about these characters I cannot avoid politics. I don't want to be a very political writer, though.

ELLIS: In your short story "Persimmons" you repeatedly weave in images of persimmons. In an early section the narrator shares a sentence of old wisdom, "If you were born a soft persimmon, you'd better stay one." Later the narrator says, "We could have made a wiser choice than Lao Da. We would have let the dead be buried and gone on living . . . There would be the pain, naturally, of waking up to the humiliation of being a soft persimmon, but humiliation does not kill a man. Nothing beats clinging to this life. Death ferries us nowhere." How did you develop the persimmon as a metaphor?

LI: There's this idiom in Chinese that if you call someone a "soft persimmon" it means this person doesn't have the bones to stand up for himself. So I took that, and at the time I saw a painting by a Japanese painter, several persimmons on a page, and I just imagined a group of men sitting around like a group of soft persimmons. That story just came once I got that image; very quickly.

ELLIS: In "Immortality" you tell the story of one particular "Great Papa," a eunuch, and span from the end of the empire in China to the twentieth century. What were the challenges of embracing such a long time period in one short story?

LI: The challenge was that I did cover two hundred years of history and in the meantime my job was to tell the story. I really had to plan the facts, the most right way to tell history. I had one sentence—then there were the two world wars, in both of which we fought on the winning side, yet winning nothing. This was what I wanted to do because I was writing about the history of this country but I couldn't go into details about why we didn't win anything, and so I just summarized everything. Is this the challenge? I don't know.

ELLIS: Ha Jin once said, "Good writers should observe and tell the story, try to reveal the complexities, the subtleties, to tell what's happening. The narrator shouldn't be intrusive." What do you see as the role of your narrators?

LI: I agree with that. I can't say it better than him.

ELLIS: Do you think about the shape or the arc of your stories before you begin?

LI: Yes, I think a lot about shapes because I have this training in mathematics, and in part of mathematics you look at the shapes. I always teach my students to look at the shape of the story. For me, if I have four characters, for example the two older couples in "After a Life," they have to be mirror images of one another. They have to be different and have similarities. I find that if you have four characters it's a very interesting story. People usually say a triangle, but I don't find a triangle exciting. The shape is set; it's a triangle. I like having four characters or more because the shape is flexible and there are interesting things you can do and it's fun.

Ellis: Which of your stories do you consider your best and why?

Li: That's a hard question. I can't answer that question because I will talk about every story. I think there's something in every story that I really love.

Ellis: Well, can you pick one of them and share what you love the most about it?

Li: I love "Immortality" because I read a lot of stories and many of them are momentary, just a brief moment in life. That is what a story is, a moment in a long passage of time. But I also think stories can be epic and I'm very happy I did that story.

Ellis: In your essay "Eat, Memory; Orange Crush" the instant drink Tang serves as a symbol for all that was American that you desired in your youth. By essay's end you write, "That was the end of my desire for a Tangy life. I realized that every dream ended with this bland, ordinary existence, where a prince would one day become a man who boiled orange peels for his family." What were the challenges you faced in writing this essay?

Li: To have the whole story, to fit everything into that space. I am kind of a messy writer and I can go on forever and ever. I think when you write for a magazine or newspaper you have to really watch out for word limit. That's one thing.
   The other thing is that orange Tang is such a small thing and I'm always happy when I can fit a big topic into something small. That's what I wanted to achieve.

Ellis: Can you compare your experience of writing nonfiction to your experience as a writer of fiction?

Li: Yes. I have different goals for fiction and nonfiction. At this moment, I think there are certain things I can only do by writing nonfiction, but they're pretty much not about me. I'm not a very autobiographical person or writer, so I think for my nonfiction I want to write about the world or other people, which is the same as my fiction.

ELLIS: What are your approaches to revision?

LI: I'm such a bad person to be asked that question because I usually don't revise enough. I think I'm kind of a one-draft writer, and if something comes right it's right. If something doesn't come out right in the first draft it's really a pain for me. The more I revise the worse a story becomes. I think a lot before I start writing. I think when I start a first draft I know the shape of the story. I pretty much know everything. I don't revise a lot.

ELLIS: Have you ever wished you could have deleted or revised part of what you wrote after it was published?

LI: Sometimes I might look at my story—I usually don't do that, and I'd think I could have used a better word here and there—but I usually don't do that. I try not to be a perfectionist. I've seen so many writers who are perfectionists which gets in the way of their writing. I try not to be like that. If something doesn't come out right then I'll say I'll do it better next time.

ELLIS: What writers have influenced your work?

LI: I'm a huge fan of William Trevor, and he is like a writing teacher on the page for me. I read him and reread him again, so he's my biggest influence. Another writer who I also like is Isaac Babel.

ELLIS: And what do you like most about their work?

LI: Isaac Babel is interesting because for one thing, he also wrote in a second language. His first language was Yiddish, and for this reason he chose to write in Russian. I thought that was fascinating. For me, he was such a masterful writer. I don't think he's a neat writer, and I really don't like neat writers.

As for William Trevor, I love everything he writes. I like his way of treating his characters, he knows them so well and presents them in a really humble way that moves me. My goal as a writer is to write like him.

The other thing I think is that both of them are very productive writers. William Trevor is probably more productive, but he's also lived longer than Isaac Babel. Trevor writes both short stories and fiction and is really good at both of them. A lot of writers can't do both well. I can go on and on and on forever and tell you how much I love William Trevor.

ELLIS: What in your childhood do you believe contributed to your becoming a writer?

LI: I read a lot. I was always a big reader. I always read ahead of time. I remember when I was seven or eight I read all these adult books, with bloody themes, or things that were too old for my age. I just loved them.

ELLIS: What made you make the decision to change from becoming a scientist to a writer?

LI: I didn't really know I wanted to be a writer. I took a community writing course just for fun and the moment I started to write a story I couldn't stop; I really couldn't stop. So I thought I would stop being a scientist.

ELLIS: Pearl S. Buck said, "I don't wait for moods. You accomplish nothing if you do that. Your mind must know it has got to get down to work." Do you write whether or not you're in the mood?

LI: That's a good question. I have two children. Two hours is precious time. I'm still doing my share of procrastinating and looking at things on the internet that have nothing to do with writing, but I'm always aware I have so much more in my life so I need to focus. I don't believe in the mood thing. I believe in hard work.

ELLIS: What have you learned not to do as a writer?

LI: I remember once I met a young, aspiring writer who was very talented. She talked about going to a coffee shop and meeting other writers and talking with them. I remember I was very surprised. One thing I learned not to do as a writer is to socialize too much, because I don't think that helps with writing, and I don't talk a lot with other people about my writing. I saw this somewhere. If you spend too much time talking about your project you've invested enough passion in the project and you probably won't do it.

ELLIS: Do you find it harder or easier to write about what you know?

LI: It's really hard for me to write about what I know. I think if you're writing about something you know you tend not to work hard enough to use your imagination. Don't write about what you know. Write about people that you don't know that you are curious about.

ELLIS: Is it difficult for you to come up with new ideas?

LI: I spend a lot of time on the internet to see if I can find little stories. For example, "Love in the Marketplace" was based on a snip of news I saw on the internet about this man going into the marketplace and he said, "I'll let you cut me once with a knife if you give me ten yuan; if you finish my life with one cut you don't owe me anything." Little things like this fascinated me and I just kept thinking about this man. I thought there would be a person, a woman, who would cut this beggar and she would think it was the right thing to do. This is how I got my ideas. I just imagined.

ELLIS: Kurt Vonnegut said, "Find a subject you care about and which in your heart you feel others should care about. It is this genuine caring, and not your games with language, that will be the most compelling and seductive element in your style." Do you agree?

LI: I can't agree more because there are a lot of talented young writers who can write a sentence really well; they can write passages using really beautiful language. For me there is an advantage that I don't write in the first language. I used to write a little bit in Chinese—just a journal. Yes, I could write really, really beautiful in Chinese because this was the language where I grew up. I read all the poetry. I got all my language training. I could write as beautifully as anybody. But underneath the language it was empty, I think. One tends to be carried away with the language and not pay attention to the story. Back to William Trevor; in every story he really cares about his characters, and that is why his stories are so good. If you don't care, there will be a distance between you and the characters, and the reader will sense the distance while they read the work.

ELLIS: When you stop writing for the day are you aware of what will happen next?

LI: Yes, pretty much because I have to think a lot.

ELLIS: You recently won the PEN/Hemingway Award and have won several other awards. What effect has this has had on you, and what do you believe about awards in general?

LI: I think if you win an award you are really lucky; it doesn't mean that you are really good. I don't think an award means anything. I think I'm really lucky.

ELLIS: What are you working on now?

LI: I'm working on a novel. I've been working on it forever. It's set in China, again.

ELLIS: And are you willing to share a little information about the topic?

LI: Well, probably no. Because it's not done. I don't want to talk about it.

ABOUT THE EDITOR

Sherry Ellis is the editor of *NOW WRITE! Fiction Writing Exercises from Today's Best Writers and Teachers*, which was selected as one of the best writing books of 2006 by *The Writer* magazine. Her book of nonfiction, *NOW WRITE! Non-Fiction* will be published in January 2010 by Tarcher. Ellis is the author of a novel entitled *The Goode Books*, a story about a biracial family of five women, which is told in their own voices. Her early interviews appeared in the *Kenyon Review*, *Glimmer Train*, the *Iowa Review*, the *Writer's Chronicle*, and other literary and arts magazines and journals. She is a writing coach who has taught in Concord, Massachusetts. Visit her website at SherryEllis.org.

www.ingramcontent.com/pod-product-compliance
Lightning Source LLC
Chambersburg PA
CBHW020329170426
43200CB00006B/324